NOTHING
BUT THE
NIGHT

NOTHING
BUT THE
NIGHT

LEOPOLD & LOEB AND
THE TRUTH BEHIND THE MURDER
THAT ROCKED 1920s AMERICA

GREG KING AND **PENNY WILSON**

ST. MARTIN'S
PRESS

NEW YORK

First published in the United States by St. Martin's Press, an imprint of St. Martin's Publishing Group

www.stmartins.com

Library of Congress Cataloging-in-Publication Data

Names: King, Greg, 1964– author. | Wilson, Penny, 1966– author.
Title: Nothing but the night : Leopold & Loeb and the truth behind the murder that rocked 1920s
    America / Greg King & Penny Wilson.
Description: First edition. | New York : St. Martin's Press, 2022. | Includes bibliographical references
    and index.
Identifiers: LCCN 2022014440 | ISBN 9781250272669 (hardcover) | ISBN 9781250272676 (ebook)
Subjects: LCSH: Leopold, Nathan Freudenthal, 1904–1971. | Loeb, Richard A., 1905–1936. |
    Murderers—Illinois—Chicago—Biography. | Murder—Illinois—Chicago—Case studies.
Classification: LCC HV6785 .K55 2022 | DDC 364.152/3092—dc23/eng/20220420
LC record available at https://lccn.loc.gov/2022014440

Our books may be purchased in bulk for promotional, educational, or business use. Please contact your local bookseller or the Macmillan Corporate and Premium Sales Department at 1-800-221-7945, extension 5442, or by email at MacmillanSpecialMarkets@macmillan.com.

First Edition: 2022

10 9 8 7 6 5 4 3 2 1

In Memory of Roger King.

And to Barbara Wilson, with gratitude.

CONTENTS

NOTHING
BUT THE
NIGHT

INTRODUCTION

IT'S BEEN A CENTURY SINCE NATHAN LEOPOLD AND RICHARD LOEB, two wealthy, Jewish Chicago teenagers, kidnapped and killed fourteen-year-old Bobby Franks. It was the original "Crime of the Century." Although other crimes had shocked the nation, the 1924 drama surrounding Leopold and Loeb was among the first to be covered as a national—even an international—media event. Newspapers and radio stations fought to report every stray fact, every bizarre assertion. While denouncing interest in the case as prurient, they eagerly printed up the latest gossip, the newest developments, and the most sensational details in efforts to satiate the seemingly unending public appetite for news about the crime and its perpetrators.

From the beginning it seemed so bizarre. Leopold and Loeb were both prodigies, graduating from college by eighteen. Leopold's father was a millionaire box manufacturer; Loeb's father, even wealthier, had been vice president of Sears, Roebuck. Their young sons, denied nothing in life, with everything to look forward to and very little to gain, upended expectation by joining together, locked in an amoral danse macabre in which they fed off each other and eventually murdered.

These two disaffected young intellectuals, it is often said, were obsessed with the work of Nietzsche and viewed themselves as supermen. That they had apparently killed just for the experience, to see if they could commit the perfect crime as if it was some kind of childish game pitting their wits against the police, was incomprehensible to Jazz Age Chicago. How had two young sons of wealthy families gone so wrong? The seeming lack of remorse left people reeling as the confessed killers grinned, gave interviews, and gave every appearance that they were enjoying their time in the spotlight. From the start there was an idea that the case offered important lessons. People tried to wrest some moral lesson from the chaos, making the murderers proxies for the clash between traditionalism and hedonism. They were held up as living warnings of juvenile delinquency and intellectual precocity.

Famed lawyer Clarence Darrow managed to save Leopold and Loeb from a date with the hangman, winning them life sentences. In 1936, a fellow inmate murdered Richard Loeb, claiming that he had done so to resist his unwanted sexual advances. This left Nathan Leopold: he rewrote history, blaming his former lover for their crimes and attempting to present himself in the best possible light in his quest for eventual parole. A smuggled straight razor wielded by another fellow convict deprived Loeb of his redemption story; Leopold, by default, claimed the mantle of remorse, won his freedom in 1958, and lived on for another thirteen years.

The case has never quite gone away, even as other more notorious crimes supplanted it in the public imagination. Writing about the case, historian Paula Fass noted that the story has an almost "Dostoevskian quality that made it at once compelling and unsolvable."[1] It has spawned films, documentaries, myriad scholarly articles, and a plethora of books—ironically the most famous, *Compulsion*, was a novel, a fictionalized recounting of events in 1924. There have been psychological explorations, historical narratives of varying accuracy, an autobiography by Nathan Leopold and, bizarrely, even two books aimed at a young adult reading audience.

Gallons of ink have been spilled over the case; sometimes the facts seem set in stone. Yet after a century, it's time to take a fresh look at the original Crime of the Century, to strip away the legends and challenge accepted history. The Leopold and Loeb case remains relevant today, encompassing as it did so many issues still in headlines: the death penalty; mental illness; anti-Semitism; homophobia; and the corrupting influence of money on the justice system. Darrow delivered an epic closing argument against the death penalty that spared his clients' young lives. A century has wrapped it in legend, extolling his brilliant advocacy. In truth, it was dishonest, disjointed, and often offensive.

Then there is the groundbreaking courtroom battle of psychiatric arguments and Freudian theories—the first time such testimony took center stage in an effort to transform villains into victims. The wealthy Leopold and Loeb families hired a veritable Who's Who of American psychiatry to examine the pair. Defense alienists proposed a litany of alleged mitigating circumstances: abusive governesses; parental neglect; improper reading materials; and a host of minor physical ailments that, under Darrow's careful machinations, skirted the truth. The portraits fell just short of insanity, leaving the popular though erroneous impression that these two young defendants were, at best, emotionally fragile and, at worst, so mentally damaged that they had been unable to resist their murderous compulsions.

Newspapers played up the fact that the Leopolds, the Loebs, and Bobby Franks's family were all Jewish. It didn't matter that the Leopolds were far from observant, that Richard Loeb's mother was Catholic, or that the Franks family had converted to Christian Science—much public opinion seems to have lumped them all together. For some, their Jewish roots made them alien: Jewish intellect, it was said, fed the crime, and Jewish money corrupted them and defeated justice.

And, from the first, whispers surrounded the nature of Leopold and Loeb's relationship. Even the most sensational newspapers refrained from printing the details, instead merely referring to the pair's "perversions." The truth burst forth in stunning testimony during their trial: Nathan was gay, and Richard had gone along with his sexual demands in order to secure him as an accomplice. The issue was deemed so shocking in 1924 that at one point the presiding judge ordered all women from his courtroom, lest details offend their refined sensibilities. It left the distasteful and inaccurate idea that the pair had killed only because of their sexuality.

Or, Darrow and others suggested, it was money that had corrupted their young minds and driven them to murder. Not want of it—until their incarcerations Leopold and Loeb lived in mansions, drove fast cars, sported the latest fashions, and freely indulged their every desire. Rather, defenders and critics alike claimed, it was this privilege that had so corrupted them and freed them from any sense of social obligation. It was perhaps the earliest example of what became known as the "affluenza defense," a strategy echoed in 2013 when sixteen-year-old Texan Ethan Crouch killed four people while driving under the influence and tried to claim that wealth had stripped him of an ability to determine right from wrong.

Here we have tried to answer the remaining questions: Did Leopold and Loeb commit other murders? Who actually killed Bobby Franks? Was he sexually assaulted? Did Nathan have a hand in Richard's murder? Here, and often for the first time, we have attempted to address these issues at length, even if much is still speculative. We've also dug deeply into the psychological relationship between Leopold and Loeb. History (and Leopold) portrayed Loeb as the psychopathic impresario, with Nathan positioned as his weak, infatuated disciple swept up in a mad folie à deux. But we discovered evidence contradicting this view. It is time to even out the scales in an attempt to understand what really happened in 1924, even if this introduces a certain imbalance in the narrative.

A century later, this tumultuous crime and its enigmatic criminals demand a fresh investigation, exploring persistent themes, exposing common fallacies, and probing for the hidden truth. By turning a critical eye to what has come before, reexamining Leopold and Loeb's personalities and relationship, and exploring controversial theories, it is possible to pull the curtain back just a little more on events that summer a hundred years ago.

—Greg King and Penny Wilson
June 2021

PART I

THE MISSING BOY

CHAPTER ONE

AT HALF PAST TWO ON THE AFTERNOON OF MAY 21, 1924, THE DOORS of Chicago's elite Harvard School for Boys flew open. Classes were over, and students spilled from the three-story brick building in the city's South Side Kenwood neighborhood. Previous days had been gray and heavy with rain; now, the thick, scudding clouds had finally begun to fade, washed away by mild but persistent winds blowing from Lake Michigan to the east. Spring was late this year: oaks and maples marching along adjoining streets still bore bare patches open to the sky. But the break in the weather offered a chance to relieve pent-up boyish energy.

Some boys climbed into family limousines sent to fetch them; others walked down Ellis Avenue, toward the rows of impressive mansions nearby. But several groups lingered: with thoughts of home and homework pushed aside, they dropped their books and organized impromptu baseball games. One team formed in the schoolyard while another started off for a nearby vacant lot. Harvard instructor J. T. Seass, who had volunteered to supervise, decided he should follow the second group.[1] Just as he walked out of the yard, a figure waved to him from the sidewalk.

Seass recognized him: everyone in the neighborhood seemed to know eighteen-year-old Richard Loeb, the handsome, charismatic son of one of Chicago's most prominent families. Richard's father, Albert, had made a fortune rumored at nearly $10 million as vice president of Sears, Roebuck & Company; the family lived just three blocks down Ellis Avenue, in an immense Elizabethan-style mansion.[2] Called Dickie by his family, young Richard was an academic prodigy: a year earlier, he'd been the youngest man to ever graduate from the University of Michigan.[3]

The instructor exchanged a few words of greeting before continuing to the vacant lot; as he left, Seass saw Richard speaking with his ten-year-old brother Tommy Loeb, who attended Harvard.[4] Then Richard stopped nine-year-old Johnny Levinson, son of a wealthy attorney. "What are you doing after school?" he called out to the boy.

"I'm going to play baseball," Johnny replied and quickly walked away.[5]

Shouts rang out from a vacant lot at 49th Street and Drexel Boulevard as Seass approached the second game. He'd barely arrived when he again saw Richard Loeb, standing off to one side, his eyes on the gathered boys. As Johnny Levinson went to bat, Loeb shouted, "Hit it up!" before finally leaving.[6] The game lasted some two hours before the boys began making their ways home.

It was a quiet afternoon; only a few cars passed along the street. Sometime after half past four, Carl Ulving, chauffeur for the Spiegel family, was driving north on Ellis when he spotted a "dark colored" touring car going south on the avenue. Something made Ulving look closer—perhaps the fact that, despite the nice weather, the car had its canvas side curtains pulled up. Ulving saw Richard Loeb "sitting behind the wheel." He'd known Richard for years—"since he was a boy"—and raised his hand to wave. Loeb saw him and waved back in acknowledgment.[7]

The second group of boys, playing baseball in the schoolyard at Harvard, ended their game at five. They might have gone longer—the sun was now shining—but most knew that their parents would be expecting them home for dinner. Fourteen-year-old Bobby Franks left the yard and began walking the three blocks to his house on Ellis Avenue—he lived just across the street from the Loebs. He hadn't yet hit a growth spurt—at five feet tall and a hundred pounds the brown-haired boy was smaller than most of his classmates, but that didn't stop him from joining their play. Bobby loved sports, with a special passion for baseball: his most prized possession was a baseball signed by Babe Ruth.[8] He hadn't played that afternoon but instead served as umpire.

Another Harvard student, Irvin Hartman Jr., followed Bobby out of the yard and down Ellis. Hartman was in no mood to rush; he lingered along the sidewalk, stopping now and then to enjoy the weather. But he could see his schoolmate walking a half block ahead of him.[9] Bobby wore a pair of wool knickers; knee-length brown stockings with argyle tops; a shirt with his school tie; a tan jacket with a black-and-gold class pin on the lapel; and a cap. Since the weather had cleared, Bobby had taken off his overcoat, and had it draped over his arm.[10]

Out of the corner of his eye, Irvin noticed a car driving down Ellis, with its canvas side curtains up. It may have been gray, he later said, and maybe it had been a Winton, but he admitted that he hadn't paid too much attention to it. Instead, he began eyeing the broad lawns sweeping up to the large houses along the avenue. The borders were planted with shrubs and beds of flowers. "My teacher had told us to look at tulips," Irvin remembered, "and I saw a big red bunch of them." He paused midway between 47th and 48th Streets. "I looked just about a minute," he said. When he raised his head, Irvin saw that the car he had spotted earlier "was coming lickety split up Ellis going north. It whizzed past me." He gazed down the avenue. Bobby Franks was no longer on the sidewalk ahead of him. In an instant he had simply disappeared.[11]

IN A CITY AWASH WITH honking automobiles, pushing crowds, and rumbling trains, the Chicago neighborhood of Kenwood was an oasis of serenity. Nature buffered it from urban sprawl: Washington Park to the west, Lake Michigan to the east, and the leafy campus of the University of Chicago and Jackson Park to the south. The large lots and quiet streets spoke of exclusivity and refinement. Ornate Italianate, Romanesque, and Elizabethan mansions of the city's wealthiest and most important Jewish families—the Adlers, the Sulzbergers, and the Rosenwalds—marched proudly along its avenues. Here, said a resident, all was "quiet and peaceful."[12] But the great houses, as Kenwood was soon to learn, were no guarantee of security. Evil could lurk anywhere, even in this privileged enclave.

Bobby Franks lived in one of these mansions, a boxy affair at 5052 Ellis Avenue. His father, Jacob, had bought the corner lot from Richard Loeb's father Albert in 1910: Richard's mother, Anna, and Bobby's mother, Flora, were first cousins, and at the time the Loebs were building their own mansion just across the avenue. Designed by architect Henry Newhouse, the Franks house, set atop a terrace adorned with lilac bushes, looked like the bastard offspring of an affair between an Italian contessa and Frank Lloyd Wright: Mediterranean arches and a clay tile roof jumbled together with Prairie-style windows and glassed-in sleeping porches.[13] The yellow brick house had cost a small fortune but, with a rumored worth of some $4 million, Jacob Franks could afford the extravagance.[14]

Born in London, Jacob Franks had come to America with his parents in 1857 at the age of two. At nineteen he founded a pawnshop, the Franks Collateral Loan Bank, with his widowed mother and won a reputation for generous lending. He soon left this venture behind—he'd later bristle at descriptions of his pawnshop days, complaining, "I only did that for two years." In 1901 he moved on to become president of the Rockford Watch Company and began buying up real estate in the city. This eventually allowed him to retire from daily business and focus on his portfolio of holdings.[15]

A quiet, reserved, serious-faced man, Jacob Franks never seemed to have made any enemies; the closest he had come to scandal was in 1903, when a woman sued him for breach of promise, insisting that he had backed out of marrying her. The suit, which he seems to have regarded as little more than blackmail, was eventually dismissed. But not until he was fifty, in 1906, did Jacob finally marry. His bride, Flora Greisheimer, was not only twenty years his junior but she had also divorced her first husband, a druggist named William Tuteur, charging him with adultery.[16]

Both Jacob and Flora were born Jewish, but shortly after marriage they converted to become Christian Scientists. This made them an anomaly in the Kenwood community, and despite their backgrounds they were never entirely welcomed by the neighborhood's Jewish elite. Perhaps there was a certain snobbery at work: a former pawnbroker didn't quite fit the refined image most Kenwood residents had of themselves.[17]

Jacob and Flora had three children: Josephine, born in 1906; Jack, born in 1908; and Bobby, born on September 19, 1909. As the youngest Bobby was treasured and indulged. He was especially close to his older brother Jack, who remembered the boy he called "Buddy" as someone with "a lot of fun in him, always ready to laugh and kid you along. He couldn't stay mad to save his life."[18]

The Franks sent Bobby to the nearby Harvard School on Ellis Avenue. From the beginning, the preparatory institution had attracted the sons of Chicago's wealthiest families. Bobby was popular at Harvard: his headmaster, Charles Pence, called him "one of our most brilliant students."[19] Intelligent and not shy about expressing his opinions, Bobby sometimes seemed smug. A few of his teachers complained that he was "too self-satisfied to make a good student," and that he harbored some "unpleasant characteristics."[20]

But Bobby also had a reputation as a thoughtful, considerate boy. A few weeks earlier, as a member of the school's debate club, he'd argued against capital punishment. Thinking that there was a link between mental illness and criminal behavior, he declared that it was wrong "to take a man, weak and mentally depraved, and coldly deprive him of his life."[21] Instead, he suggested "would it not better serve the community to put mentally weak criminals into institutions where, removed from society, they would no longer be a menace? Punishment should be reformative, never vindictive."[22]

AROUND SIX THAT EVENING, AND some twenty miles southeast of Kenwood, a car stopped at the Dew Drop Inn, a scruffy looking roadside shack in Hammond, Indiana. Richard Loeb sat inside while his nineteen-year-old friend Nathan Leopold ordered hot dogs and root beers. The son of a millionaire, Nathan also lived in Kenwood, but the Leopolds weren't as wealthy or socially prominent as the Loeb family. With his short frame, full lips, bushy eyebrows and dark features, Nathan couldn't compete with his friend Richard's dashing looks, but he was more than his intellectual equal: he'd graduated from the University of Chicago the previous year with a degree in philosophy and a Phi Beta Kappa key.[23] Now, the pair ate dinner as soft amber light filled the sky, watching as the sun began its long descent behind the trees.

In the big yellow house on Ellis Avenue, the Franks family, too, was preparing to eat. Since the Harvard School was only three blocks from his house, Bobby usually walked home for lunch. He'd done so that Wednesday at noon: nothing was unusual.[24] But now, as dinner approached, Bobby hadn't returned from school. "If he was ten minutes late," Jacob recalled, "he would phone my wife." But that afternoon there had been no telephone call.[25] Still, he was a fourteen-year-old boy: the weather had improved, so perhaps Bobby had lingered with his friends after school.

The minutes ticked by. Jacob and Flora Franks sat down to dinner, expecting Bobby to burst through the door at any moment.[26] But when the meal was over, and there was still no sign of Bobby, they telephoned a few of his son's classmates. Flora rang Robert Asher, one of Bobby's friends and president of their freshman class at Harvard. Did he know where Bobby was? Asher hadn't seen him since school had let out.[27] No one had. It was quiet and growing darker, and there was still no sign of Bobby. Finally, a worried Jacob rang his friend and Kenwood neighbor, retired corporate attorney and state senator Samuel Ettelson, for advice. Ettelson said he would come over immediately.[28]

Twenty miles away, a local cinema let out at nine that night. Lucille Smith and her young daughter Jeannette left the theater to walk home in the growing darkness. They stopped for a few minutes to buy some candy before continuing along Ewing Avenue. At 108th Street, the Smiths turned onto a dirt road leading west toward the wildlife preserve at Eggers Woods. Suddenly, a car came racing out of the desolate area. "It was a large dark touring car we met," Smith remembered, "and had side curtains on. . . . They had bright lights and they blinded us and we stepped into the grass and waited until they drove past us."[29]

SAMUEL ETTELSON ARRIVED AT THE Franks house shortly after nine.[30] Jacob wondered if Bobby might have accidentally locked himself inside the Harvard School. It was a long shot, but he phoned headmaster Charles E. Pence, asking for keys to the building. Pence thought it would be quicker to ask the janitor, but the two couldn't reach him by phone.[31] Finally, he traced Richard Williams, Harvard's athletic director, to another pupil's house. Williams said that he had last seen Bobby when the boy left the baseball game that afternoon and started walking home. Still, Williams said he would come to the Franks house and help search.[32]

When Williams arrived, he accompanied Bobby's father and Ettelson on the walk to the Harvard School, following the arc of halos cast by streetlamps along Ellis Avenue. Darkness had now fallen, wrapping the streets in shadow. They found the school doors locked but discovered that a basement window was open. They climbed in and began wandering the dark corridors, shouting Bobby's name. There was no answer.[33]

An anxious Flora Franks was waiting for her husband to return when, about half past ten, the telephone rang. Flora rushed to answer.

The caller asked for Jacob Franks; Flora said that he was not at home, but that she was Mrs. Franks. The man at the other end of the line, she later said, had "more of a cultured voice than a gruff voice."

"Your son has been kidnapped," the caller declared flatly. "He is all right. Further news in the morning."

"Who is it?" a stunned Flora asked.

"George Johnson" came the reply before the connection ended.[34]

Jacob learned of the call when he returned with Samuel Ettelson and found his wife hysterical. He put Flora to bed and then pondered what to do. At least he knew that Bobby was alive. But now new worries set in. Would the kidnappers harm him? Surely, they only wanted money. But Jacob couldn't relax until he again held his son in his arms. He discussed the situation with Ettelson. "I was afraid to do one little thing," Ettelson said, "that would incur the wrath of the kidnappers and thereby endanger the life of the boy." But doing nothing seemed even riskier. Ettelson rang the telephone company, asking them to trace any incoming calls to the Franks house.[35]

As the hours passed, the tension finally became too much. About two in the morning Franks and Ettelson went to the local police station. Ettelson knew both Chief of Detectives Michael Hughes and Deputy Police Captain William Shoemacher but, not surprisingly, neither man was on duty at this hour. Reluctantly, Ettelson told Acting Lieutenant Robert Welling of the kidnapping but, fearing for Bobby's life, asked him not to make a formal report. Welling agreed, saying that he would quietly inform detectives so that they could begin a search.[36] Ettelson escorted Jacob Franks back to his house, to continue the unnerving wait.

A few blocks away, watchman Bernard Hunt had been on his nightly patrol in Kenwood. It was normally a quiet, uneventful neighborhood, especially after midnight. But around half past one that morning, as Hunt walked toward the intersection of 49th Street and Greenwood Avenue, a red car sped by; there was a loud metallic clink as it passed. Curious, Hunt investigated. He found a chisel on the pavement. One end had been wrapped with tape; the other end, Hunt saw, was smeared with something that looked like dried blood. Hunt put it in his pocket and turned it over to the local police station when his patrol ended.[37]

Frantic searches, mysterious phone calls, cars coming and going, a bloody tool tossed into the street—it all played out while most of Kenwood's privileged residents slept soundly. Richard Loeb, too, had finally gone home, quietly entering his darkened house and tumbling into bed while across Ellis Avenue, the windows of the Franks home blazed with light as the long night wore on.

CHAPTER TWO

Just after nine on the morning of May 22, the postman rang the doorbell of the Franks house and handed over a letter. Someone had affixed two six-cent stamps on it to ensure speedy delivery and underlined the word "Special" on the envelope. Worn out by his sleepless night, Jacob quickly opened and read the letter within:

Dear Sir:

As you no doubt know by this time your son has been kidnapped. Allow us to assure you that he is at present well and safe. You need not fear any physical harm for him provided you live up carefully to the following instructions and such others as you will receive by future communications. Should you, however, disobey any of our instructions, even slightly, his death will be the penalty.

1. For obvious reasons make absolutely no attempt to communicate with either the police authorities or any private agency. Should you

already have communicated with the police, allow
them to continue their investigations, but do
not mention this letter.

2. Secure before noon today $10,000. This
money must be composed entirely of old bills
of the following denominations: $2,000 in $20
bills, $8,000 in $50 bills. The money must be
old. Any attempt to include new or marked bills
will render the entire venture futile.

3. The money should be placed in a large
cigar box or, if such is impossible, in a heavy
cardboard box securely closed and wrapped in
white paper. The wrapping paper should be sealed
at all openings with sealing wax.

4. Have the money thus prepared as directed
above and remain at home after 1 o'clock p. m.
See that the telephone is not in use. You will
receive a future communication instructing you
as to your future course.

As a final word of warning, this is a strictly
commercial proposition, and we are prepared
to put our threats into execution should we
have reasonable ground to believe that you
have committed an infraction of the above
instructions. However, should you carefully
follow out our instructions to the letter, we
can assure you that your son will be safely
returned to you within six hours of our receipt
of the money.

Yours truly, George Johnson.[1]

"Its deliberate tone struck terror into our hearts," said Samuel Ettelson, who had stayed with the family through the agonizing night.[2]
The letter was typed; the paper was of good quality, linen stock.

It was obviously written by someone educated—the phrases and language had a curious, almost legal tinge to them. In contrast, the address handwritten on the envelope was crudely lettered, as if done by someone attempting to disguise their usual style. Still, the letter seemed to confirm the telephone call, promising Bobby's safe return if the ransom was paid. The $10,000 demanded was little for a man of Jacob Franks's wealth, and he would do anything to get his son back. Ettelson advised him to follow the instructions and get the money from his bank. This Jacob did.[3]

Franks and Ettelson had hoped to keep the kidnapping a secret. Someone, though—it was never entirely clear who—alerted the *Chicago Daily News* that a wealthy young boy had been kidnapped and that former senator Samuel Ettelson was somehow involved in the negotiations. Young reporter James Mulroy was given the unenviable task of chasing Ettelson for information. He caught him at his office that morning when the lawyer briefly stopped by to check in on business. Ettelson was upset that word of the kidnapping had leaked, but he finally gave Mulroy the bare details in exchange for a promise that the newspaper would not publish the information and risk Bobby's life.[4]

A FEW HOURS EARLIER AND some twenty miles southeast of Kenwood, a slight, middle-aged man finished his night shift at the American Maize Products Company. Since emigrating from Poland, Antoni Mankowski had adopted the more American-sounding name of Tony Minke. Now he was on his way to nearby Hegewisch, Illinois, to pick up a watch, following a path called Indian Ridge through the desolate prairie near Wolf Lake.

Surrounded by Eggers Woods, the area straddled a marsh between Hegewisch and Hammond, Indiana, its languid lakes ringed by dense clumps of trees. As he walked along in the chill, damp air, Minke skirted a shallow drainage ditch, some ten feet wide, linking Hyde Lake to the east with Wolf Lake to the west. Ahead of him it narrowed, passing through a concrete culvert beneath an embankment crossed by a length of track belonging to the Pennsylvania Railroad. As Minke neared the embankment, a flash of white caught his eye. Something seemed to be caught in the culvert. He scampered down for a closer look and immediately recoiled: two small, bare feet were barely visible inside the pipe.[5]

Minke stumbled back up the embankment in a panic. In the distance, he saw a handcar with several men approaching on the railroad tracks, and ran toward it, frantically waving his arms.[6] When they stopped, Minke shouted at them in Polish, which they couldn't understand; finally, he pointed to the feet in the culvert. "Look!" he said in broken English. "There is something in the pipe! There is a pair of feet sticking out!"[7]

The men jumped from the handcar and raced down the embankment, thinking that someone had drowned. The body lay facedown inside the culvert, in roughly two feet of muddy water. Grabbing the bare feet, the group managed to pull it out and turned it over. Only now did they see it was a young boy, perhaps ten or twelve years old. He was naked; there were two large gashes on his forehead, and his face and genitals were streaked with ugly, rust-colored stains. His eyes were open, staring, vacant, lifeless.[8]

The men placed the body on the handcar and covered it with a tarp; railway worker Paul Korff didn't see any nearby clothing, but he did spot a pair of glasses, abandoned in the dirt some thirty feet from the culvert.[9] Someone ran off to telephone the police. Officer Tony Shapino—another immigrant from Poland—arrived on the scene about half past nine and got the full story from Minke. He made a quick search, finding a single tan sock, several hundred feet along the dirt road.[10] Soon a police wagon arrived to take the body off to a nearby funeral home owned by Stanley Olejniczek; assuming that the glasses had belonged to the victim, Shapino put them on the boy.[11]

BACK IN CHICAGO, JACOB FRANKS anxiously waited in his mansion for the kidnappers to contact him. Ettelson was there, and so was reporter James Mulroy. He had come to the Franks house following his encounter with Ettelson, willing to abide by the lawyer's request to temporarily keep the story of Bobby's kidnapping a secret but unwilling to give the story up. For a time, he had stood on the sidewalk, waiting for developments. The spectacle of a reporter hovering outside the house, though, was sure to attract unwelcome attention, and Jacob finally agreed that he could wait inside.

On learning that the body of a young boy had been found near Wolf Lake, an editor at the *Chicago Daily News* asked reporter Alvin Goldstein to go to the funeral home at Hegewisch to view the corpse. No one knew his identity. Bobby Franks, the editor knew from Mulroy, had been kidnapped; surely whoever had taken him would exchange him for a ransom, not kill him. And yet . . . a young boy was missing, and the body of a young boy had been found. Thinking that there might be a link, Goldstein's editor told him to call the Franks house from the funeral home and speak to his colleague James Mulroy. After viewing the body, Goldstein gave Mulroy the details: a boy perhaps ten to twelve years old, some five feet tall and a hundred pounds, with no distinguishing marks aside from the discoloration on the face and genitals. The only clue seemed to be that he wore glasses. Mulroy described it all to Jacob Franks, who was relieved: Bobby didn't wear glasses.[12]

But as the minutes ticked past, anxiety rose. Finally, Ettelson decided that the family ought to send someone down to the morgue to view the body. "It's probably not him," he said, "but we better not take a chance."[13] Ettelson asked Jacob's brother-in-law Edwin Gresham to go. It was about three when Gresham entered the room where the corpse rested on a white medical table. "The body had absolutely no clothing on," he recalled. "It was lying on its back. It had on the glasses. I removed the glasses to make sure that it was the boy. I looked further to see that there were marks on the boy's teeth. When the boy was a child, he had rickets, and that had left marks or pearls in the teeth and I looked at the teeth to make sure that the pearls were there. They were there. It was beyond the question of a doubt in my mind that the boy was Robert."[14]

Gresham rang the Franks home and conveyed the sad news to Ettelson, who in turn broke word of Bobby's death to Jacob.[15]

Within a few minutes, the telephone again rang in the Franks house. Ettelson ran to answer, perhaps thinking, hoping, that there had been a mistake. But the caller wasn't Gresham: instead, he identified himself as "George Johnson," the kidnapper. "I knew my boy was dead," Jacob said, but still he took the call.[16] "Johnson" spoke as if Bobby were still alive. He told Jacob that a taxi from the Yellow Cab Company would soon arrive at his house: Jacob was to enter it, taking the ransom with him, and go to a drugstore at 1465 East 63rd Street. There, he was to wait by the pay phone for further instructions. Perhaps hoping to contact the police, Jacob asked for more time, but "Johnson" refused.[17] In the panic of the moment, Jacob neglected to write down the address of the drugstore, and could not remember where he was supposed to go.

A dispatcher at the Yellow Cab Company had handed driver Charles Robinson a fare slip marked "at once." He was to go to 5052 Ellis Avenue. "I rang the bell as usual," Robinson said, "and a lady came to the door and said she did not think anyone ordered a cab." After a few moments, Ettelson asked Robinson who had sent him and where he was supposed to go; Robinson had no idea. After being paid, Robinson left without his fare.[18]

It was a little after three when the public telephone at the Van de Bogert & Ross Drugstore on East 63rd Street rang. James Kemp stopped sweeping and ran to answer it.

"Is Mr. Franks there?" the caller asked.

"There is no Mr. Franks here," Kemp replied.

"Probably I have the wrong number," the caller said before hanging up.[19]

A few minutes later the telephone again rang. This time, druggist Percy Van de Bogert answered.

"Is Mr. Franks there?" the caller inquired.

"Who?"

"Mr. Franks," came the reply.

"I don't know a Mr. Franks," Van de Bogert said. The caller described him and asked the man to look around the store. In a few moments, though, the druggist returned to the telephone; no one resembled the caller's description, and no one had answered to the name of Franks.[20]

Early on the evening of Thursday, May 22, after word came that Bobby had positively been identified, neighbors, reporters, and curiosity seekers gathered on the sidewalk outside the Franks house, trying to make sense of the primal darkness that had struck Kenwood. Bobby's second cousin Richard Loeb wandered across Ellis from his father's mansion to join the crowd. Reporter Alvin Goldstein was on the sidewalk, taking notes, when he saw Loeb; he knew him from the University of Chicago, which they both attended. After Goldstein described the condition of the boy's body, Loeb seemed upset. It was, he told Goldstein, "a terrible crime" and the perpetrator deserved to be punished—"strung up" was how Loeb expressed it.[21]

Finally, the doors of the Franks house, where Bobby's mother lay "prostrated with grief," opened and Samuel Ettelson came out to make a statement on the family's behalf.[22] The crowd swelled around him to listen. "It all happened in such a short time," an exhausted Ettelson said. "The events swept before us like a rushing river. We did the best we knew how."[23]

From the first, newspapers seemed to give equal weight to every rumor, every theory. "Someone living or walking along Ellis Avenue," declared the *Daily Tribune* on May 23, "must have seen the kidnapping."[2] Scenarios and possible solutions appeared daily, especially after rewards had been offered—$5,000 from Jacob Franks, $1,000 from the police, and $5,000 each from the *Daily Tribune* and the *Herald and Examiner*.[3] Hearst's *Herald and Examiner* even ran a tasteless contest, with fifty dollars awarded to the best theory. "Somewhere in Chicago," the newspaper wrote, "behind a desk, or in a street car, or in a foundry, may be a keen analytical mind adapted but not trained to detection and the reconstruction of past events, as a hunter reconstructs the story of the chase from the muddy records of the spoor."[4]

Chicago police opened a file on the murder of Bobby Franks: it was Case 6034. Police Chief Morgan Collins said that Bobby's death was "one of the most brutal murders with which we have had to deal. Never before have we come in contact with such cold blooded and willful taking of life. . . . The children of our schools must be protected against the possibility of any such crime as this. . . . We intend to hunt down the slayers if it takes every man in the police department to do it. . . . We'll run down anything that looks like a clue."[5]

Robert Crowe, state's attorney for Cook County, promised swift action. It would fall to Crowe to assemble a case—if and when the perpetrators were arrested—and prosecute it before the court. With his pudgy, boyish face and jaunty bow ties, the forty-five-year-old Crowe looked more like a high school teacher than an intimidating legal powerhouse. But behind his tortoiseshell-rimmed glasses lurked an iron will, "blunt, stormy, dangerous," as one contemporary called him.[6] After graduating from Yale Law in 1901, Crowe had served as chief justice of the Cook County Criminal Court, earning a reputation as a fierce defender of law and order even as he first allied himself with the city's corrupt mayor, Bill Thompson. Crowe was smart enough to cast Thompson aside to advance his own career: in April 1924 he'd been elected state's attorney for Cook County, equivalent to

CHAPTER THREE

"Kidnappers Slay Millionaire's Son as $10,000 Ransom Waits" ran the headline in the *Chicago Herald and Examiner* on Friday, May 23.[1] Chicago was accustomed to violence, especially after the Eighteenth Amendment enforcing Prohibition came into force in 1920. Bootleggers sold bathtub gin from squalid speakeasies and served up copious rations of illegal liquor in the city's illicit brothels and gambling dens. These were the early days of Al Capone, who initially joined forces with existing mobsters to corner Chicago's South Side market. Turf wars between Italian and Irish gangs, bloody executions, and bombings became common.

But kidnapping was rare, and the story exploded in the city's papers. The kidnapping and murder of a young boy was sensational enough, but the Franks family's wealth somehow made it even more shocking. Chicago's six daily newspapers stumbled over themselves in morning editions, evening editions, and special editions as they attempted to ferret out details, interview friends and relatives, and indulge in rampant speculation. The *Chicago Daily Tribune* and the *Chicago Daily News* largely kept to their respectable reputations, but the two papers owned by tycoon William Randolph Hearst, the *Chicago Herald and Examiner* and the *Chicago Evening American,* offered readers more tantalizing, often lurid, accounts of the crime.

the position of district attorney.[7] Crowe seemed amiable enough but he could be ruthless and made no secret of his desire to one day run for higher office. Solving the Bobby Franks case would, he knew, go a long way toward that goal.

Crowe gathered a crack team to help him investigate the crime and evaluate evidence gathered by the police. Three of his assistant state's attorneys, Bert Cronson, Joseph Savage, and John Sbarbaro, hunted down leads and questioned suspects. They worked closely with a handful of detectives, who interviewed the alleged witnesses who came out of the woodwork: some described seeing a number of men, sometimes accompanied by a woman, in the area around Wolf Lake early on the morning of May 22.[8] Police investigated every "George Johnson" in the city, but to no avail. After Irvin Hartman Jr. mentioned the car he'd seen on the day Bobby was kidnapped, police began searching registrations for gray Wintons.[9] Various suspects—"drug fiends," "morons," convicted criminals, and alleged "perverts"—were arrested, interrogated, and then released as the mystery deepened.[10]

The case was a puzzle. Had the kidnappers meant to go through with their plot, collect a ransom, and return Bobby unharmed to his family? Perhaps the boy had struggled and been accidentally killed. That, at least, made a certain amount of sense. But suspicions began drifting toward other possibilities. The fact that the body was naked suggested a sexual motive. The *Daily Tribune* openly wondered if Bobby had been the victim of a "male annoyer of boys," a "degenerate who sought to cloak his act and the boy's presumed accidental death by the demands for money."[11] Thus in the first days, as historian Paul Franklin notes, "the myth of the male homosexual as child molester held sway."[12]

Police had few clues. Bobby had been kidnapped in Kenwood; this suggested that the killer was either familiar with the area or perhaps lived there. Because his body was found some twenty miles away, it was obvious a car had been involved. Irvin Hartman Jr., walking a half block behind Bobby on Ellis that May 21 afternoon, had heard nothing; if Bobby had been forcibly abducted, wouldn't he have screamed or cried out? That indicated that Bobby had voluntarily entered the car—and if so, he must have known his kidnapper. And that also pointed to a Kenwood resident: Bobby's universe was not large and was largely confined to his own neighborhood.

The site where the body was dumped might indicate that the killer or killers were familiar with the area. Then there was the bloodstained chisel. Although no one could yet say for certain that it was the murder weapon, by May 22 it was not an unreasonable conclusion. And this again pointed back to a Kenwood resident. It was possible to envision Bobby being abducted, killed, and dumped at Wolf Lake, but if the chisel was tied to the crime, it meant that the killer or killers had literally later returned to the scene of the crime to toss out a key piece of evidence. If Bobby was kidnapped by a local resident, this chain of circumstantial evidence made sense. Had these things been considered, the police might early on have sought a possible killer who lived in Kenwood and was familiar with the area around Wolf Lake. But they apparently never pursued this idea.

Instead, police focused on more obvious clues. The ransom letter seemed particularly important. The wording indicated that it had been written by someone with a "more than ordinary education," a "scholarly person, a master of English." Police called in Hugh Sutton of the Royal Typewriter Company to examine the document. Sutton determined that the letter had likely been typed on an Underwood portable, by someone who essentially hunted and pecked given the variations in pressure in pushing certain keys. In addition, the lowercase "t" and "f" on the machine used were slightly defective, meaning that the letter could likely be matched to a suspect's typewriter if it was ever found.[13]

Detective James Gortland discovered what he thought was a startling similarity between the story "The Kidnapping Syndicate" in the May 3 issue of *Detective Story Magazine* and the style and content of the ransom letter Jacob Franks had received. The *Daily Tribune* published both letters side by side, suggesting that it was likely Bobby's kidnapper had read the story.[14] But how could the police trace readers of a popular magazine?

The glasses found near the body, though, offered the most promising clue. Several newspapers published photographs of them; since they didn't belong to Bobby, police assumed that the killer had accidentally dropped them. Articles described in detail their Xylonite frames, thick lenses, and measurements. The *Daily Tribune* offered up an analysis under the headline, "Glasses Near Body Not Such as Man Wears." An optician declared, "It would be a strange kind of man, a little bit of a wizened faced fellow, who could wear these."[15] And Chief of Detectives Michael Hughes said: "They were not purchased by a laboring man, or a man who is employed with his hands." Instead, he believed that the owner must be "a scholarly person, one who reads a great deal or was under considerable eye strain. . . . I am told it must have been a highly intelligent person who wore these glasses. A high strung, nervous temperament."[16] Although the prescription was common, Crowe announced that assistant state's attorney Joseph Savage was to "devote every effort toward tracing ownership."[17]

OUT OF RESPECT FOR BOBBY Franks, the Harvard School canceled classes on Friday, May 23.[18] It was a desolate day: rain fell across the brick building, driven sideways by gusts of wind. The playground was deserted. A few morbid tourists looked on before making their ways down Ellis Avenue, to gaze in silence at the mansion where the murdered boy had lived and where police now stood guard.

A mile away and around noon that Friday, Howard Mayer, campus reporter for the *Chicago Evening American,* dropped by his Zeta Beta Tau fraternity house at the University of Chicago. By coincidence, Richard Loeb happened to be there: he'd belonged to the University of Michigan chapter. Loeb was in a talkative mood, and freely shared his theories about the death of his second cousin Bobby Franks with Mayer. Newspapers had reported that Jacob Franks couldn't recall the address of the drugstore that the kidnappers had directed him to. Wherever it was, Loeb said, he was sure that it wouldn't have been the final destination: "You know," Loeb said, "these kidnappers would not meet a man on a busy street like that, that's common sense." It was, Loeb thought, worth investigating. "Why don't you make the rounds at some of these drug stores on East 63rd Street," he proposed to Mayer, "and see if you can't find the one at which some word was left for Mr. Franks?"[19]

Mayer wasn't keen on the idea: it was still pouring rain outside. Soon, and by coincidence, fellow reporters Alvin Goldstein and James Mulroy from the *Chicago Daily News* also appeared at the fraternity, apparently stopping for lunch. With a new audience to convince, Loeb suggested that Goldstein and Mulroy search for the drugstore. They agreed and soon the quartet—Loeb, Goldstein, Mulroy, and a reluctant Mayer—were off. They went from one store to another along 63rd Street (the only detail Jacob Franks could recall) until reaching Van de Bogert & Ross. Loeb and Mayer entered and asked if the store had received any calls for a Mr. Franks the previous day. When told that they had, Richard shouted in excitement, "You see, I told you we could find it! Now you have got a scoop!" This, Loeb insisted, "is what comes from reading detective stories."[20]

The reporters first telephoned the discovery to their respective editors so that the story would make the latest editions, and then called the police. Chief of Detectives Michael Hughes responded; the reporters filled him in while Loeb lingered silently in the background, sipping on a soda.[21] Although his apparent intuition had led to this break, Loeb didn't want to be publicly associated with it—"For God's sake," he implored Mulroy, "don't use my name!" On the drive back to the university, the reporters asked Loeb about his second cousin, thinking that he could add some human interest to Bobby's story. But Richard shocked them with his reply: "If I were going to murder anyone," he said, "I would murder just such a cocky little son of a bitch as Bobby Franks."[22] Loeb had a reputation for being glib; perhaps the remark was nothing more than an insensitive joke, but it seemed a harsh, odd thing to say.

At half past two that Friday afternoon, the same quartet—Loeb, Mayer, Goldstein, and Mulroy—attended the inquest on Bobby's death. Loeb had invited himself along, apparently wanting to know all of the details. A contingent of reporters crowded the room but kept a respectful distance from Bobby's father, who sat forlornly at a table. He was still in shock. "No one at the inquest," the *Tribune* reported, was "less emotional than the boy's father, Jacob Franks. . . . In a clear, unemotional voice he told of the events following the disappearance of his son."[23]

Coroner A. F. Benson, assisted by coroner's physician Joseph Springer, had conducted an autopsy the previous day. Their report noted that four significant wounds had been inflicted to Bobby's head by some blunt instrument: a three-quarter-inch gash on the right forehead; a half-inch cut just above the left eyebrow; and two deep blows to the back of the head. The latter had penetrated to the bone and led to swelling of the brain. There were scratches on the left side of Bobby's forehead and on his right shoulder, probably made as he struggled with the killer, with more scratches across the left shoulder extending down his back as well as on his right buttock. All had bled, indicating that Bobby had been alive and his heart still pumping blood when they were inflicted.[24]

Acid of some kind had been poured over the boy. Bobby's face "presented a peculiar appearance," the autopsy report noted, "with a marbled outline around the nose and mouth and part of the chin, the color of the skin in this area being pale. The rest of the face presented a flushed and streaked appearance, such as would result from acid fumes." The area around Bobby's mouth had turned a copper color, and there were similar streaks extending down the left side of his face, and his left shoulder to his elbow. The acid had also been poured on his genitals—no one could say why.[25]

Something, perhaps a rag soaked in ether, had been shoved deeply down Bobby's throat, probably in an effort to silence his cries. The tongue was swollen; fumes had discolored the windpipe and entered the lungs.[26] Bobby had suffocated to death; no water was found in his lungs, meaning that he was dead when he was placed facedown into the culvert.[27]

But it was another finding that Benson and Springer noted that caused horrified reactions: Bobby's "rectum was dilated, and would admit easily one middle finger." The pair, though, failed to detect any signs of "recent forcible dilation."[28] The coroner expressed doubt that Bobby had been sexually assaulted, but he added "it is difficult to determine this. Attempts to attack him might have been made, and some forms of attacks accomplished without leaving external evidence of violence." The idea hung in Jacob Franks's head. He suggested that if Bobby was "killed by a pervert, or several of them, he probably was killed accidentally in a struggle."[29]

"One instructor at the Harvard School," Samuel Ettelson flatly declared, "killed Robert Franks. Another wrote the polished letter demanding $10,000 from the family. The instructor who wrote the letter was a cultured man, a man with perverted tendencies; the man who committed the actual crime is a man who needed money and who had mercenary motives."[30] Police apparently agreed, for they focused on several of Bobby's teachers, subjecting at least one to harsh interrogation and beatings.[31] In the end, the instructors were released without charges.[32] The police seemed no closer to catching the killer as one potential suspect after another faded from consideration.

As HIS COUSIN'S BODY LAY in the morgue, Richard Loeb went dancing. It had been a long day—running around with reporters, finding the drugstore where the kidnappers had intended to contact Jacob Franks, and then the inquest on Bobby's death—but then Richard was eighteen and full of youthful energy. Why stay home and mourn? He and Bobby hadn't been that close and, as Richard had brusquely told the reporters earlier that afternoon, he hadn't even liked his cousin all that much. And, after all, it was a Friday night.

And a Friday night in Jazz Age Chicago—even in the middle of Prohibition—promised excitement. Richard had his own circle of Bright Young Things: would-be flappers with bobbed hair, crimson lipstick, and shapeless dresses, and suave gentlemen like himself, wealthy, immaculate, with slicked-back hair in imitation of Rudolph Valentino. Rather than the illicit thrills of bathtub gin in a crowded speakeasy, Richard opted for elegance: a night at the Edgewater Beach Hotel on Chicago's North Sheridan Road. By day, and in good weather, it boasted expansive beaches and busy tennis courts; by night, its gilded ballroom and lavish restaurant catered to a refined crowd that foxtrotted across the floor to lively music from a jazz combo.[33]

Dapper as always, Richard strolled into the hotel with a pretty young woman on his arm. Germaine Reinhardt was the latest in a long string of his interchangeable girlfriends. Known as "Patches" or "Bud," the young woman typified the era, with her black bobbed hair and modeling career.[34] They'd met in February: "I suppose he had a flock of girls," Reinhardt said. "Well, at first he would only give me the bad nights of the week, the Tuesdays and the Thursdays, you know. That was at first. . . . And in the end I was getting the big nights."[35]

At Richard's side—almost inevitably—was Nathan Leopold. He'd brought his own date, Susan Lurie. A senior majoring in philosophy at the University of Chicago, she enjoyed her time with him but, as she was careful to point out, she and Nathan were "just friends." Richard shone as usual, wandering about the room and charming his friends; even the usually misanthropic Nathan, Lurie recalled, "seemed gay" that night. "Not once," she said, "did he mention the sensation that was sweeping the city."[36]

Bobby's small, private funeral took place on Sunday, May 25, in his parents' house on Ellis Avenue. Only a handful of relatives, some family friends, and twenty of Bobby's fellow students from the Harvard School were invited to the house "where grief is mingled with horror," as the *Daily Tribune* wrote. Veiled and dressed in black, Flora sat next to her daughter, Josephine, while Jacob and his only surviving son, Jack, stood alongside.[37] Looking at his brother's coffin, Jack thought that it was all so surreal. He didn't, he later said, think kidnappings "happened outside the moving pictures."[38]

Bobby's white coffin rested in front of the library fireplace. A blanket of red rosebuds covered the top of the casket; arrangements of lilies of the valley, orchids, roses, and peonies hid the mantelpiece.[39] The arrival of one wreath caught everyone's attention: an arrangement of tiger lilies, with a card reading "Sympathy from Mr. Johnson." Police wondered if this could have come from the kidnapper, who had identified himself as George Johnson. But no one was ever able to trace the sender, whom the florist described a tall, older man.[40]

The short service was conducted according to Christian Science rites. Elwood Emory, first reader of the Fifth Church of Christ, Scientist, and second reader Maybelle Armstrong, intoned prayers and read from the scriptures, and a soloist sang hymns. At the end of the service, Flora arose from her seat, walked up to the group of Bobby's classmates, and "ran her hands hungrily over their faces."[41] Eight of the boys picked up the coffin and carried it from the library into the hall; above them, dim light from the gray day streamed through a stained glass window on the staircase landing, illuminating its depictions of Josephine, Jack, and Bobby Franks, all dressed in angelic white.[42] The boys walked out the front door, and down the terrace stairs to the waiting hearse, watched by some three hundred people who had gathered beneath the leaden sky to witness this sad farewell.[43]

Across Ellis Avenue that Sunday, Richard Loeb happened to leave his house just as the funeral service for his second cousin concluded. He hadn't attended—none of his family had. He watched for a moment as Bobby's coffin was carried to the hearse by the group of "bright faced boys."[44]

Police on motorcycles escorted the procession of twenty-five cars ten miles to Rosehill Cemetery. Sometime earlier Jacob Franks had built a granite mausoleum in the Jewish section of the cemetery: above the leaded glass doors, the name "Jacob Franks" had been carved in stone. A velvet carpet, strewn with flowers, led from the roadway to the open mausoleum doors. There were more readings from scripture and more prayers. Flora Franks "trembled, turned away and went back to the car, where she gave way to her grief in pitiful little moans and sobs. Her daughter, a pretty, dark-eyed girl, tried to comfort her and so did her husband, though he, too, was on the verge of breaking down."[45] The mausoleum doors were closed and locked. Here, behind a slab inscribed "God is Infinite, Indestructible, and Eternal," Bobby would rest for eternity.

A few days later, the *Tribune* published an interview with a grieving Jacob Franks. "They tell me I bear up under the strain very well, but they do not know. I know it will not help that baby any to keep brooding. I try to put things out of my mind, but they come back. My wife keeps showing me pictures of him. And I lay awake until dawn thinking about it all, thinking about that baby. . . . I have been racking my brains trying to think who they could be. Robert knew the murderers. That is why they choked him to death. And since Robert knew them, I must know them. Whoever it was who kidnapped my boy did so for the ransom. It was the money they were after. They knew his habits. They knew my love for him and that I would willingly pay any sum to have him back. But Robert recognized them, and they grew afraid and strangled him."[46] Jacob Franks was soon to learn just how prescient his words were.

CHAPTER FOUR

AFTER BOBBY FRANKS WAS KILLED, CHICAGO POLICE CAPTAIN THOMAS Wolfe questioned residents of the few isolated houses near Wolf Lake. The stories about mysterious cars, strange comings and goings, and shadowy men and women wandering through the prairie in the early morning hours of May 22 were so contradictory as to be useless. Finally, he visited Oscar Staff, deputy game warden for the area.[1] Did Staff recall any frequent visitors to the preserve—perhaps someone had seen something important? In looking over his station book, Staff saw that a man named Nathan Leopold had often come to the lake, watching for birds.[2] It seemed like a long shot, but police were tracing every possible lead. Perhaps this Nathan Leopold would have some ideas.

At eleven on the morning of Sunday, May 25, Wolfe drove to the big, gabled house at 4754 South Greenwood Avenue in Kenwood, where young Nathan Leopold Jr. lived with his father and namesake; eerily, it was just three blocks from the Franks mansion. Wolfe asked to see the son but was told that he was still asleep. Wolfe insisted. It took a few minutes but finally a sleepy young man appeared. Wolfe wanted to know if he had ever visited the area around Wolf Lake;

when Leopold said yes, the police captain asked him to accompany him back to the 8th District Station to answer a few questions in the investigation.[3]

Wolfe assured young Leopold that he wasn't a suspect: police just wanted information. And indeed, why would he suspect this awkward nineteen-year-old law student at the University of Chicago? Leopold certainly didn't need the money police believed led to the crime: his father was a millionaire. Young Nathan, called "Babe" by his friends and family, was an intellectual prodigy, with a talent for languages and a passion for ornithology. He was soft-spoken, measured, polite, and seemingly honest when Wolfe questioned him. Leopold admitted that he had often visited the area around Eggers Woods and Wolf Lake to watch birds. Wolfe casually asked if he wore glasses: Nathan said that he did not. The captain then wanted the names of any other people Nathan might have seen around Wolf Lake wearing glasses; Leopold identified a few of his friends who had joined him bird-watching.[4]

Before leaving, Wolfe asked Leopold to write out a brief statement: "I have been going to the general locality of 180th Street and Avenue F for six years. I have been in the locality about five or six times this year. The last two times were Saturday May 17 and Sunday May 18." He had a precise recall—down to the minute—about events that weekend.[5] Wolfe thanked him and sent Leopold on his way, the issue apparently at an end and no suspicions raised about the young man. Once again, a potential lead had seemingly fizzled out.

At least until Thursday, May 29. Police had spent the past week attempting to trace the owner of the glasses found near the body, visiting optometrists throughout the city. Although the prescription was not uncommon, police learned that the Xylonite frame had a new and distinctive hinge, manufactured by the Bobrow Optical Company in Brooklyn. Only one Chicago firm, Almer & Coe, sold glasses with this hinge. It was a time-consuming process to search through tens of thousands of records, but eventually the company found that they had sold only three pairs of glasses with Bobrow hinges in Chicago. One was purchased by an attorney who had been away in Europe for some time, another by a woman who quickly produced the pair she owned, and the third by Nathan Leopold Jr.[6]

Hearing this, state's attorney Robert Crowe wanted to speak to Leopold. But he moved cautiously. Prejudice weighed in Leopold's favor: he was intelligent and from a wealthy family. It seemed unthinkable that he would have been involved in the crime, but he might be able to resolve ownership of the glasses. And so, at half past two on the afternoon of Thursday, May 29, Crowe sent Detective Sergeant William Crot and Detective Frank Johnson to the Leopold house. Maid Elizabeth Sattler answered the door and asked them to wait in the library while she fetched Nathan.[7]

When Leopold appeared the two men asked if he wore glasses; Nathan now admitted that he did. They wanted to see them; Nathan didn't know where they were but insisted that they must be in the house. Since he couldn't produce the glasses, the officers asked Nathan to accompany them to a meeting with state's attorney Robert Crowe. Leopold protested: he was scheduled to lead a bird-watching group in a few hours. But the men insisted.[8]

To avoid embarrassing a member of one of the city's wealthiest families, Crowe had Leopold brought to room 1618 at Chicago's La-Salle Hotel. He showed Leopold the glasses found near the body; Nathan admitted that they resembled his but insisted that he had not lost his pair.[9] Under questioning, Leopold agreed that whoever wrote the ransom letter must have been educated. "I should not think it would be necessary that he be a college graduate," he opined. "I should think a high school graduate or a man with some college training would be capable of writing such a letter." He also agreed that the killer must have been familiar with the area around Wolf Lake to locate the nearly hidden culvert into which Bobby's body had been jammed. Crowe asked if Nathan owned a typewriter. He confirmed that he did, saying that he had a Hammond Multiplex at home. But, he added, he didn't own a portable typewriter.[10]

Where had Leopold been on May 21? He couldn't really remember—a week had passed and there was nothing special about that day.[11] But this young man clearly had a remarkable memory and Crowe pressed him. Finally, Leopold admitted that he knew exactly how he had spent May 21. He was embarrassed. He had finished his morning law classes at the University of Chicago and met his friend Richard Loeb; the pair drove downtown in his bright red Willys-Knight motorcar and had lunch at Marshall Field's Grill. After this, they went to Lincoln Park—ostensibly to watch birds, Leopold said, but really to drink: Richard had a flask of gin and Nathan had a flask of Scotch. "I should say we might have been a little bit happy," he admitted, "but neither of us was drunk." After a few hours Richard didn't want to go home—his father disapproved of drinking and his breath smelled of alcohol. And so the pair went to a restaurant, the Cocoanut Grove, and had dinner to sober up. They then drove aimlessly around, Leopold said, and picked up two girls, Edna and Mae, who agreed to have sex with them. But the girls "didn't come across," and Richard and Nathan turned them out of the car. Finally, sometime after ten, they had returned to Nathan's house.[12] But beyond these details Leopold was vague: he couldn't recall when they had eaten dinner, didn't know the girls' last names, nor could he say when he and Richard had finally returned to the Leopold house. In his memoirs Nathan placed the time he gave this story as around 10:00 p.m. that Thursday.[13] But it is clear that he did so much earlier. Sergeant William Crot and Detective James Gortland both testified that he repeated the alibi during their visit to the Franks house to see Samuel Ettelson, which took place shortly before six that evening.[14] That this is the correct timeline is verified by the fact that police picked up Richard Loeb for questioning around 6:00 p.m. that evening, precisely because Nathan had already implicated him in his alibi. Had Nathan not given his alibi until later that night, the police would have had no cause to pick Richard up earlier.

Crowe wasn't sure what to make of this story about drinking and picking up girls, but he knew that he wanted to see those glasses: if Leopold produced them, then those found near the body must belong to someone else, someone who hadn't bought them in Chicago.

And so, at six that evening Detectives Crot, Gortland, and Johnson drove Leopold back to his father's home. "I am being questioned to this Franks murder," Nathan explained to his eldest brother, Mike, saying that the glasses found near the body closely resembled the pair he owned. "My glasses must be in the house."[15] A search began. The effort turned up a case marked "Almer Coe & Co.," but there were no glasses within.[16]

Mike Leopold asked his brother if he might not have lost his glasses at Wolf Lake during one of his bird-watching expeditions; Nathan agreed this was possible. It seemed like a minor point, but Mike thought it best—given the notoriety of the crime being investigated—that Nathan consult a lawyer. His choice, ironically, was Samuel Ettelson. Ettelson's office said he was at the Franks home. And so Nathan, Mike, and the detectives drove the three blocks over to the big yellow mansion on Ellis Avenue.[17]

Jacob Franks was in the parlor with Ettelson when the group was shown in. "You know Babe, don't you?" Mike asked Ettelson.

"Yes, I have known him since he was a small boy," the lawyer replied, adding, "I always thought well of him."[18]

Ettelson listened as Mike explained how his brother could have lost the glasses on a previous bird-watching expedition; the lawyer agreed that this was the most likely explanation. When asked where he had been on May 21, Leopold repeated his story about drinking and picking up girls with his friend Richard Loeb.[19] Ettelson advised Nathan to go with the detectives and answer their questions, but he also warned that he would follow developments closely lest Crowe overreach.[20]

The group returned to the hotel; Crowe left the questioning to his assistants John Sbarbaro and Joseph Savage. After several hours, Leopold finally admitted that the glasses found near the body were almost certainly his. He must, he explained, have lost them the weekend before Bobby was murdered, when he had spent both Saturday and Sunday at Wolf Lake. He'd had on a pair of rubber boots, and as he ran after a bird he had stumbled: the glasses must have fallen unnoticed out of his jacket pocket.[21] This seemed plausible, but there was a problem. Five days had passed between the time Leopold said he had lost his glasses and the morning of May 22 when they were found. It had rained over those days, and the glasses should have been dirty, or at the very least had dust or mud on them: but they were pristine, as if dropped a few hours earlier.[22] Savage handed Leopold the glasses and asked him to demonstrate how they could have fallen out of his pocket. Nathan tucked them into the breast pocket of his coat and went through several pratfalls, stumbling, tripping, and falling in front of the attorney. But the glasses always remained in his pocket.

As this was taking place, police returned to the Leopold house. They wanted to again search for the missing glasses, but now they also wanted any typewriter in the house as well as samples of Nathan's handwriting, to compare against the ransom letter and its envelope. They found the Hammond typewriter Leopold had said that he owned. But then maid Elizabeth Sattler volunteered that there had also been a portable typewriter in the library—"I seen it two weeks ago," she told police. Now it was missing. The search uncovered a number of bottles of strychnine, ether, and arsenic, as well as two unlicensed revolvers, a .32 caliber Remington automatic and a .38 caliber Remington, both loaded.[23]

The questioning of Leopold now became more intense as Crowe focused in on this strange young man. Leopold admitted that he wasn't religious—"I do not believe there is a God," he declared. When Crowe asked if there was any difference between the death of a man and the death of a dog, Nathan told the startled attorney, "No, Sir."[24] Four more hours of questioning followed: the harder the attorneys pressed, the cockier Leopold seemed to become. There was something odd about him, and his answers did nothing to clear him of suspicion. Rather than let him return home, authorities escorted him to the Central Police Station, so that Nathan could rest.[25]

BECAUSE LEOPOLD HAD IMPLICATED HIM in his alibi that Thursday afternoon, police also wanted to speak to Richard Loeb. They had arrived at his father's mansion around six on Thursday evening and asked him to come down to the LaSalle Hotel for questioning without revealing what Leopold had said. His father Albert was in bed—he'd had a heart attack on May 18—when Richard went to see him. "They want to ask me some questions, dad," he told his father. "I'll be back in two or three hours."[26]

The detectives took Richard to a separate hotel room for questioning. Crowe asked where he had been on the day Bobby was kidnapped, but Richard said he couldn't remember—"that was more than a week ago," he told Crowe.[27] Crowe was suspicious; he hadn't told Richard that his friend had named him in his alibi, but if it was true, why didn't Loeb mention it? If he had indeed been with Leopold drinking and picking up girls, there was no reason to lie about it. The questioning continued throughout the night and into the next morning. Crowe wasn't willing to send him back home; a nagging sense that something was wrong led him to move Richard to the Central Police Station to rest. Still, the charming, genial Loeb seemed even less likely to be involved in any crime than his peculiar friend.

Despite the fact that the evidence piling up against the pair was circumstantial, police were sure that they were on the right track. And so early that Friday morning, May 30, they brought Richard back to his house to conduct a search for any incriminating evidence. Reporter Howard Mayer got a tip about the investigation and raced to the Loeb mansion in time to see Richard being led inside. Richard was unperturbed—he seemed most excited about having been able to ride in a police car. In searching Richard's desk, police found two letters that Nathan had sent to him the previous autumn. Just a quick glance revealed that their content was bizarre, and so police took them as possible evidence.

Learning that Leopold was being detained, Mayer drove downtown and was allowed to speak to him. Nathan professed his innocence, offering up the alibi he had already given to Crowe. Leopold was surprised that Richard hadn't told police how they had spent the afternoon and evening of May 21 drinking and picking up girls. "Tell him to remember what happened on Wednesday," Nathan urged Mayer.

Mayer rushed off and found Richard at a police station near Kenwood. He told Loeb that he'd just come from seeing Leopold, who wanted Richard to tell the truth about what they had done on May 21.[28] Soon, Loeb repeated the same story as his friend about drinking and trying to pay two girls for sex.

Word soon got out that police had taken the sons of two of Chicago's wealthiest families into custody. The *Daily Tribune* seemed astonished that Leopold, the "nineteen-year-old student marvel, son of a millionaire," was being held in the kidnapping and murder of Bobby Franks. As for Loeb, the newspaper insisted that, although he had been taken in for questioning, "suspicion was in no way directed against him."[29]

"In Nathan Leopold and Richard Loeb, the University of Chicago students on whom the shadow of the Franks murder mystery fell today," reported the *Chicago Daily News,* "the police and the state's attorney's staff have a type entirely new to them—a baffling type, too agile intellectually to be handled as bootleggers and bandits and confidence men are handled. Inquisitors skilled at talking secrets out of sharp gangsters couldn't dent the bland assurance of Leopold . . . and Loeb, his little less prodigious chum."[30]

One reporter briefly interviewed Nathan's father, who said, "While it is a terrible ordeal both to my boy and myself to have him under even a possibility of suspicion, yet our attitude will be one of helping the investigation rather than retarding it. And even though my son is subjected to hardships and embarrassment of being kept from his family until the authorities are thoroughly satisfied . . . yet my son should be willing to make the sacrifice and I am also willing for the sake of justice and truth. . . . The suggestion that he had anything to do with this case is too absurd to merit comment." Nathan's brother Mike dismissed it as "too silly to discuss. The family is not particularly alarmed for we know just what he did the night the Franks boy disappeared; we know just how he occupied his time and we know that he can account of himself. If he can help any in solving the crime so much the better. We know so well where he was that night, we know our brother so well, that are in no way alarmed at his examination by the police."[31] And Richard's mother Anna Loeb assured a reporter, "We have absolute confidence that Richard is telling the truth. The implication that either he or the young Leopold are involved in the Franks case is impossible on its face. No matter the circumstances of the spectacles, the idea of connecting them with the crime is absurd."[32]

But the noose was slowly tightening and would be stretched taut through the actions of reporters Mulroy and Goldstein. They learned that Nathan belonged to a small study group of law students, and that he regularly typed up notes, which they called "dope sheets," so that they could prepare for examinations.[33] The two reporters found student Arnold Maremont, who offered them copies of these typed notes. Maremont also recalled that once Nathan had used a different, portable typewriter from his usual Hammond in preparing a set of notes.[34]

Goldstein took Maremont's notes back to the *Daily News,* which asked Hugh Sutton, the expert working for the Royal Typewriter Company, to compare them against the ransom letter. Sutton saw that one set of typewritten notes looked different from the others, suggesting that they had been composed on a different machine. On close inspection, he was sure that the typeface on the ransom letter and on this set of Maremont's notes was identical. One typewriter had produced both documents.[35]

The two reporters ran to state's attorney Robert Crowe with this damning information. Although it was a Friday evening, Crowe had several of the law students immediately called into his office and questioned them in Leopold's presence: each remembered that at least once Nathan had used a portable typewriter to compose the study notes. Nathan tried to deny it. Finally, he admitted that he might once have used a portable typewriter, but insisted that it wasn't his: instead, he'd borrowed from his friend Leon Mandel who, unfortunately, was away in Europe. And so once again police escorted Nathan back to his house, this time to search for the machine. No one could find a portable typewriter, but Captain Shoemacher reminded maid Elizabeth Sattler of her comment that she had seen one in the library a few weeks earlier. "I think you must be mistaken, Elizabeth," Nathan shot back, but by now the evidence that he had until recently had a portable typewriter was overwhelming.[36]

Authorities were surprisingly indulgent in their treatment of Leopold and Loeb. They were allowed to meet privately with family members, who brought them fresh clothing and linens for their beds; officials took them out to dinner at the Drake Hotel; and they even let the pair speak freely to the press.[37] "I don't blame the police for holding me," Nathan told a reporter from the *Daily Tribune* that Friday evening. "I was at the culvert the Saturday and Sunday before the glasses were found and it is quite possible I lost my glasses there. I'm sorry this happened only because it will worry my family. But I'll certainly be glad to do what I can to help the police."[38]

But Crowe's suspicions against the pair had escalated. He was particularly interested in the first of the two, strange letters Leopold had written to Loeb that police had found in Richard's bedroom. Dated October 9, 1923, it referred to "our former relations," and was full of threats. Leopold complained that Loeb had betrayed him. But it was Nathan's hint that if they publicly fought it would be put down to "a falling out of a pair of cocksuckers" that most intrigued Crowe.[39] Leopold had told police that he and Loeb had spent the evening of May 21 picking up two girls so that they could have sex with them. This letter suggested that Leopold and Loeb were gay. Something wasn't right.

The state's attorney questioned Richard about this letter. Richard put it down to a rumor that had gone around about them. "We did everything in our power to avoid any possible scandal," he explained, adding, "we were very careful never to be seen alone together."[40]

Crowe then tried with Nathan, slowly circling in on his sexuality. Leopold said that he read Sappho, Havelock Ellis, and Oscar Wilde, but he denied that he had ever "committed any acts of perversion" with Loeb. Crowe then asked Leopold about the letter. Nathan tried to explain away the reference by claiming that all of his friends called each other "cocksucker."[41]

"I have heard of 'son of a bitch' being used as a term of endearment," Crowe said, "but I have never heard a man call another man a 'cocksucker.' Is it the habit among you boys to call each other 'cocksucker?'"

"Sure," Leopold insisted.[42]

It was a talk late Friday night that finally ended the investigation. Leopold family chauffeur Sven Englund wanted to help his boss's son. Employed by the family since 1906, Englund lived with his wife Alma and their young daughter in an apartment above the Leopold garage, caring for five cars—a Packard, two Lincolns, and two Willys-Knights. He had spent much of May 21, the day of Bobby's kidnapping, working on the brakes of Nathan's distinctive red Willys-Knight. The car hadn't left the garage; Nathan, he therefore reasoned, couldn't have been involved in the crime. Englund told this to Crowe's assistant Bert Cronson, thinking that the information would set the young man free. Englund didn't know that Nathan had already told police he had spent that Wednesday afternoon in his own car with Richard, driving around, drinking, and picking up girls. Cronson asked if the man was absolutely certain about the date. Englund was—his wife had taken their sick daughter to the doctor and had a prescription filled that Wednesday afternoon. Englund's wife still had the bottle with the date on it. And he remembered that on May 22, he had found Leopold and Loeb attempting to clean some stains from the seats and floorboards of a different car, one he hadn't seen before.[43]

Cronson rushed to Crowe and told him of Englund's account. After spending time with both young men, Crowe decided that Loeb was the weaker of the pair, and the most likely to crack under pressure. He stepped into the room where Richard sat. The Leopold chauffeur, he said, had just come in and told how he had worked on the brakes of

Nathan's car on May 21. Was he lying? "Yes, he is a liar or mistaken," Richard replied.[44]

Richard was visibly nervous. Crowe left the room and sent in Joseph Sbarbaro. "Why are you holding me here for?" Richard asked.

"You realize you are in custody, do you not?" Sbarbaro said.

"Yes," Richard replied. "You haven't got anything on me, you are not asking me anything about this, and what are you keeping me here for?"

Sbarbaro then struck. Authorities knew that Richard and Nathan had lied about their alibi for May 21; the pair had a second car that day. The glasses near the body belonged to Nathan; the ransom note matched a portable typewriter Nathan had once used; and his handwriting matched that on the ransom envelope.[45]

"My God, my God," Richard cried. "This is terrible." He turned pale. Shaking, he burst into tears and slumped in his chair.[46] After a few minutes, Richard asked to speak with Crowe: over the next hour, he confessed that he and Nathan Leopold had kidnapped and killed Bobby Franks.

After hearing Richard's story, Crowe walked into the room where Nathan was being held. Leopold remained unbowed, cocky. He eyed Crowe and said, "Let me ask you a hypothetical question. Supposing John Doe had committed this murder, and John Doe's family was as wealthy and influential as mine is and could hire able lawyers and get a friendly judge and bribe the jury—don't you think he could beat it?"

"Well Nathan," Crowe replied, "I will let you try to find out."

"What do you mean?"

"I'm going to charge you with murder," Crowe told him.

Nathan looked at him incredulously. "Why," he exclaimed, "you don't have anything on me except some flimsy circumstances, and that will never do."

"You don't know, Nathan Leopold," Crowe shot back, "your pal Dick Loeb is telling the details of this murder, do you?"

"No, my God, he is not doing that," Leopold insisted. "He would stand til Hell freezes over!"[47]

Crowe then pulled the trigger: Loeb had described everything in detail: how they had established a fake identity to rent a car; how they had rented rooms at hotels to further the charade; how they had cruised around looking for a victim; and how they had kidnapped and killed Bobby. Leopold turned red in anger. "I was stunned," Nathan later insisted. "I couldn't think; my world lay in fragments at my feet."[48] But at the time he seemed unnaturally calm about it all. He slowly lit up a cigarette, inhaled deeply, looked at Crowe, and said coldly, "Well, if Loeb is talking, I will tell you the real truth."[49]

Bobby's killers had been caught.

PART II

UNLIKELY KILLERS

CHAPTER FIVE

EARLY ON THE MORNING OF SATURDAY, MAY 31, 1924, STATE'S ATTORNEY Robert Crowe stood before the gaggle of reporters who had collected on hearing the news that the sons of two of Chicago's wealthiest citizens were being questioned in the murder of Bobby Franks. They expected an update; instead, they got a shock. "The Franks murder mystery," Crowe told them, "has been solved. The murderers are in custody. Nathan Leopold and Richard Loeb have completely and voluntarily confessed."[1]

The news broke over Chicago like a sudden storm. Crowe selectively gave out portions of the two confessions that left the city stunned. The idea that these two brilliant young men, who had everything in life that their fathers' money could provide, would kidnap and murder a boy was shocking. That they had selected Richard's second cousin as a victim was even more chilling. The utter randomness was underlined by the apparent lack of any real motive. The pair seemed to have committed their crime merely for a thrill. It had all been some kind of twisted game, so cold-blooded and beyond comprehension that many assumed that Leopold and Loeb must be insane.

Newspapers and radio broadcasts reported every stray fact, every bizarre assertion, creating the first criminal media circus of the modern age. While denouncing interest in the case as prurient, they printed up the latest gossip, the newest developments, and the most sensational details in efforts to satiate the seemingly unending public appetite for news about the crime and its perpetrators. The *Chicago Herald and Examiner* reported: "In that conspiracy and plot, devoid of every vestige of impulsiveness, every mitigating grace of expediency or passion, the talents of these two combined in what authorities of the law call the most cold-blooded and motiveless crime that has ever found mention in the pages of records or of history."[2]

The rival *Chicago Daily Tribune,* noting that "Loeb as the name of a murderer falls strangely on Chicago ears," described the few known facts: "The diabolical spirit evinced in the planned kidnapping and murder; the wealth and prominence of the families whose sons are involved; the high mental attainments of the youths, the suggestions of perversion; the strange quirks indicated in the confession that the child was slain for ransom, for experience, for the satisfaction of a desire for 'deep plotting,' combine to set the case in a class by itself. . . . Were they bored by a life which left them nothing to be desired, no obstacles to overcome, no goal to attain? Were they jaded by the jazz life of gin and girls, so that they needed so terrible a thing as murder to give them new thrills?"[3]

The reactions from the three families most concerned—the Leopolds, the Loebs, and the Franks—mingled disbelief with horror. To reporters gathered outside his house and through his tears, Nathan's father insisted that it was "impossible, ridiculous, Nathan—my boy, my boy—I can't believe it, I won't believe it."[4] It was, he declared, "a lie" that Nathan had confessed, adding, "that boy can not be guilty."[5] The Loeb family, too, protested that Richard was "innocent, and confessed merely to get some sleep. It can be refuted when he comes to trial." Albert Loeb's boss, Sears president Julius Rosenwald, said he was stunned: "It does not seem possible that two boys, with so much money at their command, should do a thing like this, especially for the motive assigned to them." And Loeb's university friend Richard Rubel declared, "It's a damned lie! I'm Dick Loeb's best friend, and he couldn't have done it. For a ransom? Why, these boys could have had all the money in the world! Why would they do that?"⁶

Across Ellis Avenue from the Loeb mansion, reporters heard different sentiments from Bobby's father. "I am relieved a bit to know who killed my boy and how he was murdered," he said. "I can't, however, understand it. Why did they do it? What could have possessed them to kill my boy, except that they are murderers at heart? Think of the smallness of it—to take my son's life for $10,000—and they were heirs to millions. If a poor man did such a kind of thing, one might say he was influenced by circumstances, but these boys, with nothing to crave for, why should they commit such a heinous crime? Young Leopold has said there is no God. He now will know there must be. He has said he is an atheist. He will now realize that God alone could have caused him to drop those glasses that the murderer of my boy might be discovered." As far as he was concerned, Jacob declared, "No punishment would be too severe for them. They are fiends. I can't see how any jury, court, or even the president could release them, the act was so atrocious. . . . They ought to hang." When asked if his wife shared his opinion, Jacob quietly said that she still seemed to be in shock. "She keeps saying that our baby isn't dead," he told the reporters. "She keeps saying that they are only hiding him. She believes that Robert will come back to her."⁷

Jacob Franks didn't know the Loebs well: despite the fact that his wife and Richard's mother were first cousins, they never really socialized, and he had only a passing acquaintance with the Leopolds. But all three families lived within four blocks of one another. Like most neighborhoods, Kenwood was not immune from gossip, and there had long been gossip about Leopold and Loeb. No one suspected that they were criminals, but they wore reputations for being "fast." "I know my son would never have grown up to be like those boys," Jacob Franks commented. "Those boys were not brought up rightly. They were given too much freedom. For two years it was common gossip in the neighborhood that they drank and ran about at all hours of the day and night."⁸

———

NATHAN FREUDENTHAL LEOPOLD JR., WAS born on November 19, 1904, the third and last child of his namesake father and his mother, the former Florence Foreman. The senior Nathan, forty-five at the time, was the millionaire owner of the Morris Paper Company and the Fiber Can Corporation. A quiet, reserved man of even temper, he had married the daughter of a wealthy Chicago banker and fellow member of the city's German-Jewish elite in 1892. People recalled Florence Leopold as gentle and loving, a woman who, like her husband, devoted herself to various Jewish charities.[9] "Happiness," Florence once said, "is a perfume you cannot sprinkle on others without getting a few drops on yourself."[10]

Nathan and Florence Leopold already had two sons, Foreman Michael, called Mike, born in 1895, and Samuel Nathan, born in 1900, when the third arrived in 1904. They named the baby Nathan Freudenthal Leopold Jr., but he was always called by the nickname "Babe." "No one," he later wrote, "ever called me Nathan except my mother," and then only when she was about to scold him.[11]

Florence's health declined after Nathan was born—there had been previous miscarriages and during her last pregnancy she contracted nephritis. She never recovered her health and was often confined to bed.[12] The boy worshipped her, calling her "an extremely feminine little lady," someone who was, he said, "patient and saintly."[13] But even had Florence been well, Nathan would largely have been brought up by a succession of nurses and nannies, following the custom practiced by wealthy families of the time.

Nathan's relationship with his father was cordial but not close. Nathan Sr. was consumed with business affairs and had little time for his children. He was present, but absent as a real influence in his son's life. This might have been a blessing, for the father treated Nathan differently from his other sons. "I was a little something of an ugly duckling," the younger Nathan recalled, adding that his father "used to kid me quite a lot."[14] No matter how lighthearted this may have been, the comments undoubtedly affected the sensitive young boy. Perhaps not surprisingly, Nathan later admitted that he loved his mother more than he did his father.[15]

The young Nathan Leopold was a precocious baby and an even more precocious child. "Ever since I can remember," he later said, "I have heard how bright I was."[16] He supposedly uttered his first words at four months; was walking by fourteen months; and said his first prayer in German, "*Ich bin klein, mein herz ist rein*" ("I am small, my heart is pure"), at the age of three.[17]

When Nathan was five, a new governess entered the household, an Irish Catholic girl named Paula. She found him a most peculiar boy and later spoke of his pronounced "meanness." Nathan kept largely to himself. Early on he engaged in some petty thefts, stealing stamps he wanted from an album belonging to one of his few playmates.[18] He apparently found the experience exciting; he would get an occasional thrill by stealing fruit from a restaurant, or by taking his brother Mike's neckties and trading them for cigar bands. Mike suspected as much and confronted his brother, but Nathan saw nothing wrong with what he had done, saying, "It's my business."[19]

The boy became obsessed with ornithology. At the age of five Nathan began studying the birds in trees outside his window. His father bought him a gun and Nathan spent hours shooting them, not for sport but so that he could collect and inspect their bodies; later he learned taxidermy and began preserving what would eventually become a collection of some three thousand birds. Although he was keenly interested in the scientific aspects, Nathan's hobby became so consuming as to seem pathological. Pauline Van den Bosch, who claimed to have worked as a nanny in the Leopold household, later said that Nathan "had a mania for killing" the defenseless animals, perhaps suggestive of some latent, violent tendencies and a desire to exert control over living things. Once he carelessly shot at a bird in a neighbor's yard and just missed hitting one of their servants; when Pauline scolded him, Nathan replied, "I should give a damn!"[20]

Florence, Nathan said, "detested" his hobby of killing birds. His mother, he recalled, "didn't like animals or butterflies or birds, but she had three boys, always bringing frogs or white mice or chameleons home. Dad was a great believer in boys should be boys—a gun, a dog, fishing, hunting, you know. Mother could have done without all that. . . . I carried things to an extreme. I turned the house into a museum."[21]

Small and weak for his age, Nathan began his education just before he turned six, when he was enrolled at Miss Spaide's School in November 1910. This had once been a coeducational facility, but by the time Nathan arrived there was only one other boy among the pupils.[22] Attending what amounted to a girls' school led to Nathan being teased and ridiculed by the few playmates he had.[23]

All in all, this first year outside the house proved miserable. Thinking that a change would help, Nathan's father enrolled him in the Douglas Public School. Instead, Nathan faltered. The fact that a governess took him to and from school every day further emphasized that he was somehow different—"I realized I was not like other children," he later recalled. The governess even forbade Nathan from using the bathroom at school; this resulted in at least one humiliating episode in which he wet his pants while sitting in the classroom.[24] His mother, or so he later thought, disliked him associating with "Negros and tough boys," and Nathan soon returned to Miss Spaide's School.[25]

Nathan was nearly eight when he returned to the Douglas School. He was more advanced than his classmates, and a teacher arranged for him to skip a grade. This again marked him out as different. Nathan had no interest in sports, and he was bullied relentlessly.[26] "He was smart and smart-alecky," a childhood acquaintance later said. "He wasn't a boy's boy. He didn't go out and play tennis and football, didn't go fishing. Most boys thought he was crazy."[27]

Nathan found it difficult to make friends. He wanted to break free of his loneliness but held back, fearing that he would only get hurt.[28] Nathan later insisted that he felt inferior, deeply insecure, and was extremely sensitive to criticism.[29] Despising his weakness, more and more he turned inward, preferring the company of books to that of people and attempting to suppress his emotions—something his parents insisted upon. No one, Nathan later recalled, ever saw his mother "weep in public," while his father "criticized open displays of emotion."[30]

With his family's money and his own intellect, Nathan felt himself superior to others, and he began putting those beliefs into practice. A sense of grandiosity fed ideas that he deserved special attention and treatment—it explained why he didn't fit in with others. Insecurity drove Nathan into his self-imposed, hardened shell: he repressed his emotions, adopting a brittle veneer to conceal his insecurities. He cared little about others except when they were useful to him. Nathan largely treated the rest of humanity with contempt. He belittled those he deemed less intelligent, was prone to sarcastic remarks, and made no attempt to disguise his arrogance.[31]

In 1915, the Leopold family moved to Chicago's Kenwood district. Their new house, at 4754 South Greenwood Avenue, had been built in 1886 by Charles Van Kirk, one of the founders of the Chicago Board of Trade.[32] It was a handsome residence, vaguely Tudor in style, of two stories topped by a steeply pitched gabled roof and ringed by porches. If not quite a mansion, it was a capacious and comfortable home, a quietly impressive statement that the Leopold family had achieved much in life.

Once ensconced in the new house, Nathan entered the nearby Harvard School, having already skipped several grades. He did well academically, but socially he remained an outcast. His father later complained that he was too rebellious, that he rejected "moral obligations," and refused to conform to expectations.[33] No one, it seems, could understand this strange young boy.

THERE WAS TURMOIL IN THE Leopold household, trauma unseen and unsuspected by Nathan's parents. In 1910, his family had hired a new governess, an Alsatian woman named Mathilda Wantz. Called Sweetie within the household, she began the position speaking only German. Since this was one of the two languages Nathan had spoken since childhood, he helped tutor her in English. The first phrase he taught Wantz was "Go to hell," which he explained meant "good morning."[34]

Mathilda Wantz was both suspicious and jealous, often complaining to Nathan and his brother Sam about other servants in the household. She especially resented the invalid Florence Leopold, and she did all in her power to drive a wedge between mother and the two sons in her care. "She had a very great influence over my brother and myself," Nathan later said. "She displaced my mother. She was a scheming woman who used the children as a barrier to shield herself."[35]

The damage was not limited to maternal alienation. At some point, Wantz began sexually abusing both Sam and Nathan. She regularly played with Sam's penis; Nathan claimed that he didn't recall such episodes but assumed that he had also been abused. She took the boys into her bathtub and flaunted her nude body in front of them, asking them to examine her closely, especially her breasts and her nipples. Wantz often wrestled naked with the boys and took a perverse delight in showing Sam and Nathan her used sanitary napkins. Soon, she convinced Nathan to strip and lay on top of her while she was facedown on the mattress, telling him to rub his penis between her legs.[36]

This sordid situation lasted until Nathan was twelve. One day, the ailing Florence went to visit her sons and found Wantz treating them roughly. Florence dismissed her on the spot.[37]

Apparently neither brother ever mentioned the abuse to anyone, especially their parents. Shame likely played its part, but the silence also suggests something of the dynamic within the Leopold household, where emotions were suppressed, unpleasant situations ignored, and a sense of isolation—at least where Nathan was concerned—hung heavily over the situation. His parents were unaware of what was happening beneath their own roof—his mother too ill and his father too consumed with business to pay much attention. Beyond this, Nathan seems to have had little in the way of family support at home. With a ten-year age gap between them, Nathan and his older brother Mike weren't especially close at the time. Indeed, Mike spent most of his time with their mutual cousin Adolph Ballenger, called "Bal" in the family, who moved into the house in 1911 after his widowed father died. And Nathan's relationship with Sam was always strained; perhaps they regarded their shared molestation as taboo and it is possible that it drove a wedge between them emotionally.

It is impossible to know how much this sexual abuse fueled Nathan's aloof manner. But it introduced him to a subject that was to dominate much of his life: sex.[38] He gradually came to realize that he preferred men to women—he later admitted that he had "never been attracted toward the opposite sex."[39] It would be a half century before Illinois decriminalized sodomy, and another decade beyond that before homosexuality lost its classification as a mental illness by the American Psychiatric Association, too late to inform Nathan's views of himself. He understood only that he was different, a "degenerate" with "shameful" sexual desires.

In 1916, at the age of eleven, Nathan attended a summer camp where he developed a crush on an older instructor. William was a "well-developed . . . very good-looking boy of eighteen," and Nathan began fantasizing about him. A year later, Nathan had his first gay experience. A boy named Henry taught Nathan how to masturbate; at first Nathan just watched, standing by with a jar—he wanted to save his friend's semen. Soon, Nathan was staying over at Henry's house and regularly masturbating him; apparently Henry returned the favor.[40]

For Nathan, a new and powerful world had opened up, and he began masturbating several times a day, although he felt inferior for giving in to his desires.[41] He idolized "large, muscular or beautiful" young men like those depicted in clothing advertisements from the Hart Schaffner & Marx company.[42]

Thanks to Henry, Nathan found a new outlet for his sexuality. The two formed a secret club and brought in a slightly younger neighborhood boy named Joe. This allowed Nathan to indulge in yet another of his secret desires. His fantasies were aggressive and violent. Now, with Joe, he introduced "a certain sadistic element" into his sexual interaction. He started by tying up Joe—Nathan liked the idea of having control over someone else—and masturbating him against his will, committing sexual assault. Soon, Nathan hit on a new way to inflict pain. He knew a boy who had accidentally spilled muscle liniment on his penis and who complained of how painful it had been. The idea appealed tremendously to Nathan, and he repeated the procedure on a helpless Joe, enjoying his agony.[43]

Nathan seems to have had an innate ability to seek out and befriend companions who apparently shared his desires or, at the very least, would not object to them; if they did, he simply dropped them. At fifteen, Nathan met regularly with a group of seven or eight friends so that they could masturbate each other. He was surprised to learn that not all boys were circumcised. He thought that being circumcised marked him out as different and, when given the choice, he preferred to be with boys who were not circumcised.[44]

Aggression, restraint, assaults, humiliation, and infliction of pain: Nathan linked violence with sexual satisfaction. He later admitted that he spent hours thinking up ways to torture those he disliked; his disturbed mind was always quick to seize on the gruesome details of famous crimes.[45] These scenarios began consuming Nathan' thoughts. He was especially interested in crucifying someone—"the idea of nailing anybody to something appealed to me tremendously," he later said.[46] Early in life, he began indulging in a peculiar fantasy about domination and submission in which one person acted as king and the other as slave. In nearly all of these variations, Nathan later admitted, he was the king, not the slave.[47] In his burgeoning sexual dreams, he fantasized about making William, his former camp counselor, a slave, and whenever he met a good-looking boy, he envisioned becoming his master.[48] At times he even dreamed about capturing boys and making them his slaves; he spoke of wanting to brand them on their calves and envisioned such humiliations taking place in the locker room at the Harvard School.[49]

Even when Nathan fantasized that he was a slave to a handsome man, he cast himself as exceptional. In these fevered sexual dreams, he pictured himself as endowed with all that he lacked in reality: he was desired, powerful and strong, always selected to do battle against other slaves and always the victor in conflicts.[50] He never envisioned himself as truly submissive. Instead, he had to be dominant, the silent power controlling the apparent master and skillfully shaping people to his way of thinking.

In 1920, at the age of fifteen, Nathan finished his senior year at the Harvard School. He remained an outcast. His classmates called him, "Flea," a not-so-subtle reference to his small size and reputation as an annoying pest. Even the Harvard yearbook humiliated the boy deemed "the crazy bird of the school." He was, it reported, the "crazed genius," "forever harping on birds," best summed up by the quote, "Of course, I am the great Nathan. When I open my lips let no dog bark!"[51]

Even if true friends were missing, Nathan did have a small circle of acquaintances, proving that he was capable of relationships, at least with other boys. But there were no crushes on girls, and very few of the awkward teenage dates that his classmates braved—and then only because he felt he had to do so for the sake of appearances. In the spring of 1920, a fellow student took pity on him, bringing Nathan along on an expedition to pick up some girls and have sex with them. The experience proved to be humiliating. A girl agreed to have sex with him in the back of a car for three dollars; Nathan tried, but he couldn't get an erection, and the girl was sent packing. Nathan swore his companion to secrecy, but he was left embarrassed.[52]

Nathan entered the University of Chicago that autumn, with an intended triple major in English, Latin, and psychology.[53] Most students avoided Nathan, and he returned the favor, alienated and alienating in his behavior. Even his father found him off-putting. Nathan got into trouble—minor trouble to be sure—fairly regularly, being cited for breaking game laws, shooting birds illegally, and even speeding in his parents' cars. His father always stepped in and paid the fines.[54] But the pattern irritated: Nathan's father supposedly thought him too arrogant for his own good. Rather than counsel against this tendency, though, Nathan Leopold Sr. deployed a more subtle weapon, down-playing his son's actual accomplishments as a way to check his sense of superiority.[55]

He was an enigmatic young man, this Nathan Leopold Jr. He seemed polite, mild-mannered if too serious, someone whose peculiarity seemed more amusing than dangerous. Photographs capture a sly or mocking look in his eyes, hinting at the turmoil within. The burdens of life—familial alienation, sexual abuse by an overbearing mother figure, and social isolation—mingled together in a mind consumed with sadistic sexual fantasies, cruelty to animals, lack of empathy, and a belief in his own superiority, creating a powder keg of suppressed emotions simmering just below the surface. It was this haughty, volatile young man who, at the age of fifteen, met another young man whose destiny he was bound to share: Richard Loeb.

CHAPTER SIX

A MERE THREE BLOCKS SEPARATED THE LEOPOLD AND LOEB HOUSES IN Kenwood. In 1910—the same year that Richard's father Albert sold the lot across the street to Jacob Franks—the Loebs commissioned prominent Chicago architect Arthur Heun to design a new house at 5017 Ellis Avenue.[1] Sitting on a spacious plot occupying the modern equivalent of a city block and ringed by a brick wall, the Loeb residence evoked Elizabethan pretensions: ivy-covered walls and leaded glass windows, with tall chimneys erupting from its steeply pitched slate roofs. Dwarfing neighboring residences, the Loeb mansion, as well as the family's social status and their wealth, made the Leopolds seem positively middle class by comparison.

Like the Leopolds, the Loeb family had come from Germany to Chicago after the Revolutions of 1848. Born in 1868, Albert Loeb studied at Johns Hopkins University before returning to Chicago, where he was admitted to the bar and partnered with Sidney Adler practicing corporate law.[2] In 1901, Julius Rosenwald, a fellow wealthy member of Chicago's German-Jewish elite and co-owner of Sears, Roebuck & Company, hired Loeb to serve as corporate secretary. The occasionally abrasive Rosenwald increasingly relied on the "calm and easygoing" Loeb, and in 1908 Albert became vice president of the growing company. It was Albert who instituted what was, at the time, a unique idea: a profit-sharing plan with the company's employees.[3] As catalog sales skyrocketed, the money poured in: by 1924, at least according to rumor, Albert had amassed a personal fortune of nearly $10 million.[4]

People described Albert Loeb as "a prince among men."[5] Indeed, the only scandal stemmed from his 1894 marriage. Anna Bohnen was the daughter of a German immigrant of modest means and had once worked as a secretary; she was also Catholic and refused to convert to Judaism. There were unkind whispers that Albert was marrying beneath him, that he was betraying his religion, and that his new wife had only wed him for his money.[6]

On June 11, 1905, Anna gave birth to her third child. They named him Richard Albert Loeb, but he was always called "Dick" or "Dickie" in the family. There were already two older sons, eight-year-old Allan and five-year-old Ernest; the youngest, Thomas, called Tommy, would be born in 1914. On the surface they seemed a happy, close-knit family; Albert's father, Moritz, had regularly beaten him, and he wanted his own children to love, not fear, him. But he was also distant: consumed with business, he didn't play with his sons and saw them rarely.[7]

Anna Loeb had certain expectations for her children. "The Loeb home," noted a contemporary account, "has been noted for its high standards of virtue and culture and a place where the task of bringing up children was viewed with unusual seriousness."[8] But, like many society women, Anna largely left the care of her children to others, and her relationship with Richard was somewhat distant—he never went to her for anything. One of Richard's early nurses insisted that Anna "never knew how sweet and good he was like I did. She never cared for him."[9]

This benign neglect preyed on young Richard's mind. He was convinced that his family didn't really care for him; he felt inferior and said that he couldn't really confide to anyone in the house.[10] He later complained that his parents never understood him or gave him much affection. They favored, he thought, his older brothers Allan and Ernest, who in turn pointedly excluded him from their activities.[11] Feeling pushed aside and ignored, he stumbled along, desperate for attention and validation.

He got both in 1910, when Richard's parents hired a new governess. Anna Struthers was thirty-six, the daughter of Scottish immigrants to Canada, when she took the position in the Loeb household.[12] But the attention came at a steep price as Struthers introduced her own un-balanced ideas into the Loeb mansion. She had little understanding of children and was extremely possessive of her young charge. Struthers wanted her influence to be total: she reinforced Richard's sense of alienation from his family, telling him that the Loebs preferred their other sons and that his brothers treated him badly. She even attempted to turn Richard against his mother.[13] Struthers usually forbid Richard from playing with others, thinking that they might corrupt him. "As a boy," he said, "I was kept under and did not do the things other boys did."[14] Extremely critical, she was always on the lookout for perceived errors on Richard's part.[15] The young boy learned to obey her—"to the minute—second," he later said. "Her word was law."[16]

Convinced that she could shape Richard into an ideal young man, Struthers constantly pushed him beyond all reasonable expecta-tions: he was to achieve more, advance farther, and outshine all other boys. A great future lay in store for him, she would say—perhaps he would be an ambassador—but only if he followed her direction. "I think she was so anxious for me to develop into the type of boy she wanted that she overdid it," Richard later reflected.[17]

Struthers never used corporal punishment, but she freely expressed her displeasure when Richard didn't meet her high expectations. She complained that he was selfish—how much of this behavior stemmed from his own insecurities or from Struthers's oppressive rule isn't known.[18] Richard never rebelled. He seems to have learned to please and to appease, whether it was his parents or his governess. With his malleable personality, he likely avoided uncomfortable situations and confrontations. Compliance and accommodation seem to have be-come deeply ingrained traits that would dominate his life.[19] But he also learned that he could lie—and lie skillfully—to evade any punishments.[20]

Richard entered the third grade at the University of Chicago Elementary School when he was seven: early lessons had left him more advanced than others his same age. Loath to lose any control, Struthers walked him to school every day; she filled his afternoons and evenings with even more lessons. Richard's activities had to be useful: in 1915, he founded his own journal, *Richard's Magazine,* which his father paid to have published. *Richard's Magazine* lasted for only two issues, but its content was revealing.[21] A year into the Great War, Richard wrote: "Daily millions of dollars are being spent in the purchase of ammunition and weapons. Think if that amount of money was spent daily in the beautifying of the world. Think if all the lives that had been lost in this war could have been spent in peaceful labor and happiness. . . . Think if Chicago was bombarded. Would not as many women and children die in the attack? Would not as many neutral foreigners die? The aeroplanes cannot pick out the men they are warring against. Such is war in the twentieth century."[22]

Albert Loeb showed a copy to Julius Rosenwald, who in turn sent it to former president Theodore Roosevelt. Roosevelt was duly impressed, dispatching a letter to Richard in May 1916: "It does me good to see young men of your stamp growing up in this country."[23]

EVEN WHEN IT CAME TO reading for pleasure, Richard couldn't pursue his own interests. Struthers selected his books, and her tastes ran to history and historical fiction like *Quo Vadis* and *Ben-Hur,* although she occasionally stretched to include the works of Charles Dickens and Thackeray, with their moral lessons. Books, she insisted, must educate, or advance him academically.[24] Richard quietly resented this constant pressure; rather than protest, he began sneaking books from his older brothers' rooms—popular mysteries and the Sherlock Holmes series—that offered escape from his regimented existence.[25]

Perhaps there was a special allure to such tales because they were forbidden, but Richard soon discovered an affinity for detective stories. These weren't tomes filled with hard-boiled criminals, bloody murders, and rough-and-tumble investigators but rather light mysteries. Among them was Maurice Leblanc's 1910 novel *813,* which featured the author's famous gentleman thief and detective Arséne Lupin using his wits to solve a case of international espionage. Equally fascinating was Wyndham Martyn's Anthony Trent, a character whose adventures first appeared in serialized form in popular magazines and then in several books. Trent, an intelligent but bored young man, becomes a master criminal out of a desire to pit his wits against those of the police.[26]

But of all these gentleman criminals, Richard was most captivated by Frank Packard's character Jimmie Dale.[27] Dale lived a double life: wealthy young man by day, the Grey Seal by night, Dale broke into homes, opened safes, and committed other offenses but being a gentleman, he never took anything. His crimes were undertaken only for the excitement, for the challenge of committing them and then escaping detection. These mysteries and detective stories were so popular that Dale, like Lupin, even appeared as a character in several films between 1917 and 1920.

Richard began fantasizing about crimes, and he soon translated dreams into reality. He followed random people—he called it "shadowing"—on the street, observing their movements as he played detective.[28] When he was nine Richard stole some money from a neighborhood boy; it was the idea that he alone knew what had happened, not the meager financial windfall, that proved most exciting.[29] One day, Richard and John Abt, a friend from school, visited a nearby shop. When they left, Richard revealed that he'd stolen a few small items of no real value—"to show me how smart he was," Abt thought.[30] This became a pattern: secretly pocketing pencils or dental floss from a store, Richard said, gave him "a tremendous thrill."[31] He stole the proceeds from a lemonade stand he briefly ran with another boy, and once joined a neighbor boy in taking a silver vase from a nearby house.[32]

Richard was careful to avoid detection, but he later admitted that the idea of being caught and punished was enticing. He pictured himself being arrested and thrown into prison, beaten by others.[33] "I was abused," he said, "but it was a very pleasant thought. . . . I enjoyed being looked at through the bars, because I was a famous criminal."[34]

What to make of this peculiar behavior? Like many others, Richard was captivated by the exploits of masked avengers and gentlemen thieves; there wasn't anything unusual in this. Nor were his crimes particularly striking: he probably committed more than his share of childhood thefts, but this sort of boyish delinquency wasn't terribly serious or even rare. He stole for no real gain or reason. Even his fantasies of arrest were immature. But it's likely that there were motivating factors behind it all, ones that even Richard didn't understand. He was desperate for excitement, and the thefts gave temporary escape from his rigidly controlled life. Perhaps he secretly hoped to be caught, even if it meant punishment: punishment would at least suggest that his parents cared about him, that they had some interest in his life. Rather than indicating some deep criminal psychosis, Richard's petty thefts and childish dreams may have been a subconscious cry for the attention—even unwelcome attention—that his parents denied him.

BY THE AGE OF TWELVE, in 1917, Richard had advanced through his studies at such a rapid pace that he entered the University of Chicago High School; this was Kenwood's other preparatory institution, a rival to the Harvard School. He struggled: Richard was a few years younger than his classmates and felt out of place, trying to act far more worldly than he really was—a student described him as "just a young punk."[35]

In time Richard settled in. He did well academically, and especially enjoyed history. For the first time he made real friends and joined several school clubs. As his popularity gradually increased, he began playing tennis and other sports with his new companions.[36] At times he seemed to be everywhere, a chameleon who dashed about, exchanging one persona for another at the drop of a hat. His entry in the school's annual *Correlator* reinforced this view: Richard, it declared, was "a drama in two acts," divided between the three characters he played,

Richard, Dick, and Dique. The first was a precocious student and afi-
cionado of fictional detective Arséne Lupin; the second was consumed
with his appearance and clothing; and the third was a languid, bored
youth who hoped to attend the Sorbonne in Paris.[37]

Struthers insisted that Richard accelerate his courses and complete
high school not in the usual four years but in two. Compliant as usual,
he pushed himself hard to achieve this unreasonable goal, taking extra credit courses in German and French, as well as correspondence
courses in history and in Latin.[38] He was also egged on by a promise
from his parents: if he graduated in two years, they told him, they
would reward him with a trip to Europe.[39]

Richard managed this academic feat, graduating from high school
in June 1919 at the age of fourteen. But disappointment soon followed. He'd fulfilled his end of the bargain, but when he mentioned
the promised holiday in Europe his parents suddenly declared that
they had changed their minds: there would be no trip. Whatever the
excuses offered—he was too young, it was too dangerous—Richard
likely took this turn of events as a betrayal, yet more evidence that his
parents didn't really care about him.[40]

The only reward came by accident. In the autumn of 1920 Richard
entered the University of Chicago at age fourteen. He was in college
now, too old to need a governess. Not wanting to dismiss Struthers, the
Loebs asked her to care for Richard's youngest brother, Tommy. But
still jealous of her relationship with Richard, Struthers refused, and the
Loebs let her go. That, at least, is the story they gave. But Struthers's
husband, lawyer Frank Bishop—whom she married on New Year's Eve
that same year—later claimed that she had been Albert Loeb's mistress,
and had tried to blackmail him.[41]

For the first time in a decade Richard was free of Struthers's overbearing influence—"when she left I sort of broke loose," he later
admitted.[42] But the University of Chicago proved to be a less than
pleasant experience for him. The curriculum was more demanding,
and he began to flail about. Instead of exceptional marks he satisfied himself with passing grades, having no taste and no discipline for

academic work. Richard took an interest only in those classes—like history—that spoke to his imagination.

Again thrust into an environment where he was several years younger than his classmates, Richard tried to prove himself: he later said that he "grew up overnight."[43] Attempting to fit in socially, Richard began spending time with older students, emulating their drinking in an effort to appear more mature. Having been denied most ordinary childhood experiences, he lost all sense of balance, gambling and playing cards with his new friends as one drunken evening passed into the next. Richard remained eager to please; although he took a leading role when it came to sports, he was happy to let others dominate. He treated his circle as elastic: it grew and shrank, as Richard quickly befriended people and then dropped them just as easily, although he was careful not to cause any hurt feelings. What he most wanted was to find one or two friends who would admire him, providing Richard with the attention and admiration he had never felt from his family.[44]

And then there was sex. Eleven-year-old Richard learned about sex not from his father or older brothers but from Leonard Tucker, the Loeb family's chauffeur.[45] He lost his virginity at fifteen, when a group of students from the University of Chicago took him to a brothel.[46] This left Richard with a case of gonorrhea; ashamed, he confided his plight to his eldest brother Allan, who secretly took Richard to a doctor for treatment so that their father wouldn't find out.[47]

The encounter probably informed Richard's ambivalent attitude about sex. Once cured, he again joined his friends as they sought out prostitutes or easily persuaded girls, but Richard had almost no interest in sex. "I could get along easily without it," he later admitted. "The actual sex act is rather unimportant to me."[48] Although Richard would occasionally brag about bedding his latest conquest, he secretly worried he might be impotent and often lied about encounters to disguise his lack of desire.[49]

———

CHARLEVOIX, NEAR LAKE MICHIGAN IN the northern part of the peninsula, had been a popular resort since the turn of the century, a place of sandy dunes, lazy stretches of water, open fields and deep forests. Summer brought refreshing breezes and the scent of pine wafting through the air. In 1917, Albert Loeb began buying up property just southeast of the town—eventually he held some 1,800 acres. He wanted a retreat where the family could escape the heat of Chicago summers, but he also envisioned developing a model farm, a place where he could raise cattle and horses and test machinery sold through Sears, Roebuck.

Loeb commissioned Arthur Heun, the same man who had built his Chicago mansion, to design the numerous farm buildings and the family summer house. There were enormous dairy and cattle barns, stables, a carriage house, and other structures meant to evoke the architecture of Normandy, with locally sourced fieldstone walls, steeply pitched roofs, and towers. Here, Albert raised prizewinning Holstein Friesian cows and Belgian draft horses, and sold butter, milk, and cream to the public on Sundays. Some ninety employees ran the complex; Loeb even built a school for their children and sponsored the farm's own softball team, called the Sodbusters.[50]

The Loeb mansion, also designed in a vaguely Norman style, crowned a hill above Pine Lake. The sprawling fieldstone house, built around an immense terrace, sported red tile roofs, loggias, and sleeping porches. The rooms within, replete with beamed ceilings and wrought iron chandeliers, evoked a kind of sparse, medieval majesty that contrasted with modern overstuffed chintz-covered sofas and wicker chairs.[51] Richard learned to sail on Pine Lake; he eventually became proficient enough that he often went out onto Lake Michigan and into the Straits of Mackinac, skillfully navigating the strong tides.[52]

The Loebs were the most prominent family to summer in Charlevoix and were greatly liked and respected for their economic contributions to the community. Richard became a well-known fixture in the area, and generally made good impressions: one local called him, "a swell kid even if he is a millionaire's son. . . . He is the most regular guy you ever knew."[53] But he also developed a bit of a reputation. A few neighbors called him "a kind of crazy kid . . . a little wild, a heavy drinker, a little noisy when he was happy."[54] He could be reckless, and there were several accidents when he went joyriding in one of the family's cars. In the summer of 1920 Richard had an accident at Charlevoix when his vehicle rammed into a horse and buggy one evening. The woman and her grandson in the buggy were injured, and Richard apparently struck his head during the impact. Still, he managed to help the pair from their carriage and escort them to a nearby hospital. Robert Bruce Armstrong, the doctor who treated him for a minor concussion, later recalled that Richard fainted several times during his examinations, probably from stress.[55]

Richard was back at the hospital the following morning, bringing the injured woman flowers, fruit, and packages of food. He visited every day, convinced his father to pay her hospital bill, and to send her on a trip to aid her recovery. He even asked his father to pay off her mortgage.[56] This suggests something of Richard's character. He'd always been sympathetic to the less fortunate. In 1916, after reading of the hardships endured by teachers in France during the Great War, he begged his father to send them seven hundred dollars.[57] He'd also donated his allowance to war relief charities.[58] His care of the woman after the Charlevoix accident fit in perfectly with perceptions of him as kind, considerate, and gentle, a thoughtful young man with a bright future ahead of him.

People in his family's circle all agreed. A friend of Richard's parents called him "one of the sweetest boys in the world. It was impossible to know him without being fond of him."[59] Yet he struggled to form meaningful relationships. He had never felt particularly close to his parents, and he carried this distant, cool approach over into other relationships. Richard had learned to please, but in the process lost himself, changing his personality by small degrees in attempts to connect with others, until he seemed more a collection of disparate parts rather than a whole person. Everything was shallow, a facade. No one really knew him well, knew of his loneliness, deep insecurities, and need for approval and affection. His disconcerting habit of cultivating and then abruptly dropping friends kept people from penetrating too deeply into his inner world.

Exactly when Nathan and Richard first met remains a mystery—they claimed they couldn't really remember. They seem to have always known of each other—"just barely" was how they described their association before 1920.[60] This isn't surprising. Both came from wealthy Jewish families and lived within three blocks of each other in the same Kenwood neighborhood. Their parents hadn't socialized, but the boys walked the same streets and probably shared some mutual friends.

But it wasn't until the fall of 1920 that circumstance threw them together in a real way. That autumn, both Richard and Nathan attended the University of Chicago. There was a certain wariness. Both were young intellectual prodigies and academic rivals, each expecting to seize a unique place on campus. Nathan, in particular, was unlikely to have welcomed the competition, and the first months were apparently uneasy. Despite their backgrounds, they seemed to have little in common: the arrogant, introverted Nathan Leopold, and the gregarious, charming Richard Loeb, one misanthropic, one outgoing. But they began sharing friends, began meeting for games of cards set against the thrill of illicit drinking. It seemed innocent enough, but early in 1921, the relationship would take a more serious and provocative turn.

CHAPTER SEVEN

FEBRUARY 1921: IN CHARLEVOIX, TEMPERATURES DIPPED, SNOW COVered the countryside, and the usual tourists from Chicago were nowhere to be seen. Yet two figures stepped from the train at the railway station: Richard Loeb and Nathan Leopold. Their destination was the nearby Loeb family estate.

The two boys had traveled alone from Chicago for a brief holiday. Over the last six months, Nathan and Richard had increasingly spent time together, a seemingly odd friendship likely based on mutual isolation and loneliness as they each sought a friend sympathetic to their private inadequacies. By the time they arrived in Charlevoix, the relationship had turned serious.

Richard and Nathan had shared a private Pullman compartment on the train; as the hours passed, they exchanged confidences, revealing secrets they dared tell no one else. Richard spoke of his interest in crime, of how he committed petty thefts to provide a thrill and outwit authorities. Nathan welcomed the admissions and then shared his own: he liked men. It was a bold thing to say to another fifteen-year-old boy, especially in 1921. Nathan risked everything: Richard could easily turn on him or worse, tell his secret to others. Yet Richard had also admitted things that Nathan could use against him. Confession laid the basis for their continued friendship: their secrets bonded them together while hovering uneasily over their heads.[1]

As the train had continued north through the desolate, snowy landscape, Richard did something extraordinary, inviting Nathan to share his Pullman berth. He may have been curious; he may have felt sorry for his friend. Perhaps Richard, after years of feeling that he never quite belonged, that no one cared about him, was genuinely moved; perhaps it was a way for him to secure power in the relationship. Whatever the motivation, it was an extraordinary thing to do, and Leopold was quick to seize the opportunity. He'd been with other boys, masturbating them, but now Loeb let him fulfill his fantasy of domination. Nathan lay on top of him and began rubbing his penis between his friend's thighs, in an echo of what he had done with his abusive governess. This experience with Richard, Nathan later admitted, "gave him more pleasure than anything else he had ever done."[2]

The relationship begun on the train continued at Charlevoix. Nathan usually avoided his sexuality, ashamed to admit that he was gay. Richard, for his part, never evinced much interest in sex with anyone, male or female, but as always, he was eager to please and win approval. He seems to have gone along with Nathan out of friendship, perhaps to see if he could find any thrill in the experience.

At first Nathan hadn't considered Richard "very good looking," although he soon came to regard him in adoring terms.[3] He said that looking at Richard's body or just touching him on the shoulder sent a thrilling shiver through him. Nathan even claimed that he was jealous of "the food and drink" that Richard consumed, because he could never share such intimacy with him.[4]

Their sexual interactions were uncertain, awkward, ruled by typical teenage confusion: the two likely masturbated each other, and Nathan performed oral sex on Richard, but claimed that it wasn't exciting enough, perhaps because it wasn't about him and his desire to control.[5] Nathan was the one who dictated the terms and acted as the sexual aggressor.[6] Throughout the relationship he usually wanted to repeat what had happened between them that first night on the train, laying on Richard's back, and thrusting his penis between his thighs to orgasm. He seemed to prefer depersonalized encounters that freed him of being looked at during sex. Yet there was also a sadistic element to these encounters: "furiously passionate," Nathan's actions were closer to a rape fantasy than to making love—he admitted that control was a driving force in his arousal, even with Richard as a willing partner.[7]

Despite his ambivalence toward sex, Richard went along with Nathan's fantasies. Almost nothing was required of him—perhaps that made it easier. All Richard had to do was lie there and feign being passed out. He probably dismissed this objectification as just another of Nathan's peculiarities. It was easier, as always, to remain compliant. And, aside from Nathan's preferences, there was nothing particularly abnormal about the relationship. It was frantic and frenzied, uncertain and worrisome like most teenage affairs, and ruled by the necessary secrecy, but sexuality did not, as some contemporary voices hinted, lead the pair to commit murder.

Richard must have wondered about Nathan—was he really interested only in men? He apparently took Nathan to a brothel, a test to see how his friend would respond. The result revealed less about his sexuality than it did about Nathan's need for control. During World War I, Nathan had read tales of atrocities committed by the kaiser's soldiers: one described how a young French girl had been tied to a table, raped, and then killed. The idea appealed tremendously to Nathan—not the actual sex with a woman, but the humiliation, the control, the sadism, and the murder. And so at the brothel he fantasized that he was committing rape—it was, he admitted, the only way he could get an erection.[8]

A lot of ink has been spilled in attempts to unravel what lay at the heart of this unlikely friendship and even more unlikely relationship. Did it just represent a moment in time, a temporary youthful abandon whose flame burned brightly but would eventually have faded? Was it a case of opposites attract? Did they recognize a certain darkness in the other that mirrored their own secret malignancies?

As is true of so much of the case, the key probably lies in Richard's damaged psyche. He'd been accustomed to disguising his insecurities, his alienation, behind a smooth, assured facade. And he'd always wanted an intense friendship, with someone he trusted and who in turn openly admired him. With Nathan, he found acceptance. For the first time in his life, Richard didn't have to put up a pretense, didn't have to measure up to expectations. It all coalesced into a powerful emotional tie: he felt appreciated, liked for himself—with all of his flaws laid bare—and able to share secrets he carefully guarded. He fell into the relationship easily: he could accept the flattery, indulge in the enthusiastic worship, and still view it for what it was: a youthful dalliance between two teenagers who each in their own ways felt alone and misunderstood.

But for Nathan, it was love, at least a kind of obsessive, possessive devotion that he took for love. Lonely and starved for affection, it must have seemed unbelievable that he had found his apparent mirror in the handsome, socially popular, charismatic Richard. Loeb had swept into Nathan's drab, ordered world like a ray of gleaming sunshine, breathing sudden life into his grim existence. He was the only real friend he had: by extending his understanding, Richard gave Nathan shelter from the storm swirling in his mind. The relationship made Nathan feel special: love, safety, self-discovery, and fulfillment all combined to reinforce his need for Richard.

In his overwrought emotional state, Nathan was all endless devotion and cloying affection. "Dick," he later enthused, "possessed more of the truly fine qualities than almost anyone else I have ever known. Not just the superficial social graces. Those of course he possessed to the nth degree. Dick could charm the birds out of the trees. He could get along with anyone, make anyone like him. He always knew how to act, what to say. In any company. With older people or those of higher social position he was respectful. Genuinely and effortlessly respectful. With age-fellows and equals he was natural, friendly, lovable. With social inferiors he never condescended."[9]

Nathan envied the ease with which Richard moved through life. At times, though, he felt overshadowed by his friend: "I'd try deliberately to copy his mannerism, to be consciously charming. I couldn't come close. More often than not I'd just alienate people, more so than if I hadn't made a conscious effort. But Dick didn't have to try. He just seemed able to push an imaginary button and turn on the charm." According to Nathan, Richard also had some unpleasant characteristics. He tended to be moody, and snobbishly looked down on others. Still, as Nathan admitted frankly, "I just liked the guy so darn much, admired him so darn much, that my mind closed automatically to anything unpleasant about him. . . . He was aces with me. I wouldn't trade his little finger for any six other people I knew."[10]

Part of that bedazzled attitude erupted in Nathan's fevered mind in the form of his king/slave fantasies. Later he cultivated the image of himself as helplessly in thrall to Richard, completely subservient to his desires.[11] If true, this would have been what Nathan wanted: to maintain the relationship, he positioned himself as subordinate, knowing that Richard would find this attractive. But even in this scenario he imagined himself as the slave who kept the king in power, silently controlling while exerting actual domination.

But was this true? In his head, Nathan might occasionally envision himself as Richard's slave but, as he later admitted, he placed himself in the role of king 90 percent of the time.[12] He liked to imagine that Richard had been injured, that he saved him, and that a grateful Loeb eagerly became his slave.[13] In another fantasy, Nathan imagined that he and Richard were shipwrecked on an island. A piano washed ashore. Because Nathan was the only person who could play it, the natives made him a noble, but Richard was enslaved. Nathan purchased his freedom and, in so doing, won Richard's lasting admiration and submission.[14] Perhaps these fantasies stemmed from frustration, from Nathan's realization that his friend didn't share his passionate feelings—it became easier to indulge in wishful thinking than to acknowledge the truth.

Richard, too, began to draw Nathan into his own fantasies of being a master criminal, in this case his petty thefts. Nathan later insisted that, when it came to crime, Richard "didn't have a single scruple of any kind. He wasn't immoral; he was just plain amoral—unmoral, that is. Right and wrong didn't exist. He'd do anything, anything. And it was all a game to him. He reminded me of an eight-year-old all wrapped up in a game of cops and robbers."[15]

But in this case, Nathan didn't have any scruples, either. Although he thought the escapades were foolish, he admitted that he enjoyed them.[16] Nathan was smart enough to recognize his power: by participating in his crimes, he ensured his place in Richard's life. Who else would agree to such risky misadventures? The thrill of this experience proved to be a catalyst, as each crime became easier yet more exciting. The pair worked out an elaborate ruse: Nathan would excuse himself for the night, go to his bedroom, and make enough noise so that the household knew where he was. After turning off the lights, he would then slip out of the house without being detected and meet Richard, who had gone through a similar ploy with his own parents. They were careful to be back in their respective beds by no later than five in the morning, to avoid being caught.[17]

Starting in the spring of 1921, the pair began committing crimes. Richard's past misadventures had all been juvenile: minor thefts and shoplifting. Once Nathan entered the picture, things accelerated. Richard needed more excitement, and Nathan was eager to please. They developed a system to cheat at card games. Then Richard discovered that the keys to his mother's Milburn electric car also worked in other Milburns; twice, he and Nathan stole Milburns and went on joyrides before crashing or abandoning them.[18]

They spent these secret nights driving around Chicago playing exciting games of cat and mouse in the dark, tossing bricks through the windshields of unoccupied cars. Once they broke a car window only to interrupt a couple having sex in the back seat. The man had a gun and shot as they fled. Unhurt and thrilled by the experience, they continued their nocturnal adventures. They were nearly caught after breaking a shop window and tripping an alarm. Police roared up and opened fire just as they jumped in Richard's car. One bullet actually struck the vehicle but, once again, they managed to evade capture.[19]

The relationship became a way to test their own limits, their devotion to each other, to see how far they could carry their subversive acts. It was childish, but it bonded Richard and Nathan together.

Richard and Nathan were back at Charlevoix when, in the summer of 1921, their intimate relationship threatened to explode. Working at the farm during the summer break was fellow University of Chicago student Hamlin Buchman. Details remain vague, but the three had apparently been drinking: because it was so hot, they decided to spend the night on a large sleeping porch. At some point, Richard went off to use the bathroom; when he returned, Buchman saw him climb into bed with Nathan.[20]

Though shocked, Buchman said nothing. But both Richard and Nathan feared that he would reveal their secret. Nathan later admitted that he spent hours thinking of "ingenious ideas of torture" to inflict on Buchman.[21] Worried about blackmail or exposure, the pair apparently decided to kill the potentially troublesome young man. It was likely Nathan who suggested this—he was, after all, the one with violent fantasies—but Richard went along with the idea. An accident, it was supposedly decided, would be best: Buchman said he didn't swim, and so the pair asked him to join them in a boating trip on Pine Lake. When they reached deep water, Richard and Nathan deliberately upset the boat, plunging everyone overboard. If they expected to idly float by in the water as Buchman went under, they were in for a surprise: the young man could swim, at least well enough to make it to shore. He went straight to Richard's brother Allan, complaining that he'd caught them in bed together.[22]

Hamlin tended to be high-strung; perhaps that made his story sound unlikely. Richard and Nathan denied everything. Allan might have had his own reasons to doubt the tale. He'd taken care of his younger brother after Richard picked up gonorrhea from a prostitute; Allan likely seized on this as proof that Richard wasn't gay. The Loebs fired Buchman: in retaliation, he went back to the University of Chicago and told classmates what had happened, including the fact that Richard and Nathan had shared a bed while nearly naked.[23]

Scandalous sexual gossip about two of the university's wealthiest and most precocious students didn't take long to spread across campus. Richard tried to ignore it and plunged himself into university life. An older botany major on campus named William Ghere befriended the young man, and he suggested that Loeb join his fraternity, Lambda Chi Alpha. But the fraternity dismissed the idea—Richard was Jewish, and they didn't accept Jews. Years later, having changed his name to Will Geer, the man who won fame portraying Grandpa Walton on the 1970s American television show *The Waltons* fondly recalled Richard as "a brilliant boy, with lilac [*sic*] eyes."[24]

The illicit nature of what was, after all, an uncertain, heady queer relationship between emotional teenagers was bound to show itself in tension, and Buchman's tales only exacerbated an already tenuous situation. The relationship had begun powerfully, a rolling wave sweeping across everything in its path as Richard and Nathan found in each other freedom from their own insecurities. The intensity was genuine, but it couldn't last. It was inevitable that the relationship would eventually sink into unhealthy battles as jealousy flourished.

The whispers finally got to Richard. In truth, he also felt restless: living at home, he complained, was too much like being in high school. He wanted the freedom and glamour of going off to college.[25] And so, in the autumn of 1921, he transferred to the University of Michigan.

Nathan refused to be separated; although they were only sixteen, the pair arranged to share an apartment in Ann Arbor. But illness kept Nathan from joining his friend for the first few weeks of college. And he had barely arrived when, in October, word came that Nathan's mother Florence had taken a turn for the worse.[26] He rushed back home and was with her when she died of nephritis on October 17. Shattered, Nathan was convinced that, since she had contracted the disease while pregnant with him, he was responsible for her death— "my presence was the cause of her absence," he said.[27]

"After my mother's death," Nathan admitted, "I realized that if I could kid myself into the belief that there was a life hereafter I would be happy but I felt I must be intellectually honest. . . . I tried to cut out the emotion. My idea was cold blooded intellect."[28] Florence's death cemented the atheism that had been growing in Nathan since he was eleven.[29] He couldn't envision a God who would make his mother suffer.[30]

By the time Nathan returned to the University of Michigan on October 19, things had changed. The differences between Leopold and Loeb came into sharper focus under the critical eyes of their classmates at Ann Arbor. Student Max Schrayer frankly told Richard that no one liked Nathan. "Most people couldn't understand why Loeb hung around him," Schrayer later said.[31]

It wasn't just Nathan's brittle, arrogant personality. Most university students disliked openly precocious intellectuals. Unpopular, conspicuous academics like Nathan were given nicknames like "wets" or "weirs," and for most students "genius" was code for "strange."[32] Even Robert Angell, then president of the University of Michigan, wrote, "To appear greatly interested in one's studies or to admit that one has put much time on them, is bad form."[33]

Between his own illness and his mother's death, Nathan hadn't managed to spend much time with Richard at Ann Arbor; now, he noticed that his friend was suddenly distant, preoccupied. Richard was out on his own for the first time, under no restraint, and wanted to find new friends and explore new possibilities. He may have come to regard Nathan as a cloying, effusive, and socially unpopular anchor around his neck; perhaps he was tired of having to soothe Nathan's fragile ego. As Richard began pulling away, it was obvious to Nathan that their relationship was at a turning point. He couldn't ignore the fact that he cared more about Richard than Richard did about him.

Things came to a head when Richard told Nathan that he wanted to pledge Zeta Beta Tau, an exclusively Jewish fraternity. There wasn't a chance that the fraternity would accept the unpopular Leopold. But there was a problem: somehow Hamlin Buchman heard that Richard planned to pledge, and he wrote to the fraternity, boldly warning that Richard and Nathan "were two cocksuckers."[34]

Fraternity member Max Schrayer remembered that someone called Allan Loeb and asked if the allegation was true; Allan was so alarmed that he rushed to Ann Arbor, declaring that Buchman had exaggerated the story.[35] He also apparently spoke to Richard.[36] Although he didn't believe the rumors, Allan warned that Richard could be hurt by them. His friendship with Nathan had gone too far: Leopold was too odd, too unpopular, and Richard risked being dragged down with him.

After Allan's intervention, the brothers at Zeta Beta Tau agreed to pledge Richard, but only on the condition that he stop seeing Nathan.[37] It was a lifeline that Richard was apparently eager to seize, and he took little time to make his choice. Never as enamored of Nathan as Nathan was of him, and unsettled by the rumors, he decided that the fraternity was more important than the friendship. Shattered and feeling rejected, Nathan finished out the year at Ann Arbor before transferring back to the University of Chicago for the fall term of 1922.

Richard promptly moved into the Zeta Beta Tau fraternity house, anxious to prove himself, but he was a typical sixteen-year-old, frenetic and still immature in his behavior and in his tastes. "He would always walk hastily," remembered one fraternity member. "He would pop into the room. In coming upstairs, he would take two or three steps at a time and run. He very seldom walked in the manner which is customarily done. Even when he lounged, he would flop down in a seat and all of a sudden jump up."[38] Other brothers noted that he read "dime novels and detective stories," and deemed Richard "childish," and "very young."[39]

The sixteen-year-old also drank heavily, in an effort to keep up with his older fraternity brothers. "There were," recalled Zeta Beta Tau member Theodore Schimberg, "many times when we were unable to tell whether Dick was drunk or sober."[40] This childish behavior led to Richard's exclusion as a mentor to junior pledges on the grounds that his actions "were not such as would incur the respect of a freshman," although his age probably also had something to do with it—it wouldn't do for a sixteen- or seventeen-year-old to serve as a mentor to a student two or three years his senior.[41]

Richard admitted that he was "intellectually lazy," and like many college students, he slid through these years "along the lines of least resistance."[42] He was a prime example of "the gentleman loafer," as social historian Paula Fass termed it, someone who attended college with no real objectives.[43] Richard's only real interest was history: he developed a passion for the American Revolution, and especially the Civil War and the lives of Henry Clay and John Calhoun. He briefly toyed with the idea of becoming a history teacher but decided that he was too lazy to make a success of it.[44]

NATHAN, MEANWHILE, RETURNED TO THE monotony of life in Chicago, surrounded by his family and hemmed in by the familiar, endless days. He sought refuge from his rejection in his studies. He filled his notebooks with drawings, some indicating a troubled mind: dissected penises; the backsides of naked young boys; severed heads; and decapitated bodies. He labeled a sketch of a gallows, "Nathan Leopold's Shrine," suggesting that death was never far from his thoughts.[45] He admitted that he deliberately took classes that marked him out as different, studying Sanskrit, Russian, and Greek along with a handful of other languages. Although he often publicly claimed that he spoke fifteen languages, he privately admitted that he was fluent in only five (English, German, French, Italian, and Spanish).[46]

At the University of Chicago, Nathan joined a club devoted to Italian studies, and launched a project to translate *Ragionamenti*, the work of an obscure sixteenth-century Italian poet, Pietro Aretino, with a college friend, Leon Mandel II. Aretino specialized in satirical, often pornographic verse that included depictions of bestiality.[47] "Aretino," Nathan coyly insisted, "has a great literary value if one can get over the first feeling of revulsion and disgust that it is absolute filth."[48] When the head of the University of Chicago's Italian department learned of this, he warned Mandel's parents against allowing him to associate with Nathan: soon Mandel was sent off to Europe.[49] This suggests that the rumors about Nathan's sexuality had spread, and had begun taking a toll on his other relationships.

Nathan's obsession with German philosopher Friedrich Nietzsche grew in these years of isolation—he later said his goal was "to become a perfect Nietzschean."[50] With their antagonism to religion and challenge to conventional morality, Nietzsche's writings were particularly faddish in the years following World War I, his theories popular subjects of debate among college students and intellectuals. He developed the idea of the Übermensch in his 1883 book *Thus Sprach Zarathustra.* Usually translated as "superman" but more properly "overman," the Übermensch was a being apart, intellectually superior to those around him, beyond concerns of good and evil since God was dead, and endowed with such extraordinary abilities that he was no longer subject to conventional morality or the laws of man.

Nathan had first encountered Nietzsche as a boy reading Jack London's 1904 novel, *The Sea Wolf.*[51] London conceived this book, at least in part, as a refutation of Nietzsche's Übermensch, but this intended moral eluded Nathan. Instead, he eagerly embraced Nietzsche's ideas, taking them as literal guides for life. They explained so much: Nathan's sense of superiority, why he felt different from others, and why he had so little empathy.

Taking these lessons to heart, Nathan was soon espousing Nietzsche-like views, with a messianic certainty of his position. Fellow student Arnold Maremont said that Nathan "believed Nietzsche literally."[52] Leopold, according to Maremont, "believed in his own happiness regardless of anyone else . . . the only wrong he could conceive of was something that did not give him happiness. . . . If it gave him pleasure to go out and murder someone it would be perfectly all right in his philosophy."[53] Student Harry Booth once discussed a murder case in law class with Nathan. Nathan insisted that if he killed someone, he could not be held responsible: "He felt himself right to do it and it would be perfectly all right."[54] And another classmate, John Abt, asserted that Nathan's "main thesis was that pleasure was the sole emblem of all conduct. Whenever he contemplated an act he would weigh the amount of pleasure, balance it up against the amount of pain he thought he would get out of it. If the pleasure was greater than the pain, he would do this act."[55]

In this twisted philosophy, and even with their relationship fractured, Nathan elevated Richard to absurd heights. To Maremont, he insisted that Richard "was a super man, that he had a brilliant mind, was handsome and irresistible to women. I tried to tell him that he didn't know what he was talking about, that Loeb was glib, superficial and lied to impress others. Leopold kept insisting I didn't understand Loeb."[56] Nathan once drew up a list of traits he deemed necessary in the ideal man: while he gave himself a score of 62, he bestowed a score of 90 on Richard.[57] This was self-delusion: Nathan knew that Richard was not a great intellect, but the object of his affection had to be raised to grandiose qualities in order for Nathan to justify their tortured relationship.

Nathan tried to convince Richard of such views. "I am going to ask a little more in an effort to explain my system of a Nietzschean philosophy with regard to you," he wrote to Richard in October 1923. "In formulating a superman, he is, on account of certain superior qualities inherent in him exempted from the ordinary laws which govern ordinary men. He is not liable for anything he may do. Whereas others would be, except for the crime that it is possible for him to commit, to make a mistake. Now, obviously any code which conferred upon an individual or upon a group extraordinary privileges without also putting on him extraordinary responsibility would be unfair and bad. Therefore, an Übermensch is held to have committed a crime every time he errs in judgment, a mistake excusable in others."[58]

Richard wasn't interested. Contrary to the usual depiction of the pair as Nietzschean-obsessed youths, only Nathan espoused his views. Richard, as he later admitted, took Nathan's endless talk about Nietzsche and his theories "with a great big dose of salt."[59]

IN THE YEARS FOLLOWING WORLD War I, hedonistic abandon seemed to overwhelm America's sons and daughters. After the bloody carnage in Europe, attitudes were jaded, creating palpable tensions between traditional expectations and modern desires. "Here," wrote F. Scott Fitzgerald in *This Side of Paradise,* "was a new generation . . . grown up to find all Gods dead, all wars fought, all faiths in man shaken."[60] Languidly elegant playboys and flappers with rolled stockings and bright lipstick became the dominant role models for a mass of disillusioned youth. Previous taboos fell by the wayside. It was the era of "free love," "petting parties," and Prohibition, with bathtub gin downed at speakeasies to the syncopated soundtrack of the latest jazz.

This was the world that greeted Richard and Nathan when, in 1923, they both graduated from college. A week after he turned eighteen, Richard received his bachelor of arts degree from the University of Michigan. The *Daily Tribune* noted that Richard was the youngest graduate in the institution's history.[61] Perhaps Richard hoped that his parents would follow through on their previous promise and send him to Europe. If so, he was to be again disappointed. Albert may not have known of his son's criminal activities, but he was probably aware that he drank too much and was often irresponsible; perhaps he'd even heard something of the rumors about Richard and Nathan's relationship. Letting Richard go off to Europe must have seemed too risky.

Nathan, too, was said to be the youngest graduate of the University of Chicago when he left that spring, having earned a bachelor's degree in philosophy and a Phi Beta Kappa key.[62] He candidly put his academic ability down to "ten percent work and study and ninety percent horseshit."[63] Nathan had no real ambition: he'd never had to work for anything, he bragged, and he didn't see why he should do so now. But to appease his father he agreed to study law.[64] And Nathan now got a splashy new car: a cherry-red Willys-Knight four-passenger Country Club sport model, with red disc wheels, nickel-plated bumpers and lamps, and a tan canvas top.[65]

The pair remained a study in contrasts. Standing five feet, nine inches tall, Richard had transformed from a moonfaced child into a handsome, slim young man, his face marred only by a barely visible scar on his chin—the result of a childhood accident.[66] He wore his dark hair slicked back in imitation of Rudolph Valentino and was careful about his appearance: he dressed impeccably and with flair, donning sporty tweeds and sleek jackets. With his collegiate good looks and smooth aura of success, he was accustomed to turning heads wherever he went. He had, one friend later recalled, "a glamorous personality."[67]

A dinner guest at the Loeb mansion recalled how Richard "delighted us by his charming personality. I regarded him as one of the finest youths I have ever known."[68] Yet that pleasant exterior concealed insecurities. He was adept at playing to expectation. In many ways, Richard personified Amory Blaine, the fictional character in *This Side of Paradise*. His friendships were casual, and his romantic relationships shallow. "He used them simply as mirrors of himself, audiences before which he might do that posing absolutely essential to him," Fitzgerald wrote of Blaine.[69] The description fit Richard perfectly.

And that was the problem: no one knew the real Richard, not even the young ladies he dated. He'd met seventeen-year-old Lorraine Nathan during a dance at his fraternity in November 1921 and the pair dated off and on. Lorraine heartily disliked Nathan Leopold and objected to Richard associating with him. But by the summer of 1923, Richard's allure seemed to have worn off. She claimed to notice "a complete change" in him, calling Richard "unusually infantile." As evidence, she pointed to an evening when he'd shown up at her house and "took introductions to some guests he had not known very flippantly. . . . He then started dancing down the middle of the room and at that time we were passing some chocolates and he put his thumb into each one of them to find a hard center, and he did this in all seriousness and then he went out in the reception hall and tried on all the hats of the guests." She didn't think that he'd been drinking; it was the sort of behavior, though, that usually accompanied his disguised inebriation.[70] Lorraine's daughter, the journalist Meg Greenfield, later recalled that her aunt Rosalind had deemed Richard "plain cuckoo. . . .

For her, the chocolate squashing represented a lapse in decorum so grave as to constitute, on its face, evidence of insanity."[71] Although they continued to occasionally see each other, Richard moved on, dating a young woman named Germaine Reinhardt.

Nathan, too, had grown in these years. Maturity did him no favors. He was short, standing five feet, five inches tall, with a dark complexion, protuberant, uneven eyes, and bushy brows that nearly met above his nose. There was something fleshy about him, a slight pudginess that his heavy lips only accentuated.

Little had changed about Nathan's personality. He had a circle of acquaintances but, as he later admitted, "no close friends."[72] Nathan wasn't completely without charm: he could be engaging and seemed to enjoy time with his companions, but many found him off-putting. John Abt said that, to Nathan, friends "were simply the means to an end and he used them for the amount of pleasure he got out of them."[73] And Arnold Maremont described Nathan as "very egocentric. Practically all the time that I was with him, in ordinary social conversation, he attempted by any sort of ruse possible to monopolize the conversation. It didn't make any difference what was being said or what was being talked about, he always attempted to get the conversation revolving around him so he could do most of the talking."[74]

Nathan later admitted that he'd never had any serious relationships and was "not in love with any girl." Although he pondered marriage as something expected, he worried if he "would be able to satisfy his wife."[75] Yet Nathan later tried to rewrite his own history, insisting that in 1924 he'd been "head over heels in love" with a girl whose true identity he concealed with a pseudonym, "Connie," in his memoirs.[76] This was Susan Lurie, a pretty, dark-haired young woman he'd met during a dance at the University of Chicago sometime in 1923. They spent their time together reading poetry and discussing philosophy, but that seemed to be the extent of the relationship. Although Nathan later insisted that they were "informally engaged," Lurie denied that they had ever been romantically involved.[77]

There were holidays in Cuba and in Hawaii that summer of 1923, but Nathan spent much of his time pursuing his interest in birds. A few years earlier he had begun teaching ornithology to small groups, leading them to isolated areas outside Chicago and guiding them in identification. And Nathan had spent several summer weeks on extended expeditions with other ornithologists to Northern Michigan, where they discovered the Kirtland's warbler, a small bird rarely seen. A jerky home movie captured Nathan feeding the nestlings with flies, and he wrote an article about the find, which was published later in *The Auk,* the journal of the American Ornithologists' Union.

Nathan and Richard had barely seen each other in these years. "We did everything in our power to avoid any possible scandal," Richard said. Because of Buchman's tales, "we were very careful never to be alone together in public, seen together any place, or to be alone together any place." This, as Richard admitted, was "on the advice of my brother, who told me to be careful and not to see too much of Leopold, and if I did to be sure somebody else was around."[78]

BY THE SUMMER OF 1923, both Richard and Nathan were back in Chicago. Bored, they fell back into their friendship and their nocturnal activities. Once, they decided to break into the house of one of Loeb's friends while he was away and steal his supply of alcohol. In preparation, they purchased rope with which to tie up anyone they might encounter, and a chisel, whose handle they wrapped with adhesive tape. They also carried guns: Nathan had illegally owned a .32 caliber Remington revolver since 1921. But when they reached the house, they found that they could not break a window and gain entry and abandoned the plan.[79]

They continued cheating at cards. When playing bridge, most of their friends wagered between a penny to three cents a point; Nathan and Richard, on the other hand, played for five to ten cents a point.[80] Enormous sums apparently changed hands, at least judging by Richard's bank accounts. Between March and December 1923 alone, he deposited some $5,573.[81] These sums far outweighed his monthly allowance of $250 or any special checks he received from his father when he ran short of funds.[82] Perhaps this financial windfall represented something as innocuous as Richard betting on football games, or perhaps part of it stemmed from the pair's criminal activities.

Richard and Nathan soon extended their crimes to calling in false alarms and to setting fires. Usually they selected shacks or vacant buildings; they would disappear once the fire was set, and then return to the scene a few minutes later, mingling with the public and enjoying the chaos and destruction they had caused.[83] Richard especially enjoyed this aspect—"the thrill of watching it and talking with the crowd, sneering at their ignorant guesses as to the cause of the fire, offering impossible solutions," gave him a great thrill.[84]

Both remained eminently respectable on the surface, enrolling for graduate work at the University of Chicago in September 1923. Richard began advanced courses in American and European history, while Nathan enrolled in constitutional history and law. The constant studying strained Nathan's eyes and he began suffering from headaches. On October 1, 1923, optometrist Emil Deutsch suggested reading glasses: Nathan got them a few weeks later from optician Almer Coe & Company, paying $11.50 for the tortoiseshell, round-framed glasses.[85] "I wish I had not gotten them," he later said.[86]

By this time, things were disintegrating. Increasingly the relationship was all Sturm und Drang, with incessant arguments and constant recriminations driven largely by Nathan's insecurities. Richard was bored by Nathan's endless talk about his intelligence and Nietzsche. It must have been emotionally exhausting. Richard even started lying to Nathan. He cheated when playing cards with him and swindled him out of money for alcohol.[87]

By this time, Richard had become close friends with fellow University of Chicago student Richard Rubel. This preyed on Nathan's mind. Although the three were often together, Nathan made no secret of his jealousy and dislike of Rubel, dismissing him as "only of fair intelligence" and derisively calling him "the bastard Jew."[88]

Nathan, for his part, also resented Richard; although he wouldn't admit it, he knew that his friend wasn't a superman. The faltering sexual relationship struck Nathan hard: he didn't want to lose the handsome young lover he had miraculously bewitched, and the emotional distance probably led to renewed feelings of isolation and loneliness. It had become a decidedly unequal relationship, a destructive cycle with one man distancing himself and the other becoming even more needy, each unable to break free of the ties that bound them together.[89]

Arguments became frequent. Once, Nathan proposed, in all seriousness, that they settle a dispute with a game of poker, the loser having to kill himself. When Richard objected, Nathan threatened to kill him. Such behavior unsettled Richard. There were too many volatile feelings at play as Nathan seemed to spiral out of control. Richard later admitted that he was afraid of his friend: "He intimidated me by threatening to expose me and I could not stand it. . . . I had always considered him a bad influence on me." Things got so bad that Richard thought about killing himself; he abandoned the idea only because he couldn't think of a way to conceal his suicide. He also idly pondered killing Nathan, perhaps shooting him, or hitting him over the head with a chisel. But ultimately, he always talked himself out of such drastic action. "The idea of murdering a fellow, especially alone," Richard explained, "I don't think I could have done it. If I could have snapped my fingers and made him pass away in a heart attack, I would have done it."[90]

Things boiled over after yet another argument in October 1923. Loeb had tentatively planned to spend the distant New Year's Eve with Nathan, but changed his mind when Richard Rubel asked that he join him on a double date. "I did not like it very much," Nathan explained, "because I did not think it was a nice thing to do."[91]

The change of plans was innocuous enough, but Nathan disliked Rubel. And, on top of the New Year's Eve issue, Richard and Nathan each accused the other of lying to Rubel over some minor issue. For the emotionally insecure and possessive Nathan it swelled into a crescendo of perceived treachery and unbridled anger. He was leaving for Boston to deliver a paper on the Kirtland's warblers, but before departing he composed a remarkable letter that gives insight into the tortured relationship with Richard. Written on October 9, this was the strange missive police later discovered when they searched Loeb's room eight months later. Nathan wrote of "our former relations" and complained that Loeb had betrayed him. "I wanted you this afternoon, and still want you, to feel that we are on equal footing legally, and, therefore, I purposely committed the same tort of which you were guilty, the only difference being that in your case the facts would be harder to prove than in mine, should I deny them." He actually enclosed some sort of evidence that he could use against Richard "in any court" if he did not accept his demands. Then came something truly astonishing: "When you came to my home this afternoon," Nathan wrote to Richard, "I expected either to break friendship with you or attempt to kill you unless you told me why you acted as you did yesterday." Richard, Nathan declared, must decide: declare that Nathan had done nothing wrong and continue the friendship, or break off the relationship. "I do not wish to influence your decision either way, but I do want to warn you that in case you deem it advisable to discontinue our friendship, that in both our interests extreme care must be had. The motif of 'A falling out of a pair of cocksuckers' would be sure to be popular, which is patently undesirable and forms an irksome but unavoidable bond between us." Richard was to call his house and leave one of two messages: "Dick says yes," if he wanted to continue the relationship, or "Dick says no" if he wanted to end it. Although Nathan ended by promising that "your decision will, of course, have no effect on my keeping to myself our confidences of the past," the tone of the letter was threatening.[92]

This letter reveals much about Nathan's rigid state of mind. Richard apparently responded by saying that he wished to continue the relationship, which prompted Nathan to compose a reply. "I was highly gratified to hear from you," he wrote, "for two reasons, the first sentimental and the second practical. The first of these is that your prompt reply conclusively proved my previous idea that the whole matter really did mean something to you, and that you respected my wishes, even though we were not very friendly. This is a great satisfaction, but the second is even greater, in that I imply from the general tenor of your letter that there is a good chance of a reconciliation between us, which I ardently desire, and this belief will give me a peace of mind on which I based my request." Yet even here Nathan was not about to let Richard escape, lecturing him pointedly of "the crime you originally committed (your mistake in judgment) from which the whole consequences flow. . . . Furthermore, even if I did not regret those consequences, it would not follow at all that I consider myself to have acted wrongly." He advised Richard to wire him with an answer clarifying whether he accepted guilt in the matter, adding a good deal of passive-aggressive thought in his conclusion: "I did not and do not wish to charge you with a crime, but I feel justified in using any of the consequences of your crime for which you were held responsible to my advantage. This and only this I did, so you see how careful you must be. Now, Dick, just one more word to sum up. Supposing you fulfill both conditions necessary for reconciliation. One, waive claim to my statement, and, two, state yourself that you no longer think me to have acted treacherously. We are going to be as good or better friends as before. I want that to come about very much, but not at the expense of your thinking that I have backed down in any way from my stand, as I am sure of that in my mind and want you to be."[93]

True to form, Richard followed the line of least resistance, acceding to Nathan's demands. The letters shatter the common perception of the relationship: that Nathan was helplessly in thrall to Richard, unable to assert himself. Nathan dictated the terms of the friendship: even a reconciliation with Richard had to follow his wishes. It was Richard who submitted, who gave in to Nathan's manipulations. Richard was, in modern terms, in an abusive relationship, too immature to recognize what was taking place but worried enough about Nathan's rage that he wanted to end it. This tortured friendship was hanging on through habit and by the thinnest of threads. And it would quickly turn deadly.

CHAPTER EIGHT

ON A CHILLY AUTUMN EVENING IN 1923, NATHAN AND RICHARD climbed into Leopold's red Willys-Knight motorcar and left Chicago, driving some 250 miles north to Ann Arbor. That Saturday, November 10, the University of Michigan's Wolverines met the Marines' team on the football field. Michigan's victory was decisive, and students celebrated across the campus.

The journey was Richard's idea: he wanted to rob his old fraternity, sure that most of the Zeta Beta Tau members would either be at parties or passed out from drinking. The escapade would be exciting, and they were antsy and uncertain as they drove. Richard could have done it alone, but he'd reconciled with Nathan after their October argument. Nathan agreed to join him if they burgled a second fraternity house of his choosing. There was probably a certain satisfaction in this for Nathan: the fraternity system in general, and Zeta Beta Tau in particular, had rejected him and forced Richard to choose between them and his friend. It was a lark for Richard; it was probably revenge for Nathan.

The drive from Chicago to Ann Arbor took six hours; Nathan and Richard didn't arrive until around three early Sunday morning. They crept through the darkness: both wore masks and held flashlights.

Richard had a chisel, its blade wrapped in tape so that it could be used as a bludgeon if needed. And both apparently carried revolvers. Nathan was prepared to shoot and kill anyone who might interrupt them.[1]

Entering by the unlocked front door, the pair crept through the fraternity, stealing things as they found them: a knife, money totaling seventy-four dollars, a self-sharpening pencil, a fountain pen, a watch. As a final thought, they picked up a portable Underwood typewriter and carried it out to Nathan's car.[2]

Richard wanted to call it a night. He'd been most interested in planning the crime; now that it was accomplished, he wasn't eager to strike another house. Nathan, though, insisted. And so they approached a second fraternity—no one knows which. They entered and stole a camera, but when Richard heard someone snoring, he panicked and insisted that they leave.[3] They climbed back into Nathan's car and set off south, for Chicago.

That six-hour return drive was a turning point in the relationship. As they sipped from flasks of illicit alcohol, Nathan unloosed his fury, accusing Richard of cowardice. He'd helped rob the first fraternity, but Richard had been half-hearted and abandoned the second effort. Nathan railed against his captive audience. He questioned Richard's commitment to him; he was mad that their sexual relationship had waned. Anger filled the car: things grew so heated that they again pondered ending their friendship. But Richard worried that if they did so, Nathan might use knowledge of their crimes against him.[4]

By the time Nathan and Richard returned to Chicago, they'd reached a formal pact to continue the relationship under certain conditions. The agreement was to last until June 1924, when Nathan planned to go to Europe for the summer. Precisely who came up with the idea is unknown, but both accepted its terms. Nathan agreed to assist Richard in any criminal schemes if Loeb invoked the phrase, "For Robert's sake." With this, Nathan ostensibly placed himself under Richard's control—this is how he portrayed the situation. Yet Nathan could reject any ideas he considered too dangerous, absurd, or damaging to his family—he was able to agree or disagree at will. In exchange, Nathan demanded sex: Richard agreed that Nathan could sleep with him three times every two months.[5]

The pair had also agreed to something else to draw them closer together: kidnapping someone for ransom. Each later blamed the idea on the other. It was Nathan, Richard said, who'd proposed the crime "as a means of having a great deal of excitement, together with getting quite a sum of money."[6] Nathan, though, insisted, "As far as the suggestion is concerned, again I am sure it was Mr. Loeb that made it, and that it was his plan."[7]

Nathan's version was almost certainly correct: the proposal likely came from Richard, who always enjoyed plotting intricate criminal schemes. But how serious was the idea? It came when a tired, deflated Richard was trapped in a car with a complaining, disgruntled Nathan: he may simply have tossed it out to appease his friend, a philosophical proposal to silence his nagging, without any real thought that it would be put into effect. This would explain why the pair waited until the following April to begin seriously planning the crime—if Richard had really wanted to do it, surely they would have acted sooner.

The idea, though, seems to have triggered something in Nathan: a desire to follow through on his belief that he, as a superman, was entitled to do whatever he wanted, to test his superior wit and will against those of the authorities. Richard wanted a crime partner; what he got was a sociopath. Nathan wanted to seize a girl, rape her, and kill her, to live out his fantasy inspired by German atrocities during World War I. He saw nothing wrong with the idea—"it was the thing to do," he explained glibly. More important, he said that he would "derive a great deal of pleasure from it."[8]

Richard, though, rejected Nathan's suggestion. He wasn't interested in rape or murder—it wasn't part of "a perfect kidnapping-ransom crime." In any case, he argued, girls were too closely watched: it would be easier to kidnap a boy.[9]

It all fit Nathan's twisted personality and the desire to humiliate others. He'd been sadistic in his fantasies and in his early sexual encounters with his playmate Joe; he could only get an erection with a woman if he imagined raping her; he dreamed up ways to torture his enemies; and he even preferred simulated rape with Richard to any other form of sexual activity. Control, pain, and humiliation were themes constantly running through Nathan's fevered brain. He might only occasionally act on them, but there is no denying that they formed an integral part of his personality. He apparently took Richard's suggestion as permission to access these ideas and put them into practice. He wanted to escalate the crime to include violence and murder: being a superman practically demanded committing the ultimate outrage. Richard never expressed views similar to his friend, that there was no good or evil, or that intellectual superiority justified killing. All of his crimes had been against property, not people, at least until Nathan came along. As renowned criminal profiler and former FBI agent John Douglas has noted, "the best indicator of future violence is past violence."[10] Although both Richard and Nathan would ultimately dip their hands in blood, Leopold was the only one with a history of violence in his past.

FOUR MONTHS PASSED. THEN, IN March 1924, Nathan and Richard had another blowup. Nathan had entered into their November agreement assuming an increase in crimes—and with them guarantees of sex with Richard. But they hadn't taken steps to advance their kidnapping plot. Perhaps Nathan thought that Richard was deliberately holding back to avoid sleeping with him, for he complained about the lack of sex. Richard, too, was dissatisfied, threatening to end the relationship and find another crime partner.[11]

The argument might have ended things. Shared secrets, trust, and love of a kind had initially drawn Richard and Nathan together. That was now gone: mistrust dominated. They clung to each other out of habit and mutual fear, each worried what the other might do or reveal. And so the lethal relationship continued—Richard, as usual, acceded to Nathan's demands, and agreed to have sex with each time they committed a crime.[12] Only now, as Richard recalled, did they seriously pursue their kidnapping scheme.[13]

Later, Nathan claimed he'd had no desire to commit the crime—he only went along with the idea because of the pact he'd made with Richard and that he'd felt forced to obey. He positioned himself as a passive, subservient, and reluctant participant, insisting that he "made numerous, impossible suggestions purely with the idea of delaying the plan," and claiming that he "didn't think the plan would ever be executed."[14]

This is nonsense: Nathan wasn't brainwashed into participating against his will—he was too intelligent and strong-willed to be so easily manipulated. Of the pair, Nathan had the superior mind, and he knew how to deploy it to maintain the relationship; he'd showed an uncanny ability to bend the weaker Richard to his will.[15] With his penchant for violence, it's not difficult to view Nathan as Richard's equal, if not the actual leader, in the plan: the power disparity in the relationship was to Nathan's advantage. It's possible he used his intellect to nominally place himself under Richard's control while actually using subtle manipulation to play a leading role.

And, when it came to the crime, Nathan was the more resolute of the pair. Whenever Richard faltered or expressed reluctance, Nathan stepped in and took charge, determined to see it through.[16] He spent a lot of time working out how to get the ransom, and enjoyed the plotting. He later admitted that he contributed various ideas "which were of value in perfecting their plan." And he had no moral objection to the idea. Nathan "merely felt it was dangerous" and that he would derive little pleasure from it.[17]

And so, the March argument behind them, Nathan and Richard began earnestly plotting their perfect crime. They met several nights a week, and frequently spoke on the telephone.[18] It was like a giant puzzle: each aspect, each piece, had to fit together to achieve the end result. Nathan's schedule dictated the time frame: on June 11 he was due to leave aboard the Cunard liner *Mauretania* for Europe, where he planned to spend three months with his friend Abel Brown before entering Harvard Law School that autumn. Any kidnapping would have to take place before the trip.

The ransom, Nathan said, was "the most difficult problem. We had several dozen different plans, all of which were not so good for one reason or another."[19] The final plan was deliberately complicated, meant to drag out the process step by step and make it more difficult for police to intervene. First, they would send the kidnapped boy's father a letter, demanding a ransom and telling him to await further news. Later, they would call him with instructions to take the ransom and enter a taxi dispatched to his house. This would deliver him to a certain address, where he should look for a set of instructions taped inside a "Keep the City Clean" wastebasket on the sidewalk.

This new message, in turn, would direct the victim's father to a drugstore on 63rd Street. There, the kidnappers would ring him on the pay telephone, telling him to purchase a ticket on the Michigan Central train to Boston that left the nearby Illinois Central Station each afternoon and made numerous stops on its route. In the last train car, he would find a previously concealed message in the telegraph box telling him to go to the rear platform. This final message would direct him to watch as the train approached the Champion Manufacturing Company at 74th Street, whose tall water tower with the word "Champion," Nathan decided, was a suitable landmark. The area was sufficiently far out of town so that danger of exposure was lessened. Once the train passed the factory, their victim's father should quickly count to five and then toss the bundled ransom from the rear of the train. Nathan and Richard would be waiting, hidden in the overgrown grass and watching through binoculars, to sweep in and retrieve it.[20]

The train idea was Richard's, probably inspired by what was, until 1924, America's most notorious kidnapping case. In 1874, two men had lured a four-year-old Pennsylvania boy named Charley Ross and his six-year-old brother, Walter, into a carriage. They let Walter go, but no one ever saw Charley again. The kidnappers demanded $20,000 from his wealthy father—among other instructions the money was to be dropped from a passing train.[21]

To ensure success, Nathan and Richard started rehearsing this scheme in April. They tied a bundle of newspapers together, to simulate the ransom package. At least once, Richard boarded the afternoon train armed with the bundle; when the train passed the factory, he counted to five and tossed it out. Nathan waited in the grass to make sure he could retrieve it. With each test they slightly adjusted their plans, until they were convinced it would work.[22]

WHEN EXACTLY THE IDEA OF murder entered into the plan, or who first suggested it, isn't known. Richard originally proposed a kidnapping for ransom; Nathan apparently agreed that the initial idea involved only "kidnapping a boy and securing ransom."[23] He suggested raping and killing a girl—perhaps the murder originated with him? But he later insisted that it was Richard who had first mentioned murder. Given Nathan's changing stories, and his repeated efforts to blame Richard for the crime, it's impossible to determine the truth, though both eventually agreed that killing their victim was inevitable to prevent their being identified. Even so, Richard said that he "did not anticipate the actual killing with any pleasure."[24]

How to kill their victim? Richard and Nathan decided they could use a chisel to knock their victim unconscious, though this might not result in death. Nathan suggested using ether as "the easiest" and "least messy" way of killing. Richard was concerned, since he didn't know anything about it.[25] He thought that they could strangle their victim, with each one holding an end of a rope to share culpability.[26] Nathan didn't like this idea.[27] Eventually they apparently agreed to take both ether and a rope with them and make the decision on the spur of the moment.

Nathan suggested how to get rid of the body. He had spent weekends at Wolf Lake, leading groups of amateur ornithologists through its isolated prairie. One day that spring of 1924, Nathan and Richard drove out to the area, parked their car, and walked around, scouting for a place where they could dispose of their victim. Nathan spotted the culvert beneath the Pennsylvania Railroad tracks and decided that this was ideal: their victim could be stuffed into the culvert and out of view, his remains left to rot in the foot or two of muddy water passing through the channel.[28]

Selecting a victim was more complicated. Richard first suggested a young man he disliked; he abandoned the idea because he was "too large and strong" and they could not work out how to get a ransom from his family.[29] Later, there were stories that Nathan and Richard mused over the possibility of kidnapping and killing their own fathers. This doesn't seem to have been seriously considered: they recognized that they would likely to be suspects in any such crime.

Nathan wanted to kidnap and kill Richard's younger brother, Tommy.[30] This may have been a way to test Richard, to see just how far he could be pushed and controlled. If so, it failed. Richard rejected the idea outright: "I could not have done it because I am tremendously fond of him," Richard said of his younger brother.[31] This in itself is telling: Richard clearly had some sort of moral compass left, one that would not allow him to kill his brother; Nathan didn't care who they killed.

Next on the list of possible victims was Richard Rubel, Loeb's self-proclaimed best friend. If Rubel was killed, Richard thought, he'd almost certainly be asked to be a pallbearer at his friend's funeral: the idea gave him "a tremendous thrill." Was this just Richard being glib, or was Rubel under serious consideration? Nathan didn't like Rubel; he may have first suggested it, thinking that this was a splendid idea. But Loeb quickly crossed him off the list. Rubel's father, he said, "was so tight we might not get any money from him."[32]

Eventually, both Richard and Nathan later claimed, they decided that the best plan was to kidnap and kill a young boy at random. The victim would have to have a wealthy father capable of paying the ransom, and would need to know either Nathan or Richard, so that they could easily lure him into their trap. They ran through a list of possibilities and decided that they would find a suitable victim among the boys attending the Harvard School. They considered Armand "Billy"

Deutsch, grandson of Julius Rosenwald, president of Sears. "I knew and trusted both boys," Deutsch would later recall.[33] Richard, though, decided that this might harm his father's business interests. More names filtered through their discussions: young Irvin Hartman Jr., whose father owned a furniture company; Johnny Levinson, whose father was a successful attorney; and Clarence Coleman and Walter Baer, two neighborhood boys also from wealthy families.[34]

Although both later insisted that Bobby Franks had been a random victim, and that he had never been under consideration, this strains credulity. Why would they neglect Richard's second cousin? Bobby Franks, after all, could easily be lured to his death, and his father certainly had the money to pay a ransom. And the afternoon before the murder, Bobby had played tennis on the Loeb court. Had he said something, made some insulting remark, that set Richard off? There were, after all, complaints from faculty at the Harvard School about Bobby, about his smug attitudes and his tendency to be "self-satisfied" and "unpleasant;" Richard described him as "a cocky little son of a bitch," probably the most important thing he ever said about the murder. Perhaps, as the pair insisted, the choice of victim was left to chance, but it is unlikely that Bobby's name didn't cross their lips as they plotted their descent into darkness.

On May 6 Richard's brother Tommy turned ten. The Loebs gave a birthday party at their mansion on Ellis Avenue, and invited a number of Tommy's friends from the Harvard School. It isn't known if Bobby Franks was among the guests—he was four years older than Tommy and may not have been particularly close to him. But nine-year-old Johnny Levinson was there. Something happened at that party that set Richard off. Perhaps it was simply bad behavior or teasing. But Richard grabbed Levinson and spanked him—hard and, as the boy remembered, in a peculiar way that somehow left him frightened—and made him avoid Richard when Loeb approached him on the fateful afternoon of May 21.[35]

WHY DID THEY DO IT? History has insisted that the kidnapping and murder was undertaken merely for the thrill, an idea born by two bored, idle degenerates who wanted to kill for excitement and to pit their wits against the authorities. Their motives were many, and certainly differed. Things had been going badly between Richard and Nathan, and perhaps each saw in this final burst of violence a way to ensure his partner's silence about their previous crimes. Neither felt he could back down. They merely had to walk away from each other, but the secrets between them were too deep now to overcome: resentment, fear, and possibly even hate became part of the equation.

Richard said that he'd committed the crime for a multitude of reasons: "the joy in planning it;" the "thrill in committing it;" the "pleasurable anticipation in waiting for the money;" the publicity; the idea that he could talk about the crime with others who wouldn't know that he had committed it; and finally, the money he hoped to get.[36] "I knew it would make a stir in the newspapers," he later said. "I got an intense thrill out of the plans. The cleverness of the crime appealed to me."[37]

Nathan, too, gave contradictory accounts of his motivations. It was for the "thrill, for the experience," he explained. He blamed Richard, saying he had only done it "because Dick wanted it done." Nathan admitted that it had been a chance to match his "wits against the police," and added that he'd also done it for the ransom money.[38]

Money: this was, Richard said, one of Nathan's principal motivations when the plot was first mentioned.[39] And there is some evidence suggesting that, for Nathan, this was a prime consideration. He received a monthly allowance of $125, and had roughly $32,000 in the bank, much of which he had inherited after his mother's death. But this was in trust, and he couldn't spend it until he turned twenty-one.[40] As Nathan explained, he "wanted a great amount of money" of his own, saying he never had enough.[41] He was about to go to Europe, where he planned to spend the ransom, and then to Harvard in the autumn. Perhaps a desire for money played a larger role in Nathan's motivation than previously suspected. When things began to fall apart, and

Bobby's body had been found, it was Nathan who would insist on continuing the effort to get the ransom.

Yet deeper motives may have been at work. Richard may have felt trapped in the relationship by both Nathan's knowledge of his criminal history and by their shared sexual liaison. Despite his general apathy toward sex, he likely didn't want to live under the threat of possible exposure. Perhaps he regarded the crime as a way to ensure Leopold's silence on their relationship.

And, for Nathan, equally nuanced motives may have influenced his decisions. Perhaps he imagined that committing the crime would once again draw him closer to Richard, bind them together in such a way that things could never be broken, an unbreakable bond signed in blood. And Richard, after all, would be tainted, ruined, with only Nathan, his fellow murderer, his fellow "pervert," left to stand by his side. It's possible that Nathan never really probed too deeply, but possession might have been an unconscious motivation of which even he was unaware.

COINCIDENTALLY OR NOT, IT WAS on Wednesday, May 7, 1924—the day after Tommy Loeb's birthday party—that Richard and Nathan took their most significant steps in the plan. They hoped to lure an unsuspecting boy into a car. This presented certain problems. Richard had recently been in an accident and his car was under repair; Nathan had his red Willys-Knight, but there was nothing inconspicuous about it, and it would be all too easy for someone in the neighborhood to identify it. Both of their families had a number of cars, but none seemed suitable. And so Nathan suggested renting a car for the kidnapping and murder.[42]

This required additional planning. They didn't want to rent the car in either of their names, and so decided to use a false identity. On Wednesday, May 7, 1924, Richard cashed a check for a hundred dollars on his account at the Hyde Park State Bank.[43] Nathan drove him to the Morrison Hotel, where Richard registered under the name of Morton D. Ballard, claiming to be a visiting businessman from Peoria. He was given room 1031; to further the charade, he carried an old suitcase, which he had filled with books. Belying their views of themselves as master criminals, at least four of the books had been checked out from the University of Chicago and one, *Journal of the Constitutional Convention,* still had a card with Richard's name in it.[44] Nathan and Richard then returned to the Hyde Park State Bank. Nathan entered, armed with Richard's hundred dollars, and opened a new account using the name of Morton Ballard, temporarily of Room 1031 at the Morrison Hotel; a few days later Richard gave him an additional four hundred dollars in cash to deposit.[45]

On May 9 the pair drove to the Rent-A-Car Company at 1426 South Michigan. Nathan gave his name as Morton Ballard, currently of the Morrison Hotel, and asked to rent a car. He showed his bank-book from the Hyde Park State Bank, but the company wanted references. Nathan explained that he was a visiting representative from the Chick Manufacturing Company of Peoria and knew only one person in Chicago, a man named Louis Mason, whose telephone number he handed over.[46]

Walter Jacobs, owner of the rental company, rang the number. He was actually calling a restaurant, Barish's Delicatessen, at 1352 Wabash Avenue, where Richard waited by the pay phone.[47] When the phone rang, Richard grabbed it and quickly identified himself as Louis Mason. He said that he had known Ballard "for years. He's a good man, thoroughly reliable. He'll return the car. There will be no problems."[48] Jacobs agreed to rent "Ballard" a car. They had several Fords or Willys-Knights available; Nathan decided to take a Willys-Knight, which cost him two more cents a mile to rent. He also had to leave a fifty-dollar deposit.[49]

Nathan and Richard had no intention of carrying out their plan that day—they'd rented the Willys-Knight, as Leopold explained, only "so we would have no difficulty in getting the car next time."[50] They drove around aimlessly for a few hours and then returned it before nightfall. Before leaving, Nathan asked that the company send his registration card, which would let him rent another car without having to again provide references, to the Morrison Hotel.

A few days later Richard returned to the Morrison Hotel and found that the suitcase he had left had been removed from Room 1031. "Apparently the fact the beds had not been used was noticed and some suspicion occurred," Nathan remembered. Worried that he might be questioned if he asked for the suitcase, Richard left without paying his bill. They decided to go to the Trenier Hotel, where Richard again registered as Ballard. Nathan telephoned the Rent-A-Car company and explained that he had moved to the Trenier Hotel, asking that his registration card be sent there instead of to the Morrison Hotel.[51]

Nathan and Richard decided to enact their plan on Wednesday, May 21. On Saturday, May 17, Richard was out in the Kenwood neighborhood when he spotted thirteen-year-old Robert Asher, who attended the Harvard School. He played catch with Asher for a while, then suggested, "You ought to come out and see a real ball game sometime." Perhaps Asher would like to attend one the following week? He even offered to give Asher a ride. But Asher declined: he had a dentist appointment that day.[52] That weekend Nathan spent both Saturday and Sunday with several friends at Wolf Lake, watching for birds.

Both Nathan and Richard claimed to have been ambivalent about the crime in the weeks leading up to May 21. Richard was especially plagued with doubts. In 1922, his father, Albert Loeb, had been forced to step back from his daily role at Sears owing to the onset of heart trouble.[53] On Sunday, May 18, Albert had a heart attack. It wasn't serious enough to require hospitalization, but it played into Richard's second thoughts.[54] "I was afraid my father, a sick man, could not withstand the shock," Richard said, if he was caught.[55] Beyond this, he admitted to "some feelings of remorse" as he pondered the crime.[56] The planning had been exciting; the idea of committing murder had no attraction as it loomed ever larger in the future.[57] Richard wanted "to withdraw" from the scheme but felt that he could not do so because "of the time spent, because of the trouble they had gone to." More tellingly, he confessed that he was "afraid" of what Nathan might think and do if he backed out.[58] And so he continued, locked in a fatal danse macabre with his explosive friend.

Nathan and Richard spent Tuesday, May 20, preparing for the following day. Nathan drove to a hardware store at 4236 Cottage Grove Avenue. Richard went in, purchasing a chisel for seventy-five cents; he also bought a length of rope, with which they could strangle their victim, from a second hardware store.[59] Next, they stopped at a drugstore. Nathan went in and attempted to purchase a bottle of hydrochloric acid, but the clerk refused to sell it to him.[60] Nathan tried again at another drugstore on Cottage Grove: this time he purchased a pint bottle from druggist Aaron Adler.[61]

The pair drove to the Leopold house, where Nathan got some rags to use with ether to incapacitate or kill their victim. He also grabbed an extra car lap rug from the garage, which they could use to wrap the body. They put it, the rags, ether, a pair of rubber boots, the rope, the acid, the chisel, and some tape that they would use to blunt its blade, into Nathan's car in preparation for the following day.[62]

Richard and Nathan had written drafts of not only the ransom letter but also of the note which was to be taped to a "Keep the City Clean" waste bin and the one to be hidden aboard the train. They even wrote out scripts to follow when telephoning news of the kidnapping to the boy's parents.[63] Richard likely composed most of the ransom letter.

A week earlier, Nathan had strolled into the store of Hokan Stromberg and examined his stock of paper and envelopes. He finally picked up a pad of *Our Leader* stationery in a white satin finish, saying, "That will do."[64] Now, sitting in his third floor study, he inserted a sheet into the portable Underwood typewriter they had stolen in Ann Arbor. "I had used a typewriter since high school," he recalled, "and was reasonably fast and accurate with it. But I depended on the hunt and peck system and used three fingers on my right hand and two on my left."[65] Richard read from the drafts, with Nathan typing out the texts.

Around eleven that night Richard returned to his own home a few blocks away. Everything was in readiness for the following day. "We thought we had it all so cleverly worked out and felt certain of not being caught," Richard would later comment, "or we would not have gone into it."[66]

CHAPTER NINE

WEDNESDAY, MAY 21, 1924, BROKE GRAY AND COOL OVER CHICAGO. At half past seven that morning, Leopold family chauffeur Sven Englund started Nathan's red Willys-Knight and backed it out of the garage, leaving it on the driveway next to a side entrance to the house.[1] A few minutes later, Nathan came out, hopped in the car, and drove off to attend his 8:00 a.m. class in criminal law at the University of Chicago. He sat in on a French class at nine and had an additional law class at ten.

Around eleven, Richard met Nathan at the university, and the pair set off for the Rent-A-Car agency; Richard drove and dropped Nathan off just down the block. Nathan entered, walked to the desk, and asked to rent a car for twenty-four hours. This time, he selected a fairly new four-door, five-passenger Willys-Knight Model 64 touring car, dark blue in color, with a canvas top.[2] He paid a thirty-five-dollar deposit and left.[3]

It was now noon, and the pair drove to Kramer's Restaurant on Cottage Grove Avenue for lunch, Richard following in Nathan's car. Before going inside, they looked the rental car over. They had decided that one of them would drive and the other would sit in the back seat directly behind their victim. To guard against exposure, Nathan and Richard raised the car's side curtains; these were actually canvas panels, with isinglass windows, that could be snapped in place.[4]

They finished lunch, Nathan thought, shortly after one, and switched cars, Richard taking the rental and following Nathan in his own car back to his house. Here, they transferred the chisel, ether, rags, a pair of rubber boots, a roll of adhesive tape, and an extra car lap rug, from the trunk of Nathan's car into the rental car.[5] Sven Englund saw them, and Nathan quickly pulled him aside. The brakes on his car, Nathan complained, were squeaking and needed to be checked. He asked Englund to fix them and, after filling the rental car with gasoline from the family's private pump, drove off with Richard.[6]

Nathan and Richard had decided to select a victim from the Harvard School. But it was only a little after one, and school was in session until half past two. To kill time, they drove to Jackson Park and parked near the golf course. Here they wrapped the blade of the chisel with the tape they had brought—as so often in this case, each claimed that the other had done so.[7]

Around 2:15 that afternoon they left Jackson Park and drove back to Kenwood, parking the car on the east side of Ingleside Avenue down the block from the Harvard School. Amazingly for a pair of self-proclaimed criminal geniuses, they made no effort to conceal themselves. Richard got out of the car and walked over the playground area at the rear of the school, speaking to instructor J. T. Seass and to his brother Tommy, even as he kept an eye out for a possible victim. After a few minutes, Nathan whistled for him and Richard returned to the car. Nathan, who claimed to be so reluctant about the plan, had also been walking the streets, looking for a possible victim. The two went down the alley behind Ingleside as Nathan told Richard that he had seen some children playing farther down on Ingelside that they might kidnap. But they decided that there were too many sets of eyes.[8]

Walking west, the pair encountered another group of children playing in a vacant lot at the corner of 49th Street and Drexel Boulevard. Richard spotted nine-year-old Johnny Levinson and spoke to him briefly, then returned to the car. "It was impossible to watch them closely unless we showed ourselves," Richard recalled. Only now did they decide that it was better to scope out potential victims from a distance. Richard drove Nathan back to his house and dropped him off; Nathan retrieved a pair of binoculars he used when bird-watching. Richard drove over to a nearby drugstore to look up Levinson's address. He also purchased several packages of Dentyne chewing gum before collecting Nathan.[9]

They again parked on Drexel. Nathan tried to pick out Levinson through his binoculars but suddenly the boys in the lot dispersed. "I went to look for him in the alley," Richard said, "but didn't see him." The pair wandered along the streets: another group of boys was playing baseball in a lot at the corner of 48th and South Greenwood just opposite Nathan's house. They briefly went into the house and watched them through a window: among them were two—Clarence Coleman and Walter Baer—whom they had earlier pondered as potential victims. But they gave up on the idea, returning to the car and driving along the route to Levinson's house, thinking that they might catch up with him as he walked home. But he was nowhere to be seen.[10]

It was getting late and, as afternoon neared early evening, they realized that neighborhood boys would soon be returning to their homes for dinner. If they couldn't find a victim soon, they would have to abandon the planned crime. Then, about five that Wednesday afternoon, as they were driving north on Ellis Avenue, Richard spotted Bobby Franks, walking south on the west side of the avenue. They passed him as he crossed 49th Street; not wanting to lose him, they turned west into 48th Street and swung the car around; according to Richard, it was at this point, as he pulled the car over to the side of the road, that Nathan climbed into the back seat before they returned to Ellis, this time headed south, as they shadowed Bobby.[11]

As Bobby neared the corner of Ellis Avenue and 49th Street the car pulled up alongside him. Both Richard and Nathan agreed that Loeb opened the front passenger door of the car to speak to the boy.[12] Richard, Nathan said, shouted out, "Hey Bob!" Bobby came over to the car, and Richard asked if he would like a ride home. Bobby declined; he was less than two blocks from his house—he could almost see it if he looked down the avenue. Richard persisted, saying, "Come in a minute. I want to talk to you about a tennis racket."[13] The Loebs had a private tennis court, and because he was a relative Bobby often used it: just the previous afternoon he'd played a few games with Richard. The older boy had taken special note of Bobby's racket, smaller and more suited to his size. He thought his brother Tommy ought to have one.[14]

Bobby approached the car. As he did so, Richard introduced him to Nathan.[15] Richard would later recall "the sight of that happy little boy, swinging down the sunlit sidewalk, swaying from side to side in his happiness, his innocence. . . . He was such a fine kid."[16] Bobby relented and climbed into the front passenger seat. He had no reason to be uneasy. As the car went down Ellis, Richard asked Bobby if they could circle the block; Bobby agreed.[17]

As soon as the car turned east on to 50th Street the killer struck. In a sudden fury, the chisel sliced through the air, striking Bobby on the right side of his forehead. A second blow landed above his left eyebrow as he turned in his seat toward his assailant in the back, shocked, confused, trying to understand what was happening.[18] Blood flew about the car. There was a struggle, and Bobby "made whimpering and moaning sounds," Richard said.[19] As the killer dragged Bobby over the seat and into the rear of the car, he scratched the left side of the boy's face and forehead before pushing him onto the floorboards; two more blows rained down on the back of his head. Finally a rag soaked in ether was shoved deeply down his throat.[20]

LEOPOLD AND LOEB: ONE WAS driving, and the other sat in the back seat. Which was which became a point of contention and remains the biggest mystery in the case. A hundred years on, the question of who actually killed Bobby seems unsolvable. Only three people were present, one a victim and the other two known liars.

Nathan pointed the finger of blame at Richard. "At the time the Franks boy entered our car, I was driving, not Mr. Loeb, and Mr. Loeb was in the back seat," he said. "It was Mr. Loeb who struck him with the chisel, and not I." According to Nathan, "as soon as we turned the corner, Richard placed his one hand over Robert's mouth to stifle his outcry, with his right beating him on the head several times with the chisel."[21]

Richard claimed that he had been driving and that it was Nathan who had struck Bobby over the head. "Leopold," he stated, "reached his arm around young Franks, grabbed his mouth, and hit him over the head with a chisel. I believe he hit him several times, I do not know the exact number."[22]

Both men agreed that Richard had opened the front passenger door to speak to Bobby. The Willys-Knight Model 64 touring car was a substantial, sizable vehicle: feet, not inches, separated the front door from the back seat, and it could not easily be opened by someone in the rear simply leaning forward. Yet Nathan claimed that Richard had clambered forward several feet, apparently crouched on the floor, opened up the front passenger door, and managed to converse with Bobby in this awkward position, draping himself over the front seat.[23] Richard always insisted that he'd simply reached across the front seat to open the passenger door. Bobby, Richard said, "was a boy that I knew. If I was sitting in the back seat, he would have gotten in the back seat with me. He was a boy I know, and I would have opened the door and motioned him in that way. As it was, he got in the front seat with me because I knew the boy and I opened the front door."[24]

The pair had ether and rags in the back seat to use on their victim. Nathan, Richard said, "was supposed to do that, because I don't know a damn thing about it. He has a number of times chloroformed birds and things like that, and he knows ornithology and I don't know a damn thing about that."[25] If the ether-soaked rags in the back were to be used on the victim, it simply makes sense that Nathan would have been the one to do so.

Richard was vague about the specifics of the attack on Bobby, as might be expected had he been driving the car at the time. But Nathan's account of the assault was inexplicably detailed. He said that there were "exactly four of the blows struck." He claimed he knew this because "I heard them and glancing over saw them." He described which hand was used to stifle Bobby's mouth and which to strike him; the way in which the chisel was used; and his surprise that there was so much blood.[26] How, one wonders, did he manage to drive and simultaneously observe all of the details of the attack?

Perhaps most compelling, the only independent eyewitness bolstered Richard's claim that he was driving. Chauffeur Carl Ulving was on Ellis Avenue within thirty minutes of the pair grabbing Bobby Franks when he spotted their car, "dark blue or dark green," with the canvas side curtains pulled up, obscuring the view into the back seat. Ulving had known Richard for years, and he clearly recognized him behind the wheel. He waved at him, and Richard waved back.[27]

The evidence, such as it is, thus supports Loeb's claim that he was the driver, and that Leopold was the actual killer. It was Nathan who harbored violent and sadistic fantasies; who had dreamed of torturing people; and who repeatedly declared that murder was no crime. It was Nathan who had wanted to kidnap, rape, and kill a young girl. He was, by nature and temperament, more likely to have engaged in violence than Richard.

If the original idea for the scheme likely originated with Richard, as Nathan claimed, it also seemed most likely that Nathan was the one who actually wielded the chisel that May afternoon.

LEOPOLD AND LOEB DROVE SOUTH, cutting through Jackson Park and then taking South Chicago Avenue along the edge of Lake Michigan out of the city and toward Wolf Lake. As they neared Hammond, Indiana, Richard said, Nathan told him to pull onto a lonely dirt road so that he could climb into the front passenger seat.[28] Behind them, Bobby lay on the rear floor, covered with the lap rug, bleeding and unconscious but not yet dead.

They left this deserted road only to turn down another. Both Nathan and Richard said that they took advantage of the quiet to partially undress Bobby, removing his shoes, socks, and pants. "We did this in order to save the trouble of too much undressing him later on," Richard claimed.[29]

This made little sense and became one of the most contentious issues in the case. Bobby had on shoes, socks, underwear, and pants below the waist; above the waist he wore a shirt with a collar and tie, sleeves and front that had to be unbuttoned, with a belted jacket over this. If speed and a desire to strip Bobby of his most cumbersome clothing was the issue, logic dictated that the pair begin with his upper torso—with arms that had to be twisted as opposed to legs from which pants could easily be pulled straight off.

State's attorney Robert Crowe would argue that they removed Bobby's pants to molest him, a fetid charge he insisted was fully in keeping with his declaration that Leopold and Loeb were "perverts." As evidence he pointed to the autopsy finding that Bobby's "rectum was dilated, and would admit easily one middle finger," although the coroner didn't see any signs of "recent forcible dilation."[30] Crowe thought that the distended rectum proved assault; any evidence, like semen, he later asserted, was "washed away" as Bobby lay in water running through the culvert.[31]

More important, though, was other evidence found on the body, and which inexplicably escaped Crowe's attention. There were bleeding scratches found across Bobby's left shoulder extending down his back, and also scratches to his right buttock.[32] As the autopsy report determined, these hadn't been caused when the body was pushed into the culvert: they could only have been made after Bobby's pants and underwear were removed, but while he was still alive and his heart was still pumping blood as they had bled.

These scratches alone prove that Bobby lived longer than previously thought. In order for the wounds to bleed, he had to have been alive at least an hour after the initial assault in Chicago. While the rag stuffed into his mouth may have rendered him unconscious, it did not immediately kill him. He may have been unconscious but still inhaling short breaths, drawing the ether down his throat until he finally suffocated.[33]

Nathan's favorite sexual activity was lying atop Richard, who feigned being unconscious, and thrusting his penis between his friend's thighs as he pretended to rape him. Did he repeat this with Bobby? He was, after all, the one with sadistic and violent sexual fantasies. Violence that left bleeding scratches was indeed inflicted on Bobby as he lay facedown and with his pants off. And before his arrest, Nathan had a curious conversation with his law professor at the University of Chicago. Would the penalty for the crime increase, he asked, if Bobby Franks had been molested?[34] It was an odd question if nothing of the kind had happened.

No one will ever know the truth about the issue. It is possible that no sexual assault took place; it is also possible that Nathan took advantage of being alone with Bobby—as Richard drove or after they had parked and undressed him—to enact one of his favorite sexual fantasies; it certainly fits in with his character and past behavior. Crowe assumed molestation meant penetration. Had he probed more closely into Nathan's sexual history he might have understood that the mere act of removing Bobby's pants, as well as the scratches on his buttock and back, were more suggestive than he realized.

RICHARD AND NATHAN WAITED FOR nightfall, cruising around aimlessly before stopping at the Dew Drop Inn to get hot dogs and root beers. They ate in the car, with Bobby sprawled on the rear floor.[35]

It was only a little after six, still too light for the killers to safely dispose of Bobby, and so Richard again drove "back and forth, and back and forth" as they waited. Nathan asked Richard to stop at a drugstore and went inside to call Susan Lurie, reminding her of a planned date the following week. When Nathan returned, according to Richard, he said, "Slip over and let me drive for a while."[36]

Sometime after half past eight, Nathan finally pulled onto the dirt road off 108th Street and Avenue F and headed toward Wolf Lake, parking the car a few hundred feet from the channel that passed through the culvert. Silence lay across the prairie; it seemed isolated from the rest of the world. "It was fairly dark, but still not pitch black," Richard said, "so that we were able to work without a flashlight." They dragged the body from the car, placed it on the lap rug, and used the lap rug as a stretcher to carry him down the embankment to the side of the culvert. The head, Richard recalled, had bled "quite freely. There was quite a bit of blood; the blanket or robe was quite saturated."[37]

Nathan sat down beside the channel, throwing off his coat and exchanging his shoes for a pair of rubber boots. In the dim light, they finished stripping the body. Richard hesitated when it came time to pour hydrochloric acid over Bobby; he said he was suddenly overcome with remorse.[38] And so Nathan emptied the bottle over Bobby's face, a scar on his abdomen, and his genitals.[39]

Richard saw the stream of acid hit Bobby. "We knew he was dead," he said, "by the fact that rigor mortis had set in, and also by his eyes. . . . We noticed no tremor, not a single tremor in his body."[40]

Nathan splashed into the water and began pushing Bobby, head-first and facedown, into the narrow culvert. "At first," Nathan said, "I thought it was rather doubtful whether it would fit at all, but after it started it was not hard at all."[41] Finally, he kicked the body until the boy's feet were barely inside the pipe.

Richard ran to the opposite side of the narrow channel: "I washed my hands, which had become bloody through carrying the body," he said.[42] After concealing the corpse, Nathan returned to the embankment, sat down, removed the boots, and put his shoes back on. He asked Richard to hand him his coat, which he had tossed aside. Richard grabbed it and gave it to Nathan; darkness had now fallen, and neither man saw that Nathan's reading glasses fell from the pocket to the ground. They took Bobby's bloody clothes and bundled them into the lap robe, carrying them back to the vehicle: they planned to dispose of them later. In the darkness, they missed one of Bobby's stockings on the ground nearby.[43]

It was, Nathan thought, sometime between 9:20 and 9:30 that night when they climbed back into the rented Willys-Knight and left Wolf Lake.[44] As they raced down the dirt road, they nearly struck Lucille Smith and her young daughter, the car's headlights blinding the pair as it quickly swept past them and disappeared into the darkness.

RICHARD AND NATHAN HAD ENACTED their choreographed dance of death. They were now bound to each other and, by extension, to Bobby, an unholy, eternal union consummated in blood. It had happened, the horrible thing so long planned, so anticipated. What did they feel? "This is terrible, this is terrible!" Nathan had shouted during the murder. Richard admitted to being excited but said that he tried to act "cool and self-possessed" to calm Nathan down. He joked with him, he said, both to reassure his friend and "possibly to calm myself, too."[45]

"It's over," Nathan later claimed musing to himself. "There's no turning back now. How on earth could I ever have got involved in this thing? It was horrible—more horrible even than I figured it was going to be." But, as he admitted, "I can recall no feeling then of remorse."[46] Richard, too, claimed conflicted feelings. "I felt sorry about the thing, about the killing of the boy," he said.[47]

Their night was not finished. They stopped at a drugstore on Stony Island Avenue, where Nathan bought a slug—pay telephones took prepaid tokens to make calls. "I looked up the address of Jacob Franks and the telephone number," Richard recalled, "and at the same time Leopold printed the address" on the envelope containing the ransom letter.[48] He affixed two six-cent postage stamps, and scrawled and underlined the word "Special" on the envelope.

Nathan dialed the Franks house, but there was a delay in the connection; worried that the police might already have put a trace on the line, Nathan hung up and the pair drove off. On their way, they passed a mailbox at 55th Street; Nathan jumped out and put the ransom letter into the box.[49] Spotting another drugstore, Nathan hopped out of the car and again rang the Franks residence. This time the connection went through, and Nathan told Flora Franks that her son had been kidnapped.

Then, it was off to Richard's house, where the pair took the bloody lap rug and Bobby's clothes, sorting through them in the basement. The clothing went into the incinerator; they held back Bobby's belt buckle and school pin to dispose of later. "We intended burning the robe [lap rug]," Nathan explained, "but it was too large to fit and would have caused an awful stench." Richard hid it beneath some bushes outside the greenhouse in his backyard. They grabbed a bucket of water, some soap, and brushes, and made a half-hearted effort to clean the rental car's interior, but finally abandoned this project because it was getting late and, as Nathan said, "we didn't want to be monkeying around too much."[50]

Nathan and Richard next drove to the Leopold house; Nathan parked the rental car on South Greenwood Avenue, then took his own vehicle out of the garage and used it to take his visiting aunt and uncle home. On returning, he and Richard had several drinks with Nathan's father and played cards until half past one in the morning.[51] Finally, Nathan drove Richard home. On the way, Richard tossed the bloody chisel, which they had taken from the rental car, out of the window.

Despite his late night, Nathan was up early on Thursday morning to attend law classes at the University of Chicago. At eleven he met Richard, and the pair lunched at the Cooper-Carlton Hotel with Richard Rubel. After a quick detour so that Richard could fetch his father's glasses, hat, and overcoat to wear as a disguise, they returned to the Leopold house. Nathan moved the rented Willys-Knight into the driveway.[52]

Now, in clear daylight, they could see that the interior of the car looked like a slaughterhouse. A nearly two-foot-long, ugly crimson stain spread across the back of the seat where Bobby had been attacked; there was blood on the adjoining door, and blood had pooled and dripped through the carpet onto the floorboards. There was more blood in the rear of the car—on the passenger-side door and on the carpet.[53] How could they possibly return it in such a condition without raising serious questions?

Richard grabbed a pail of water in one hand and a can of Bon Ami cleanser in the other and joined Nathan in attempting to clean

the car's interior.[54] As they tried to scrub the bloodstains away, Sven Englund, the Leopold family chauffeur, came out of the garage. He thought it was odd: he'd never seen either young man clean a car before.[55] Curious, he walked over: before they could stop him he peered inside and apparently saw the stains.

"It looks like blood," Englund said.

"No, it isn't blood," Richard assured him.

"We've been doing a little bootlegging," Nathan told Englund with a smile. "We don't want the folks to find out. Don't say anything about it."[56] The pair continued on but were either too preoccupied or too lazy to make a thorough job of it: they would return the car with the red stains clearly visible on the upholstery and on the floor.

After Nathan fetched the two previously typed sets of instructions that would send their victim's father on his circuitous route to avoid his being followed, the pair drove off. They stopped at the corner of Vincennes Avenue and Pershing Road, where they wanted to leave a note inside a "Keep the City Clean" trash bin directing Jacob Franks to wait for a telephone call at a nearby drugstore, where he would receive further directions. The note, though, wouldn't stick: "fearing that it might blow away or somebody might open the box and have it blow away," Richard recalled, "we decided that the best thing to do was to entirely omit this letter from our calculations."[57] Instead, they decided to simply telephone the Franks house with instructions directing Jacob to a nearby drugstore, where he was to wait by the pay telephone for a call that would send him to the Illinois Central Railway Station later that afternoon.

At the station, Richard—wearing the long coat, hat, and glasses as a disguise—purchased a seventy-five-cent ticket for the next train to Michigan City, Indiana.[58] He hopped aboard, made his way to the last Pullman car, and placed an envelope, addressed to Jacob Franks, in the telegraph box: "Dear Sir: Proceed immediately to the back of the platform of the train, watch the east side of the track, have your package ready, look for the first large red brick factory situated immediately adjoining the tracks on the east. On top of this factory is a large black

water tower with the word 'Champion' written on it. Wait until you have completely passed the south end of the factory, count five very rapidly and then immediately throw the package as far east as you can. Remember, this is the only chance to recover your son. Yours truly, George Johnson." Scrawled on the envelope was a message: "Mr. Jacob Franks. Should somebody else find this note, please leave it alone. The letter is very important."[59]

Task over, Richard disembarked, tore up his ticket, and joined Nathan at a phone booth. Leopold asked that a taxi from the Yellow Cab Company go immediately to the Franks residence to collect a fare. But before Nathan could call the Franks house with the address of the drugstore where Jacob was to wait, they saw the afternoon newspaper and its headline, "Unidentified Boy Found In Swamp."[60] Richard decided that it was all over—"I was not very anxious to go on with the matter," he said. He argued that they should abandon the entire scheme.[61] Nathan objected: "I insisted," he said, "that it could do no harm to call the drugstore."[62] Richard gave in, and Nathan rang the Franks house with instructions for Jacob to go to the Van de Bogert & Ross Drugstore at 1465 East 63rd Street.

A half hour later, when Nathan twice rang the number for Van de Bogert & Ross and asked for "Mr. Franks," he was told that there was no such person in the store. With the second failure, Nathan said, "we gave it up as a bad job." It was sometime between five and five thirty that afternoon that Nathan returned the rental car, making sure to get the rest of his deposit back. On their way back home, Nathan and Richard stopped for a soda.[63]

IN THE DAYS AFTER THE murder, Richard seemingly couldn't keep from involving himself in the story. On May 24 he'd corralled his reporter friends and actually led them, through a process of elimination, to Van de Bogert & Ross Drugstore; that afternoon, he'd joined them at the coroner's inquest on Bobby's death. He said he "got a tremendous kick" in discussing the case with others, especially his own

family. Over dinner, his mother declared that whoever had committed the crime deserved to be tarred and feathered; "this," Richard later said, "tickled my sense of humor, to think that she was saying this about her own son." Albert Loeb, recovering from his heart attack, said little; Richard worried that perhaps his father somehow suspected him. Amid all of this talk, Richard admitted that he felt "some slight remorse."[64]

On Friday night both Richard and Nathan went dancing at the Edgewater Beach Hotel: Richard took his occasional girlfriend Germaine Reinhardt, while Nathan brought his friend Susan Lurie. When Nathan introduced Loeb to another guest, Richard grinned and supposedly said, "You've just enjoyed the treat of shaking hands with a murderer."[65] Was Richard really so careless? His attempts to involve himself in the investigation were reckless, but here we have only the word of the other guest, in this case Abel Brown. Brown was one of Nathan's few friends. Later on he would make numerous questionable statements depicting Richard as little short of a psychopath who had manipulated poor Leopold into a single, tragic mistake, rendering his account of this alleged comment suspect.

Nathan seemed to be in a good mood that night. Thoughts of the murder, he admitted, "did not mingle with nor affect my daily doings."[66] He supposedly told acquaintances that if he was suddenly struck by lightning and killed, he would have no regrets—"I already have experienced everything that life has to offer," he declared.[67] Privately, though, he was fretting. He had seen the photograph of the glasses found near the body and quickly realized that they were his. When Nathan told Richard, his friend erupted: "How the hell could you be such a stupe? Look, can they trace them, do you think?"

"There must be a jillion pairs like them in the city," Nathan replied. "So, I don't think there's much chance of their being traced. On the other hand, I've got all the alibi in the world for their being found there. You know I go birding out there all the time." But when he proposed going to the police Richard strenuously objected: "I think that'd be a fool caper. Don't get mixed up in the case at all." This was rich coming from a man who had already mixed himself up in the case, but Richard insisted: "Hell, let it go. You don't know your glasses are gone. Make 'em come to you. Then, if wurst comes to sausage, you can be so surprised that the glasses are yours. Then's the time to tell your story about losing 'em birding."[68]

Entitlement had always surrounded Richard and Nathan, a kind of safety net ensured by their fathers' money and prestige. They fully expected to get away with it, clinging to notions that they had enacted a brilliant crime. For all of their planning, though, they'd made mistake after mistake. Richard had lingered around the Harvard School on the afternoon of Bobby's disappearance and injected himself into the investigation by "assisting" reporters. Nathan hadn't taken enough care to conceal Bobby's body from discovery and had dropped his glasses. They acted recklessly, almost impulsively, as might be expected from two teenagers.

Still, worried that authorities might investigate, the pair met around two on the morning of Sunday, May 25, to get rid of the remaining evidence: the bloody lap rug and the stolen Underwood portable typewriter. They drove to Jackson Park, stopping on a bridge over the lagoon; watching over them in the dim light was the immense gold statue of Columbia, a remnant of the 1893 exposition. Richard used a pair of pliers to twist the keys off the typewriter and "threw them off the bridge." After this, they drove to a secluded spot at the edge of Lake Michigan, soaked the lap rug with gasoline, and set it on fire.[69]

They also agreed on an alibi. They would say that they had spent the afternoon and evening of May 21 together, drinking, eating, and picking up girls. Nathan argued that they should use the alibi if either of them was questioned up to the end of the first week of June. "Hell, no!" Richard shot back. "That's way too long." He insisted that no one could possibly remember their exact whereabouts on what was supposed to have been an uneventful day if that much time had passed. He suggested five days; Nathan thought that this was too short. Finally, they agreed upon a week. But they never determined precisely what a week meant: Richard interpreted the termination as Wednesday, May 28, one week from the kidnapping and murder; Nathan, though, decided it really meant Thursday, May 29, one week after their failure to reach Jacob Franks at the drugstore ended the scheme.[70]

It was just a few hours later that things began unraveling, when police picked up Nathan and questioned him about his frequent visits to Wolf Lake and the glasses found near the body. If not quite as incautious as Richard, Nathan, too, seemingly couldn't resist discussing the crime. "I got some kick from reading the papers," he admitted.[71] After leaving the police station, Nathan met Susan Lurie and spent the afternoon with her. Over lunch he pulled out the newspapers, smiled, and said, "Let's see what has happened in the Franks case." When Susan jokingly suggested that Nathan should confess to get the reward money, "he laughed gaily."[72]

Nathan took—and passed—his law examinations on Monday, May 26, asking that the results be forwarded to Harvard, where he planned to enroll that autumn.[73] Two days later, and although he had finished with his coursework, Nathan cornered his law professor, Ernst W. Puttkammer, in his University of Chicago office. Nathan wanted to talk about the Franks case; Puttkammer wasn't interested, but Leopold wouldn't give up and launched into a series of questions. What, he asked, would the law be if "the little boy were taken into the car with the intention of killing him?" Puttkammer told him that "it was perfectly obvious that there, the intention would be to take a human life, and human life was actually taken, and that it would be murder, very clearly." Nathan followed up with: "Suppose the intent was simply to kidnap, nothing else?" It wouldn't matter, Puttkammer explained. In Illinois, kidnapping, like murder, was considered a capital crime, subject to the death penalty. Then Nathan asked the most peculiar—and perhaps revealing—question: "Suppose that the intent were simply to take improper liberties with the boy? I understand that this is a misdemeanor here in Illinois." But Puttkammer pointed out that while molestation might be a misdemeanor, the actual kidnapping automatically could be charged as a capital case—the reason didn't matter.[74]

On Thursday May 29, police picked up both Leopold and Loeb and brought them to the LaSalle Hotel for questioning. In just thirty hours, Richard would confess to the crime.

PART III

ENTER THE EXPERTS

CHAPTER TEN

RICHARD HAD BROKEN FIRST—THAT FACT SAID MUCH ABOUT LEO-
pold and Loeb and the power dynamic in their relationship. Nathan
was disgusted that his friend lacked the backbone to stand up under
questioning, that he'd collapsed so quickly under pressure. And that
antipathy spilled over in the confessions.

State's attorney Robert Crowe listened as Richard and Nathan
poured out their stories early on the morning of Saturday, May 31.
Both gave similar outlines of the plot: the idea of kidnapping a child,
the subterfuge of renting a car, and the complicated arrangements for
collecting the ransom. But when it came to who had actually struck
Bobby with the chisel, each blamed the other. Nathan said he was
driving: "As soon as we turned the corner, Richard placed his one
hand over Robert's mouth to stifle his outcry, with his right beating
him on the head several times with a chisel, especially prepared for the
purpose. The boy did not succumb as readily as we had believed so
for fear of being observed Richard seized him and pulled him into the
back seat. Here he forced a cloth into his mouth. Apparently, the boy
died instantly by suffocation shortly thereafter."[1]

Richard, though, said Nathan had struck Bobby, who "began to
bleed and was not entirely unconscious. He was moaning. I proceeded

further east on 50th and turned, I believe, at Dorchester. At this time Leopold grabbed Franks and carried him over back of the front seat and threw him on a rug in the car. He then took one of the rags and gagged him by sticking it down his throat, I believe." He ended by saying, "I offer no excuse, but I am fully convinced that neither the idea nor the act would have occurred to me, had it not been for the suggestion and stimulus of Leopold. Furthermore, I do not believe I would have been capable of having killed Franks."[2]

At the end of their separate confessions, Crowe brought Richard and Nathan together in the same room and had their respective statements read aloud. A storm erupted as soon as the issue of who struck Bobby arose: according to the *Chicago Daily News,* the former friends "cursed each other, shouted hysterical charges, and denials, and threats."[3] From a legal standpoint it made no difference: in the eyes of the law, both Richard and Nathan were equally guilty of murder. But neither wanted the moral opprobrium that would fall on the actual killer. Several times during questioning that weekend, Nathan made some heavy-handed attempts to blame Richard for Bobby's death. "Dick, you know you have always read detective stories and always wanted to commit a perfect crime," he interjected during one interview.[4]

Crowe persisted, repeatedly asking who had struck Bobby. "Nathan Leopold, Jr.," Richard said. "He was sitting up in the front seat. I said he was sitting in the front seat. I mean I was sitting up in the front seat. That is obviously a mistake. I am getting excited. This Franks boy got up in the front seat. Now he was a boy that I knew. If I was sitting in the back seat, he would have gotten in the back seat with me. . . . I would have opened the door and motioned him in that way. As it was, he got in the front seat with me because I knew the boy and I opened the front door."[5]

This wasn't an admission of guilt: Richard had been answering a question about Bobby and, though clumsily worded, he was clearly saying that Bobby had been in the front seat and that Nathan had struck the blow. It wasn't the only time Richard gave confusing answers:

the longer he spoke the more exhausted he became. He corrected his own statements while making them, and backtracked to clarify nearly a dozen times, using similar language: "I mean," "No, wait a minute," "pardon me," and "now that I think about it."[6]

Richard continued to insist that he had been driving. At one point, he turned to Nathan and asked, "If I were not at the wheel, how could I have got him to sit alongside of me? He wouldn't have done so with a stranger at the wheel. If the front door was open and I was in the back and the side curtains were up he wouldn't have seen me."[7]

Nathan deemed Richard's account "absurd dirty lies," adding, "he is trying to get out of this mess. I can explain to you myself exactly how I opened the door to let the Franks boy in, and he [Loeb] got up from the back seat, leaned over forward, and spoke to the boy from the back." He then shot Richard a condescending look, saying that he was "sorry" that his friend had "stepped into everything and broke down and all that."[8]

Richard was furious that Nathan had broken their agreement and used their alibi after it was to have expired. "I stepped in to try to help you out," he said to Nathan. "I think it is a damned sight more than you would have done for me. I tried to help you out, because I thought that you at least, if the worse comes to the worst, would admit what you had done and not try to drag me into the thing in that manner," he said.[9]

Still glowering at each other, Nathan and Richard were led off to separate cells to get a few hours' sleep.

AT NINE ON THE MORNING of Saturday, May 31, Crowe arranged for a contingent of detectives to take Nathan and Richard around Chicago, so that they could pinpoint where events had taken place during the planning, kidnap, murder, and aftermath. Richard wanted nothing to do with Nathan, and Nathan wanted nothing to do with Richard; neither was speaking to the other, and police kept them in separate cars as the procession set off.

The first stop was the Rent-A-Car company; a clerk recalled Nathan renting the Willys-Knight and produced the paperwork.[10] Then it was on to the restaurant where Richard had waited by the phone to give "Morton Ballard" a reference so that he could rent the car. When owner Gertrude Barish identified Richard, he turned pale, shook, and fainted.[11] Nathan sneered as his friend was taken away to rest. A few hours later, Richard spoke to Robert Crowe: he wanted to know if he could telephone his mother. When Crowe agreed, Richard burst into tears.[12]

With Richard temporarily absent, police visited the hardware store where the chisel had been purchased before entering Aaron Adler's drugstore farther along the route. The clerk here readily identified Nathan as the man who had purchased a bottle of hydrochloric acid.[13] The group stopped to uncover the ashes of the lap rug which had been burned, and at the deserted area around Wolf Lake where they had buried Bobby's shoes.[14] That night, one of the Leopold servants arrived with silk pajamas for both of the prisoners, which the police allowed them to use. They ate a turkey dinner sent from a local restaurant, and turned in. Both Nathan and Richard, according to a police sergeant, were soon "sleeping like babies."[15]

The tour continued the next day. Richard directed the police to the bridge over the lagoon at Jackson Park, from which the typewriter and its keys had been thrown. "When I got out," he told detectives, "I had them in my hand and I just scattered them like you would throw seed. . . . I don't believe you will be able to find them in there."[16] When they arrived at the area around Wolf Lake, Richard asked where Bobby's shoes had been found, saying that his belt buckle must be nearby. Police gave him a rake and after a few minutes Richard unearthed not only the belt buckle but also Bobby's class pin.[17]

Rather amazingly, police allowed reporters to join the two killers and interview them throughout this second day. Richard seemed exceptionally immature about what his future held. "This thing will be the making of me," he declared. "I'll spend a few years in jail, and I'll be released and come out to a new life. I'll go to work and I'll work hard, and I'll amount to something, have a career."

"But you have taken a life," Captain William Shoemacher told him. "You've killed a boy. The best you could possibly expect would be a life sentence to an insane asylum." Hearing this, Richard lost his cockiness. He seemed affected by the realization of what he had done, calling Bobby "such a fine kid" and saying he kept thinking about him. He was asked if he had been under Nathan's control. "I wouldn't say that exactly," Richard declared. "Of course, he's smart. He's one of the smartest and best educated men I know. Perhaps he did dominate me. . . . Leopold suggested the whole thing. . . . I went along with him. . . . I guess I 'Yessed' Babe a lot." Richard grew increasingly nervous as the tour continued, smoking cigarette after cigarette. Finally, he spoke of remorse: "I've an appreciation of things now. Not all the time, but every once in a while the realization of what we have done comes to my mind." By the time the tour had ended, a reporter said that Richard "is slowly slipping from his lofty pinnacle. He is no longer the sure-footed, well-poised steeplejack, scaling the spires of vagrant imagination . . . and the descent is terrifying."[18]

The differences between Richard and Nathan were starkly apparent. Richard's statements somehow seemed more heartfelt, even when he was admitting to murder, than the stilted words that left Nathan's mouth. While at times Richard seemed stricken by what he had done, Nathan enjoyed recounting the grisly details with what the *Daily Tribune* deemed his "typical sneering smile."[19] "I don't see how that little bastard can sit in that other car and laugh over the whole thing," Richard told a reporter.[20]

Nathan continually bragged about both his intelligence and the crime—"it would be a good idea to have a memory such as I have," he boasted to reporter Wallace Sullivan.[21] He was, reported the *Tribune*, all cynicism, talking "glibly of Nietzsche's philosophy and sadism in the early centuries." Nathan tried to insist: "Once a man on the defensive has adopted a certain policy, he's got to stick to it." A reporter pronounced him "as sophisticated as an F. Scott Fitzgerald hero who's showing off after his first drink of gin." Nathan claimed proudly that the ransom letter had served its purpose—"it instilled terror."[22] When Sullivan's knee accidentally brushed against his in the rear of the car, Nathan laughed, "Now you're contaminated. You've been touched by a murderer."[23]

"I can't understand," Nathan announced, "why the papers say this is such an atrocious murder." When asked why Bobby had been killed, Nathan said coldly, "Well, he knew Dick Loeb, and we couldn't afford to take a chance to have him come back and say it was Dick. . . . I lived in the neighborhood, and it was just a question of time before he would see me."[24]

"Did you kill Robert Franks, or did Loeb kill him?" Sullivan asked Nathan.

"Loeb killed him," Nathan shot back. Sullivan took advantage of a stop and ran back to the other car to question Richard. "Nathan said you killed Bobby Franks," he told Loeb. "Is it true?"

"No," was Richard's terse reply.

Sullivan returned to the car where Nathan sat. "It looks pretty bad for you," he told Leopold. "Loeb has the confidence of all the reporters and everyone, and he seems to have convinced everyone that you are the real perpetrator of the crime, the one who really struck the boy."

"I can prove that it was I who was driving the car," Nathan declared, "insomuch that Loeb admits that the boy was sitting in the front seat and was struck from behind. I can prove that it was I who was driving the car." His proof? He had rented the car, and that they had filled it up with gasoline at the Leopold family garage, neither of which actually offered the proof of which he had spoken.

Sullivan continued the game of back-and-forth, telling Richard what Nathan had said. But Richard had his own answer: "He doesn't know him," he said. "I mean Bobby Franks. I introduced him to him, and it is more likely that he would be sitting next to me in the car than it would be for him to sit next to Leopold."

Nathan greeted this with contempt. He said to Sullivan: "You go and tell Loeb that I am surprised that he would falter before the State's Attorney. I am surprised that he confessed. Tell him I am more surprised that he fainted. . . . Loeb knows that the striking of a human being by me is so repugnant and against my nature that he knows it is he who did that." And then he made two important admissions: "I regret that I took him as my accomplice," Nathan said of Richard.[25] He added, "If I had thought he would squeak I'd be in this alone."[26] These offhand comments seemingly placed Nathan in charge of the plan, something he would always deny. He ended by condemning Richard as "just a weakling, after all."[27]

But the same man insisting that he was incapable of violence dismissed Bobby's death as nothing more than "an experiment." "Causing pain to the subject is highly commendable," Nathan said, "irrespective of the pain or injury caused the subject if in the experimenting the experimenter advances his own knowledge." He likened Bobby's murder to a boy pulling the wings off a fly, or an entomologist impaling a beetle on a pin. It was, he summed up, "an exemplary and commendable thing."[28] Many years later, faced with this statement, Nathan wrote that he had been misquoted, misunderstood, and "goaded" into the outburst. In his book, he deliberately altered the quote before disputing it. "What I meant was, of course, that no doubt they, the reporters, could ease their consciences for the prying, probing questioning of me they were doing on the grounds of scientific curiosity. . . . I was being sarcastic. I was telling them that they were showing me, a human being—and a human being in a tough spot—no more consideration than a scientist showed an insect or a microbe."[29] But this isn't convincing, especially given Nathan's attitude and demeanor in these first days after his arrest. As the *Daily Tribune* noted, ironically "the young scientist who revels in human thrills, who boasted that murder was a justifiable experience, is equally boastful of his inability to do an un-beautiful murder."[30]

There was another, visible example of the differences between the pair when Crowe had the rented Willys-Knight brought into the courtyard of the Criminal Courts Building and asked Richard and

Nathan to identify it. Again, reporters were present. "Yes, this is the car," Nathan said. "I know it from the scratches on the front door."[31] He "ran and got into the front seat" when photographers asked him to pose and motioned for Richard to join him.[32] "Not while that fellow's in the car," Richard shot back. "Doesn't that man think I have any feelings?"[33]

Richard finally agreed to get in the car if he could do so alone and if he could sit in the driver's seat—he didn't want anyone to think that he'd been in the back and struck Bobby with the chisel. But he exited "white and pathetic," as the *Daily Tribune* reported. When a photographer's flash went off, Richard swooned against a wall and nearly fainted.[34] "Poor weakling," Nathan smirked.[35]

The contrast between Richard and Nathan grew more acute in these first days after their arrest. It is usually said that Richard displayed no emotion and showed no remorse over his crime. This isn't true. That Sunday afternoon, police and members of the state's attorney's office continued questioning the pair. While Nathan remained contemptuous, Richard repeatedly expressed remorse. To Crowe, he admitted, "I feel so sorry. I have asked myself this question a million times. How did I possibly go into that thing?" He admitted that "the condition of my folks" and the fact that his father was so sick kept "running through my mind."[36]

When questioned by assistant state's attorney Joseph Savage, Richard admitted: "I felt sorry about the thing, about the killing of the boy—oh, well, that very night. But then the excitement, the accounts in the papers, the fact that we had gotten away with it and that they did not suspect us, that it was given so much publicity and all that sort of thing, naturally went to the question of not feeling as much remorse as otherwise I think I would have." Had the crime not received so much press attention, he said, "I think I would have felt a great deal more remorse. I think since I have spent some time alone these last two or three days it has dwelt in my mind a great deal; not the question of my folks, about me, and the disgrace has not been the only thing I thought of."[37]

THE CAVALIER ATTITUDES—OR AT LEAST the cavalier attitude Nathan maintained—along with the random nature of the crime and the lack of any clear motive beyond excitement led Crowe to suspect that once Richard and Nathan went to trial, their attorneys would plead them not guilty by reason of insanity. Illinois courts followed the M'Naughton rule. In 1843, a man named Daniel M'Naughton had tried to kill British prime minister Robert Peel but instead shot his secretary. At his trial, M'Naughton claimed insanity. The court determined that such a plea was justified as, at the time, the accused hadn't been able to differentiate between right or wrong or appreciate the consequences of his actions.[38]

In the case of Leopold and Loeb, such a plea seemed exceedingly unlikely: their meticulous planning alone mitigated against such an option. They knew that they were committing a crime and knew what the possible consequences would be if they were apprehended. But Crowe later said he worried that they would use their families' wealth to somehow evade justice. To forestall this, he arranged for a number of psychiatrists to sit in on the state's interviews and to question the killers before they could change their stories or attempt a unified defense.

The Leopold and Loeb case would become one of the first in which psychiatric testimony, from both sides, took a central role. Psychiatry was then in a great state of flux. Among its practitioners, called alienists in the parlance of the day, two schools of thought dominated. The first was the more traditional, which studied mental illness as a symptom of organic impairment. Such symptoms could readily be seen and observed, diagnosed, and blamed for any criminality. Against this was the school of psychoanalytic thought, expounded by Sigmund Freud and Carl Jung, which sought to interpret subconscious ideas and unsuspected emotions to postulate theories about behavior and explain motivations.[39]

The men Crowe called in to examine Richard and Nathan all belonged to the traditional school. Hugh T. Patrick, professor emeritus of nervous and mental diseases at Northwestern University, had previously served as president of the American Neurological Society.[40] Patrick's colleague Archibald Church was head of the Department of Nervous and Mental Diseases at Northwestern; he'd previously served as vice president of the American Neurological Association and section chair on mental and nervous diseases for the American Medical Association. Crowe also brought in Dr. William O. Krohn, a psychiatrist attached to the University of Illinois and a member of the Insanity Commission of the Cook County Criminal Courts, and Harold Singer, former vice president of the American Neurological Association, director of the Illinois State Psychiatric Institution, and Krohn's coauthor on a book, *Insanity and the Law: A Treatise on Forensic Psychiatry.*

Nathan was contemptuous about the examinations. "You won't be able to find in this anything that will help us," he warned Church, "not a thing."[41] He clearly enjoyed the experience of pitting his intellect against these psychiatrists, and of being able to discuss psychology and his crime. Singer noted that Nathan often laughed when speaking about events, and mimicked others in the room.[42]

When asked why he had committed the crime, Nathan, according to Church, temporarily lost control of himself. His "face trembled, he almost broke into tears, and he said he didn't know why in the world he ever did such a thing."[43] But he quickly recovered, and gave out a jumbled explanation of the crime offering up a variety of motives ranging from excitement and a chance to match wits against the police to pressure from Richard and a desire to get the ransom money.[44] Church was struck by "the distinct lack of emotion on the part of Leopold," who repeatedly insisted that he felt no remorse for what had happened.[45]

"The emotional manifestations," Church found, "were entirely on the part of Loeb." Richard "showed distinct emotion" when discussing the crime. In recounting the disposal of Bobby's body, Richard recalled his hesitation to pour acid over his face and said that he had felt remorse.[46] Singer noted that Richard was "quiet, restless, and his face had the appearance of being worried." He spoke of his trepidation in the week leading up to the crime and how he had wanted to back out but did not do so because he "did not want to appear a quitter" and because he was worried about what Nathan might say or do.[47] He was also quite aware of the fact that these psychiatrists were assessing both he and Nathan. "I leave it to you gentlemen," Richard told them, "to say who has the brightest mind here. I will leave it to you to judge, yourselves, from what has taken place here this afternoon as to which of the two has the brighter mind, and who has the dominating mind of the two."[48]

Singer had no doubts about the dynamic in the relationship. "In my opinion," he said, "Leopold was the real criminal, the plotter of the whole crime, and Loeb was his tool." According to Singer, Richard "was weak, and easily influenced. If he had not known Leopold, he might have got by in life under sane circumstances without committing a major crime. Leopold, no, he would not."[49]

The doctors discussed the crime with both men. The examinations were conducted under less-than-ideal circumstances, attended by police and stenographers, and were cursory in nature. Under questioning, Nathan admitted that he knew he was committing a crime and was aware of the possible penalties. Richard, too, assured the psychiatrists that he knew that what they had done was wrong, and the consequences of their action.[50]

All of the psychiatrists called in by Crowe agreed that neither Richard nor Nathan exhibited any signs of mental illness. There was nothing organically wrong with them—no malfunctions of the brain, no diseases that would impair their judgment. They gave detailed answers about the planning and commission of their crime; they gave their accounts in a logical manner and their memories were exceptional; they had no sensory defects; they exhibited no evidence of dissociation; and they were aware of their surroundings at all times.[51]

Crowe was satisfied. "I have a hanging case," he told reporters, adding, "I shall present the facts, including the confessions, to the grand jury early in the week."[52] Both men had given detailed confessions.

"We have the most conclusive evidence I've ever seen in a criminal case," Crowe said, "either as a judge or prosecutor. We have the shoes and portions of the clothing young Franks wore when he was murdered. We found these things in every instance at the places where Loeb and Leopold led us, places where they told us they would be found. The case against these two young men is absolutely conclusive. I can't see how they can get away from it. Our whole afternoon was spent in checking and organizing the evidence. I have no hesitation in saying I would be ready to go to trial tomorrow."[53]

THAT LONG WEEKEND ENDED WITH yet another trip for the confessed killers. Police escorted Richard and Nathan to dinner at separate restaurants. Richard's mood alternated between charm and worry, but Nathan made the most of the experience, chatting happily and treating the entire thing as an adventure.[54] Seeing a nearby couple looking at him suspiciously, he strode up to their table and declared, "I beg your pardon, Madam, but I'm not Nathan Leopold."[55] He then returned to his own table, looked at Sergeant Frank Johnson, who was guarding him, laughed, and said, "How would you like to be able to lie like that?"[56]

Nathan later claimed: "It had been my own personal preference at the outset to make no attempt to avoid the extreme penalty. I had desired to plead not guilty and, by refraining from offering any defense whatsoever, positively to court execution." He thought that "speedy execution of the death penalty would be much easier for us defendants than the slow, day-by-day torture of spending the rest of our lives in prison. Second, I felt that the pain to our families and the humiliation and shame they must suffer would, in the long run, be less if we were hanged than if we were sentenced to life imprisonment."[57]

But this was a bit of retrospective amelioration. At the time, Nathan felt differently. He had shocked one police officer by saying that, "if I knew that Loeb was going to peach" he would have killed himself "and while I was doing it I could have took a couple of coppers." Asked why he would want to kill the police, Nathan smirked. "What is the difference?"[58]

Nathan had an even more startling conversation that Sunday night with Detective James Gortland. Nathan, said the detective, declared that he was "not at all" sorry that he had killed Bobby Franks. Nor did he care that the victim's family was suffering, adding that he didn't "give a damn" about them. "Murder in my code is not a crime," he added. "My crime was getting caught."

Gortland was shocked at the lack of remorse, and asked Nathan why he had confessed. "He said," the detective later declared, "that it became manifestly impossible to maintain his story. I said the people are probably not satisfied with the motive expressed in this case—of adventure, excitement and money. And I says, 'Is there any other motive?' And he says, 'Well, adventure and money.'" What came next would became the subject of controversy. According to Gortland, Nathan declared, "You don't think I am entirely a fool? Don't you think I am entitled to reserve something for my defense?"

"Well, what do you think your defense will be?" Gortland asked.

And Nathan, in words that almost exactly echoed what he had said to Crowe just two days earlier, declared, "Well, that will depend on the wishes of my father and the lawyers. Of course if they wish me to hang I will plead not guilty and the jury will hang me or I will plead guilty before a friendly judge and get life imprisonment."[59] The remark was to prove almost uncannily prescient.

CHAPTER ELEVEN

CLARENCE DARROW WAS ASLEEP ON THE NIGHT OF SATURDAY, MAY 31, when the doorbell of his Chicago apartment started to buzz incessantly. His wife, Ruby, answered the door: a frustrated Jacob Loeb, Richard's uncle, had come to see the famed trial attorney. Both the Leopold and Loeb families had been surprisingly cavalier about the position of their sons, apparently unable to understand just how much trouble Richard and Nathan were in. There was, in 1924, no Miranda law that defendants had to be warned about making statements or had a right to legal counsel while being questioned, and the pair spoke freely, confessing, helping to gather evidence that could be used against them, and unwittingly sealing their fates.

The *Chicago Daily Tribune* reported that Charles Adler, Albert Loeb's former legal partner, was in discussions to act as defense counsel.[1] In the end the two families hired Benjamin Bachrach, an attorney who in the past had defended murderers, arsonists, kidnappers, and gangsters as well as heavyweight champion boxer Jack Johnson when he was accused of violating the Mann Act in 1912.[2] They would also employ Benjamin's brother and fellow attorney Walter Bachrach, who had a special interest in psychology and who, incidentally, had married Richard's cousin. Nathan was typically dismissive: later, he unfairly derided the two brothers as having no qualifications except for the fact "that they belonged to the Standard Club with my father."[3]

But the families also wanted a legal powerhouse. And so, Jacob Loeb and several others had gone to the Midway Apartments in Chicago to plead with Clarence Darrow. Ruby didn't want to admit them: "I found myself confronted by four men who seemed like masked desperadoes, clutching at their upturned collars." But they forced their way in. "Mr. Darrow is asleep," Ruby shouted as they barged through the door. "He isn't well—he should not be disturbed." Not to be put off, Loeb stormed into the bedroom, waking a startled Darrow, falling on his knees and pleading with him to take the case of the two young killers. "Save their lives," he implored. "Get them a life sentence instead of a death sentence. That's all we ask of you. Money's no object. We'll pay you anything you ask. Only for God's sake, don't let them be hung."[4]

"The terrible deed had been committed," Darrow recalled. "The two boys were in the shadow of the gallows; their confession had been made; their families were in the depths of despair, and they came to me to assist the lawyers already employed. My feelings were much upset; I wanted to lend a hand, and I wanted to stay out of the case. The act was a shocking and bizarre performance; the public and the press were almost solidly against them." But Darrow knew that taking on the defense of Leopold and Loeb would help cement his reputation as America's most famous attorney, and that he could use the case to argue against a death penalty he believed to be barbaric. He also admitted, "I felt that I would get a fair fee if I went into the case," an important consideration for a man who, despite his fame, constantly struggled with his own finances and was deeply in debt.[5] And so he agreed to represent Nathan and Richard.

Darrow was sixty-seven, tired and suffering from a variety of health issues, including crippling rheumatism, fatigue, decaying teeth, and weak lungs after decades of smoking.[6] Born in Ohio in 1857, he'd entered law in 1878 and made a name for himself in turn-of-the-century Chicago. Over the years he defended labor unions, socialist leader

Eugene Debs, and a variety of killers and corrupt politicians. His reputation had suffered after 1911, when he was accused of bribing jurors while defending the McNamara brothers in the bombing of the offices of the *Los Angeles Times,* in which twenty were killed. The first trial ended in a hung jury, and Darrow escaped a second go-round by agreeing to never again practice law in California. Although Darrow insisted that he was innocent, evidence suggests that he at least knew of the bribery and may well have been guilty of it himself.[7]

Darrow was still a formidable figure, and his courtroom appearances remained legendary. He disguised his shrewd demeanor behind a folksy charm and rumpled exterior of wrinkled clothes frequently stained with the remnants of his last meal, throwing his courtroom opponents off balance with his surprise tactics and his oratorical flights of fancy. "The picture of Darrow drawling in front of a jury box was a notable scene," recalled famed journalist Ben Hecht. "The great barrister artfully gotten up in baggy pants, frayed linen and string tie, and 'playing dumb' for a jury as if he were no lawyer at all but a cracker-barrel philosopher groping for a bit of human truth."[8] Convinced that the judicial system was rigged against the poor, he was as willing as Robert Crowe to bend the law and twist facts to win cases.

The famous lawyer had a most peculiar view of crime. Two years before Leopold and Loeb, Darrow published a book, *Crime: Its Cause and Treatment,* in which he had embraced a jumble of bizarre ideas. Insisting that genetics, and particularly endocrine glands, caused criminal behavior, he wrote that there was no such thing as free will: an individual who committed crimes was powerless to resist because the impulses of his "machine" had been predetermined. "Responsibility," he declared, "is a gross error."[9] There could be no moral responsibility for crime, he argued; as such, there could be no punishment, merely treatment. Not surprisingly, Robert Crowe regarded Darrow with contempt, believing that his philosophy was extreme and dangerous, a threat to law and justice.

Darrow tried to visit Nathan and Richard on Sunday, June 1, but the two were away under police escort visiting various sites related to Bobby's kidnapping and murder. The next morning, Darrow demanded that Crowe move them to the Cook County Jail and grant him access to his clients. Crowe refused, wanting his group of psychiatrists to finish their interviews. And so, on Monday morning, Darrow, together with Benjamin Bachrach, brought a writ of habeas corpus before Judge John Caverly, chief justice of the Criminal Court. This won the transfer and access to their clients.[10]

"The day was warm," Nathan later wrote of their first meeting, "and Darrow was wearing a light seersucker jacket. Nothing wrong with that, surely. Only this one looked as if he had slept in it. His shirt was wrinkled, too, and he must have had eggs for breakfast that morning. I could see the vestiges. Or perhaps he hadn't changed shirts since the day before. His tie was askew. . . . His unruly shock of lusterless, almost mousy hair kept falling over his right eye. Impatiently, he'd brush it back with his hand. He looked for all the world like an innocent hayseed, a bumpkin who might have difficulty finding his way around the city."[11]

Darrow, for his part, seemed impressed by the two young men. Richard, he later said, was "not only a kindly looking boy, but he was and is a kindly boy. He was never too busy to personally do a favor for anyone that he chanced to know." As for Nathan, Darrow said that he possessed "the most brilliant intellect I have ever met in a boy."[12]

As soon as he had his clients alone, Darrow lost no time trying to counteract the damage they had already done. They were, he insisted, not to answer any further questions from the state's attorney—nothing. "Mr. Darrow," Richard said, "your slightest wish will be law to me."[13] After this, both Richard and Nathan obeyed: when asked even the most innocent of questions, they inevitably replied, "I refuse to answer on the advice of counsel."[14]

Word that the Leopold and Loeb families had hired Clarence Darrow opened the floodgates of criticism. Darrow had a reputation as a defender of the poor and had frequently blamed crime on poverty. Yet here he was, abandoning such beliefs to represent two wealthy murderers who had freely confessed. Worries that family money—Jewish money—would subvert justice prevailed.[15] It was widely rumored that the Leopold and Loeb families had promised Darrow $1 million to save their sons. "The general consensus," declared the *Chicago Herald and Examiner,* "seems to be that it would be a battle of wealth versus the law."[16] "The fathers of these boys," the *Chicago Daily Tribune* speculated, "have an estimated fortune of 15 million and we suppose it will be millions versus the death penalty."[17]

This speculation led the families to issue a joint statement:

In view of the many statements that large sums of money will be used in the defense of Nathan F. Leopold, Jr., and Richard A. Loeb, the families of the accused boys desire to say that they have lived in Chicago for more than fifty years, and the public can judge whether they have conducted themselves in their relations with the community in such a way as to earn a standing as truthful, decent, upright, law-abiding citizens, conscious of their duties and responsibilities to the community in which they live. They have not the slightest inclination nor intention to use their means to stage an unsightly legal battle with an elaborate array of counsel and an army of high-priced alienists in an attempt to defeat justice. Only such defense as that to which every human being is entitled will be provided for their sons. Assuming that the facts in this case are substantially as published, then the only proceeding they favor is a simple, solemn investigation under the law touching the mental responsibility of their accused sons. They emphatically state that no counsel for the accused boys will be retained other than those lawyers now representing them, with the possible, but not probable, retention of one additional local lawyer. There will be no large sums of money spent either for legal or medical talent. The fees to be paid to medical experts will be only such fees as are ordinary and usual for similar testimony. The lawyers representing the accused boys have agreed that the amount of their fees shall be determined by a committee composed of the officers of the Chicago Bar association. If the accused boys are found by a jury to be not mentally responsible, their families, in accordance with their conscious duty toward the community, agree that the public must be fully protected from any future menace by these boys. In no event will the families of the accused boys use money in any attempt to defeat justice.[18]

In the end, the statement promised too much. Once the defense began, enormous sums indeed went to save the lives of Leopold and Loeb, including small fortunes to medical and psychiatric experts.

NATHAN AND RICHARD WERE ASSIGNED Prisoner Nos. 50 and 51 after being transferred to the Cook County Jail to await trial. They were separated, kept in cells on two different floors to prevent communication.[19] With his genial personality and charm, Richard slipped seamlessly into the jail routine, befriending other prisoners and joining in their games. Nathan found the changes more difficult. He saw no reason to mingle with other inmates and, when he did, was apparently back to his usual habit of boasting about his intelligence. "He'd better lay off that ritzy stuff and get down to earth," one prisoner was quoted as saying, "or he'll find himself in a hell of a situation."[20]

Despite their arrests, Leopold and Loeb were not uncomfortable. Police allowed their parents to send in meals from Joe Stein's Restaurant, along with packs of cigarettes. At least one friendly reporter, hoping for continued scoops, regularly smuggled in liquor for the prisoners.[21]

Richard and Nathan, the *Daily Tribune* reported, were now "open enemies," at least for the first few days following their arrests.[22] After outright animosity between them, though, the breach was healed. Apparently, and perhaps not surprisingly, it was the weaker Richard who made the first move. A newspaper reported that he managed to see Nathan and told him, "What the hell's the use? We're both in for the same ride, so we might as well ride together."

"Yes, Dickie," Nathan supposedly replied. "We have quarreled before and made up, and now when we are standing at the home stretch of the greatest gauntlet we will ever have to run, it is right we should go along together."[23]

In his book Nathan claimed that he confronted Richard, asking him to "tell the truth" and admit that he had struck Bobby. Richard, he insisted, answered: "I figure it will be much easier for each of our families if they believe the other fellow is the actual murderer. I know Mompsie feels less terrible than she might thinking you did it. I'm not going to take that shred of comfort away from her."[24]

Taking Nathan's word for anything, especially words he attributed to Richard long after Loeb's death, is problematic. The pair did reconcile, though probably for reasons they kept to themselves. Each had tried to blame the other for originating the crime, plotting it, and carrying it out. Each knew the others' secrets, including details of their past crimes. Neither could risk exposure. Fearing what the other might say, they settled their differences to maintain a precarious equilibrium meant to save them both.

On June 5, divers found the Underwood portable typewriter in the Jackson Park lagoon. Police experts had already matched Nathan's handwriting to that on the ransom envelope, and Dr. William Mc-Nally, a toxicologist for the coroner of Cook Country, had examined the inside of the rented Willys-Knight and found considerable blood in the car.[25] Armed with these findings and the pair's confessions, Crowe presented his case to a grand jury. After hearing from a number of people—Jacob Franks, Tony Minke, and Sven Englund among them—the panel returned with eleven counts of murder (which covered all possible methods by which Bobby could have died), and sixteen counts of kidnapping. Each count was a capital offense if proved in court, eligible for the death penalty.[26]

On June 11, Richard turned nineteen. Instead of celebrations, both he and Nathan stood in a sixth-floor courtroom in the Criminal Courts Building as they were formally arraigned on each count of murder and kidnapping. Thousands of curious spectators descended on the courthouse, hoping to witness this first act in the Leopold and Loeb legal drama. Some fifteen armed deputies guarded the entrance, but they couldn't stop the surging crowd, which tore the courthouse doors off their hinges before being beaten back with nightsticks.[27] Inside the packed courtroom, both defendants offered pleas of not guilty. Crowe asked for a trial date of July 15 but Darrow objected; Judge John Caverly finally set the trial date for August 4, with motions to be heard beginning July 21.[28]

Versions of Richard's and Nathan's confessions had by now been published in Chicago newspapers and set off yet another firestorm as reporters and the public tried to come to terms with these two strange young men and their horrific crime. Not a day went by without the case appearing on the front page of the city's newspapers. They turned to the fads of the day, phrenology and astrology, hoping to discover what had caused the pair to go bad. The *Herald and Examiner* offered up Charles A. Bonniwell, identified as a "nationally known psychoanalyst" who claimed he could decipher the pair's criminology merely by examining their photographs. According to him, Richard was "a good, average youngster," with his features offering a "fine balance between a feminine and masculine type." His eyebrows suggested passion. His eyes, selfishness, and his nose "animal qualities." As for Nathan, Bonniwell insisted that he was jealous, brilliant, and selfish; his long face suggested that feminine instincts dominated.[29]

Not to be outdone, the *Daily Tribune* employed its own phrenologist, James Fitzgerald, who it proclaimed was an "expert in character analysis." Fitzgerald thought that Richard was "of a feminine type of mind, eager for applause and easily led." Nathan, he thought, had a lower sexual drive than did Richard; felt himself superior to others; and lacked any sense of morality. Nathan's nose, Fitzgerald added, showed him to be an aggressive individual. According to Fitzgerald, Nathan was the mastermind behind the crime: "It has been Leopold all along. His is the ego that allowed no law but his own desire. Loeb was clay in the hands of potter Leopold."[30]

Astrologer Belle Bart chimed in on the pages of the *Herald and Examiner*. According to his horoscope, she said, Richard had a split personality. He had a "seething restlessness, a keen desire for knowledge, but rather of the superficial type than of the profound." Nathan, she thought, was prone to cruelty and violence. "With a horoscope such as he possesses," she opined, "he would brook no interference."[31] Interestingly—and coincidentally—most of these opinions, with the exception of Nathan's alleged low sex drive, actually turned out to be close to reality.

Newspaper editorial boards, self-appointed experts, and popular figures of the day stumbled over one another dissecting the pair and their motivations, to somehow make sense of this apparently senseless act. Their crime was put down to corrupting modern influences: their nonchalant attitudes toward murder, their illicit drinking, and their rumored "perversions" hinted at some sort of nihilistic threat to the existing order. Tensions epitomizing the 1920s gelled in the Leopold and Loeb case: tradition versus modernity, conservatism versus liberalism, strict parenting versus neglectful laxity. As examples of all that was thought wrong of the Roaring Twenties, Leopold and Loeb were held up as warnings to a generation. "No single event in our memory," opined the *Herald and Examiner*, "has cast such fear and awe over all classes of people. The murder has become more than a mere crime. It has become a portentous and ominous social fact. The deed confessed by Nathan E. Leopold, Jr., and Richard Loeb meets no parallel in the police records of this nation." It warned: "We have striven to free our youth, to put upon them little or no responsibilities; we have permitted and encouraged the casting off of restraints, a contempt for old codes and morals. We have become supine before the spirit of experiment and the sneer at not being 'new.' And two of the most gifted and brilliant products of the experiments of today are held by the State's Attorney, charged with the most revolting crime of the century."[32]

Richard and Nathan had been indulged, and their precocity, it was claimed, had led to disaster. Billy Sunday, the former outfielder for the Chicago White Sox turned popular evangelist, declared, "I have absolutely no sympathy for them. I think this hideous crime can be traced to the moral miasma which contaminates some of our 'young intellectuals.' It is now considered fashionable for higher education to scoff at God." He blamed "precocious brains, salacious books, and infidel minds" for leading the pair astray.[33] In a prescient echo of the strategy the defense would employ, the *Daily Tribune* sarcastically referred to Richard as "the victim of a well defined disease, an ailment understood in medical circles, but one which the law defines as a crime. He has been raised in surroundings of wealth and has never found it necessary to curb or suppress his emotional outlet."[34]

It didn't take long before anti-Semitism reared its ugly head. The *Tribune* noted that "the three principals in the tragedy are of one race."[35] The Leopolds, the Loebs, and the Franks all had Jewish roots, with ancestors who had migrated from Germany to Chicago the previous century. The city's Eastern European immigrant Jews, as author Meyer Levin recalled, regarded the arrests of Leopold and Loeb with a kind of "vengeful satisfaction—these were the sons of German Jews, these two wealthy degenerates who had committed the vicious crime and were even boasting about it. . . . Now you could see what those over-proud German Jews, with their superiority and their exclusiveness, were like."[36]

The implications were not lost on the larger Jewish community. "There was one gruesome note of relief in the affair," recalled Levin. "One heard it uttered only amongst ourselves—a relief that the victim, too, had been Jewish."[37] Certain elements tried to turn this to advantage. The problem, they insisted, wasn't that Leopold and Loeb were Jewish; instead, they had committed their crime because they had separated themselves from their Jewish roots. The Leopolds and the Loebs belonged to Chicago's Sinai Reformed Temple, but both families had been nonchalant about religion—Nathan later said that he attended only on high holidays and that he never learned Hebrew beyond a few prayers—while Richard set foot in the building only twice in his life.[38]

"The truth," insisted Dr. S. M. Melamed, "is that these two Jewish boys were not under the influence of Judaism, and they are not Jewish products, and the Jewish people has no moral control over them. . . . If the parents of these two boys had given the children a

Jewish education, if the boys had borne on their shoulders individual responsibility, if they had interested themselves in Jewish problems, if their hearts had bled for their people, if they had been consciously Jewish with Jewish souls, they would certainly not have devoted their entire time to 'pleasure and good times.' . . . You can't convince me that if these two capable Jewish boys had interested themselves in Jewish problems . . . that they would have surrendered themselves to wild and unnatural passions. . . . The two sons of the Jewish millionaires, who grew up without any ideals in life—moral 'do nothings'—are only a sad example of a life of moral anarchy. I always feared for the rich Jews who had no Jewish ideals."[39]

And then there were the discussions about the peculiar relationship between Richard and Nathan—as the *Daily Tribune* delicately put it, "the suggestions of perversions."[40] There were almost romantic portraits of Richard in jail, with his "lambent eyes and tender chin," his "gentle, disarming way and moist, soft-looking lips." Scores of young women, it was said, "had wept since Dick confessed."[41] Somehow a few young women managed entry to the Cook County Jail so that they could watch as Richard exercised. "Isn't he too dear for words, and so handsome!" they crooned.[42] Nathan seemed forgotten: there were no female admirers for him—indeed, as the *Tribune* reported, "girls who admit that they have been half in love with Babe Leopold are not so easy to find."[43]

It began weaving itself together as soon as Bobby's body was discovered, with fears that he had been kidnapped merely to satisfy some "unnatural" lust. After Leopold and Loeb's arrest, the *Tribune* shockingly reported "vague hints that this strange and direful crime may have some relation to necrophilism, that morbid fondness for being in the presence of dead bodies and the unwholesome pleasure derived from the experience."[44]

"All through their childhood and college days," said the *Tribune* in heavily coded language, "'Babe' Leopold and 'Dickie' Loeb were constant companions in the 'fussing' parties they staged, in their campus activities, and the bright south side college life."[45] Learning that Nathan had read Havelock Ellis, Oscar Wilde, and Sappho, newspapers tied him to "erotic" books and raised suspicions about the relationship.[46] The crime was supposedly rooted in "perversion," the common and unmistakable code for homosexuality.[47] As one historian noted, "what went unsaid in the course of the investigation and prosecution of Leopold and Loeb did so precisely because it went without saying. These youths were construed to be two Jewish teens whose Jewishness 'naturally' predisposed them to homosexuality, a 'crime against nature' that incited them to commit further crimes against humanity."[48]

Public opinion inevitably favored Richard over Nathan. "Mr. Leopold," the *Herald and Examiner* informed its readers, "is undoubtedly the brains of the combination, the breadth and scope of his knowledge alone would be sufficient to sweep the other boy along."[49] The *Daily Tribune* agreed: "Leopold seems to have the more dominating personality and the training, not by practice, but by philosophical thought, that would best fit him to plan such a crime. . . . And to this shadowy world, where he ruled as king, he admitted Loeb, for 'Narcissus' must have his mirror! By nature, too, Leopold had not only the more dominating personality, but a steadiness the younger boy lacked."[50]

Prejudice was at work. With his Catholic mother, fair complexion, and collegiate good looks, Richard seemed more sympathetic than the clearly Jewish Nathan, with his dark features, thick lips, and heavy eyes. It was easy for the public to believe that Richard had fallen victim to the misanthropic Nathan, who had openly boasted about the murder and shown no remorse. The *Tribune* reported that Nathan actually seemed to be enjoying his unenviable situation, as it offered him "a marvelous opportunity to study his own reactions."[51] A family friend of the Loebs summed it up two days after the arrests: Nathan, he insisted, had "dominated Richard and I suspect he was the influence in this awful affair."[52] This remark was likelier closer to the truth than many realized.

CHAPTER TWELVE

"From the beginning," Clarence Darrow later wrote, "we never tried to do anything but save the lives of the two defendants."[1] A murder conviction could be punished by a term of incarceration starting at a mandatory fourteen years; by life imprisonment; or by death. Robert Crowe had announced that he was seeking the death penalty.

Darrow's options were limited. Leopold and Loeb could plead not guilty, but who would believe it? They had both confessed with detailed statements, and had even helped police locate evidence against them. A not guilty plea also meant trial by jury. "We spent considerable time deliberating as to what we should do," Darrow recalled. "The feeling was so tense, and the trial was so near that we felt we could not save the boys' lives with a jury. It seemed out of the question to find a single man who had not read all about the case and formed a definite opinion."[2]

The whole case seemed so peculiar and the crime without apparent motive—surely that suggested an insanity defense. Indeed, Darrow let it slip that he was considering just such a strategy, hinting that there was hereditary insanity in both the Leopold and Loeb families.[3] Crowe dismissed the idea. "The report that Leopold and Loeb are insane," he declared, "is nothing more than propaganda sent out by the defense to throw dust into the eyes of men who may be called to serve on the jury."[4]

But an insanity defense was fraught with danger. Leopold and Loeb had spent months meticulously planning their scheme; they were intelligent and knew that killing Bobby was a crime. They were not suffering from delusions and went to great pains to disguise their involvement in the crime. How, then, could they claim insanity? Even more worrisome, an insanity defense automatically meant a jury would hear the case—something Darrow was desperate to avoid.

Before making any decision, Darrow needed to know if such a defense was even viable. Soon after taking the case, he sent lawyer Walter Bachrach (soon to join the defense team) to the American Psychiatric Association's annual convention in Atlantic City. Bachrach was to find experts who would agree to examine Nathan and Richard and testify about their mental states in court.[5]

There was some irony in this. "All superior men," Nietzsche had written, "who were irresistibly drawn to throw off the yoke of any kind of morality and to frame new laws had, if they were not actually mad, no alternative but to make themselves or pretend to be mad."[6] This bit of cynicism surely appealed to Nathan. Privately, he said, "I think this medical 'psychiatric' stuff is all horseshit."[7]

Even Darrow had previously expressed skepticism about such expert psychiatric opinion. He noted that "all sorts of experts testify for the side that employs them, give very excellent reasons for their positive and contradictory opinions. . . . The expert is like the lawyer: he takes the case of the side that employs him, and does the best he can. . . . Of course scientific men do not need to be told that the receipt of or expectation of a fee is not conducive to arriving at scientific results. Every psychologist knows that, as a rule, men believe what they wish to believe, and that the hope of reward is an excellent reason for wanting to believe. . . . Furthermore, the contending lawyers are willing to assist them in arriving at the conclusions that the lawyer wants."[8]

Yet Darrow willingly ignored his own warnings when it came to the Leopold and Loeb case. Bachrach rounded up an impressive slate of psychiatrists. Most were members of the emerging school of Jungian and Freudian thought, at odds with the traditionalists Crowe had consulted. Like the state psychiatrists, they received $250 a day for their work.

William Alanson White was the superintendent of St. Elizabeth's Hospital in Washington D.C., America's largest mental institution, and also served as president of the American Psychiatric Association. Bernard A. Glueck, who had trained under White, had been a psychiatrist at Sing Sing prison in New York for a year before becoming director of the Mental Hygiene Department of the New York School of Social Work in 1919.[9] William Healy was the director of the Judge Baker Foundation in Boston, which specialized in treating juvenile delinquents. All three would testify during the trial. But Bachrach also hired other analysts—Nathan recalled as many as fourteen—most of whom never took the stand.[10] Ralph Hamill, a neuropsychiatrist in Chicago and associate professor of Neurology and Mental Diseases at Northwestern University, interviewed the accused and worked with the defense team to assemble a psychiatric report. Chicago psychiatrist James Whitney Hall was also brought in to conduct interviews and opine on the mental state of the defendants.

White, Healy, Hall, and Glueck all conducted limited interviews with Nathan and Richard, but their interpretations relied heavily on the work of two additional doctors hired by the defense, Karl Bowman and Harold Hulbert. Bowman was an assistant medical professor at Harvard, specializing in mental disease, while Hulbert, after working at the Michigan State Psychiatric Hospital, had a private practice in Chicago. Bowman and Hulbert began examining the defendants in the middle of June: they spent a week conducting interviews, asking questions, and seeking additional information from their families.[11] Their report, compiled with the assistance of Dr. Hamill, was—as the doctors noted—undertaken "in order to determine whether or not insanity was a justifiable plea for defense."[12]

The Bowman-Hulbert report delved into nearly every aspect of the private lives of the two young men set to go on trial. Although it occasionally quoted both Leopold and Loeb, most of the time it defaulted to summations based on the doctors' opinions, which in turn came from speculation and inference. The results were questionable: the Bowman-Hulbert report relied almost exclusively on information provided by the two defendants, in this case two highly intelligent defendants with the ability to assess their answers and tailor their responses in ways calculated to help achieve the desired results. The doctors rarely challenged the pair and seem to have believed whatever Nathan and Richard said. This credulous acceptance rendered many of their opinions suspect.[13]

Darrow had warned, "Experts called for the defense cannot always be sure that the patient truthfully answers the questions."[14] Both Richard and Nathan, the doctors noted, frequently lied during their interviews. Bowman and Hulbert found that Nathan "undoubtedly omits certain data regarding some of his past experiences. He lied rather plausibly at times. Later, when he realized that it was known that he was lying, he appeared perfectly unconcerned. A number of times, he inquired whether his story agreed with his companion's, and seemed to show a great deal of concern about this matter. In fact, he did this so crudely that it was apparent that he was concerned lest there be some failure of their stories to coincide."[15] And Richard, the report declared, was "frank and open with others, as long as he feels there is nothing he wants to conceal, but if he feels it is to his interest to hold anything back, he does so. He therefore gives an appearance of great frankness, which is not true."[16] When questioned about his lack of candor, Richard explained that he "failed to mention certain things because either he thought it advisable not to mention them or because he had been advised not to mention them."[17]

Lies and omissions clouded revelation of the pair's crimes. Yet none of the defense psychiatrists probed too deeply or pressed too hard about important details—the defense's goal, after all, was to save Richard and Nathan from the gallows. This lack of follow-up was most apparent when it came to the question of who had actually killed Bobby. Amazingly, neither White nor Healy even asked Nathan or Richard about this central issue.[18]

Richard found the questions boring; more than once he fell asleep while being interviewed. Nathan, though, viewed the sessions as intellectual exercises, a chance to pit his wits against those of the doctors. "He apparently enjoyed being the center of attention, discussing his personality and past history," the psychiatrists noted.[19] He loved nothing more than talking about himself, and evinced repeated fascination with psychiatry in general and with these men in particular. He went so far as to admit that he thought he would enjoy his own trial as it would "be intensely interesting" and he could "learn a good deal."[20]

Unlike Richard, Nathan played to the psychiatrists. On being introduced to William White, Nathan said, "I am so glad to meet you, Dr. White. I know the exact number of lines you take up in *Who's Who*."[21] He flattered the doctors, caressed their egos, and skillfully ingratiated himself. This influenced the report: personal opinion replaced dispassionate fact as the doctors favored Nathan over Richard and tended to believe his version of events.[22]

Richard was relatively open about his personality. He admitted that he was often lazy and hadn't gone out of his way to study during college. He liked attention and admiration and could be selfish. Yet as the doctors found, he was "not bothered if someone else happens to be dominating the particular situation and he is compelled to assume a minor role."[23]

Anna Struthers, Richard's former nanny, offered to assist but her comments, like her influence on the young man, were less than helpful. Richard, she complained, had been a perfect boy until he had gone off to college, where he had been "de-feminized" and taught to drink and pursue girls. "She definitely gives the impression of a paranoid personality," Bowman and Hulbert reported. "Her general viewpoint is the conventional one and she shows no real insights into childhood psychology and is quite plainly a person devoid of the understanding necessary to deal properly with children."[24]

Of the pair, it was Nathan who proved surprisingly reflective. He had a high degree of self-awareness, although he adopted "a super-cilious attitude" toward the doctors.[25] Nathan admitted that he had always been sensitive to criticism and had found it difficult to make friends.[26] "He poses as an individual of high intelligence," the report noted, "cold blooded, scientific, with no interest except that of a sci-entist, whereas as a matter of fact he appreciates that he is a very sen-sitive, thin skinned individual, with a marked feeling of inferiority."[27] Nathan insisted that he made "cutting and sarcastic remarks" about others largely as a defense mechanism.[28] After his mother's death, he said, "I tried to cut out the emotional. My ideal was cold blooded intellect."[29]

The doctors were surprised at the prisoners' lack of remorse. Al-though Nathan later claimed that he'd immediately regretted the crime, his contemporary comments destroy such views. "He feels sorry that he has been caught, but not sorry for what he has done," Bowman and Hulbert noted.[30] Nathan admitted that he had "no real objection, or no moral scruple," against the murder.[31] Indeed, he declared that he had been very interested in "observing himself as a murderer."[32]

Nathan "denies any feeling of remorse at having committed this crime," psychiatrists found. "He states that he has no feeling of having done anything morally wrong because he doesn't feel that there is such a thing as morals in the ordinary sense of the word. He maintains that anything which gives him pleasure is right and the only way in which he can do any wrong is to do something which will be unpleasant to himself." Fear of being caught, he explained, was the only reason he would not kill again—"there would be no question of remorse or guilt entering into the thing," he said.[33] Yet these were the words from the man the defense psychiatrists insisted was an easily dominated, meek follower.

Richard was different. He'd already expressed remorse during nu-merous police and media interviews. Richard was clearly the more emotional of the pair: he was the first to confess; he had fainted on being identified; interrogators and reporters described him as pale and trembling when he recounted the crime; he had expressed disgust when Nathan smiled and laughed with reporters. At one point Richard said that he would go through with the crime again "if he could get the money," but he couldn't match Nathan's steely facade.[34] He admitted that in the week leading to the crime he'd wanted to back out; he had an "expression of disgust" when he spoke of the murder, adding that he had not anticipated "the actual killing with any pleasure."[35] Richard said that he was "very, very sorry for his family's sake," though he admitted that he "should be sorrier."[36] But he repeatedly spoke of remorse: when it came time to pour acid on the body; when he'd caught sight of Bobby's coffin being carried from the Franks's house; in the days after the murder; and, when talking to the doctors about returning the rental car after Bobby's death, Richard "choked up, and wiped his nose with his finger."[37]

Doctors showed Richard an interview with Bobby's mother. "There is no hatred in my heart for the boys who killed my son," Flora Franks said. But she expressed a desire to meet with them, so that she could ask whether Bobby had suffered in his last minutes.[38] How, doctors asked, did this make Richard feel?

"My first feeling," Richard said, "was joy, that it might help us, her not feeling vindictive, then a little remorse, not much, perhaps a little bit. But then I forgot it right away in reading another paper." He tried to explain: "What would make me sad would be to see Mrs. Franks in pain, but it does not make me sad to think about her or anyone being in pain. It is uncomfortable for me to see someone in pain."[39] His responses seemed less intellectual, more reliant on personal interactions. In discussing the crime, he could only focus on the abstract. "I did not have much of any feeling from the first," he admitted, adding numbly, "there was nothing inside to stop me."[40]

Nathan, Bowman and Hulbert found, "has a marked sex drive. Psychologically sex has played an enormous role in his life."[41] The report explored the sexual abuse Nathan suffered at the hands of his governess; his compulsive masturbation; his same-sex encounters; and his sadistic sexual fantasies. It also delved deeply into Nathan's slave/king fantasies that he said formed an intrinsic part of his relationship with Richard. Bowman and Hulbert claimed that these reflected Nathan's actual subservience to Richard, and that Leopold had been the slave fully 90 percent of the time.[42]

This was how Nathan wanted to be seen, someone under the irresistible control of Richard's malign character, but it wasn't true. He didn't correct the doctors' misinterpretation, which he thought was an attempt to offer some reasonable explanation for this otherwise inexplicable crime. Only later did Nathan clarify that the doctors had misunderstood him: it was he, not Richard, who had played the king role 90 percent of the time in his fantasies.[43]

Bowman and Hulbert also conducted extensive physical examinations of the two defendants, seeking some organic basis for their criminal behavior. In this, they echoed Darrow's view that endocrinology explained mental illness and influenced criminal tendencies.[44] The quest was somewhat less than successful, at least as far as Richard was concerned. They noted that he still had three of his baby teeth, and only needed to shave every other day, none of which proved their case.[45] He had a low basal metabolism rate, but even this was not rare.[46] And yet the doctors concluded that Richard's endocrine system had led to his bad judgment, arrogance, and murderous compulsions.

Even so, Richard was a model of health when compared to Nathan, at least as far as these doctors were concerned. They noted everything as a possible contributory cause to his criminal behavior: he had flat feet; too much body hair; his facial features were uneven; his spine was slightly curved; his eyes were too prominent and asymmetrical; his shoulders were too round; his stomach protruded. They determined that Nathan had a calcified pineal gland, an overactive thyroid, and circulatory difficulties.[47]

Not all of the psychiatrists agreed on how to interpret these results, as James Whitney Hall later admitted. Hall, who never testified during the case, believed that Nathan was most to blame for the crime. He was, Hall said, "fundamentally a criminal and psychopathic personality." He thought that Richard might not have ever committed murder but for his association with Nathan, who he called the more dangerous of the pair.[48]

But the defense psychiatrists had to make decisions. Combining these interviews and physical examinations, they reached some extraordinary conclusions. Nathan, doctors said, suffered from a "delusional, disordered personality," while Richard had "a disordered mentality."[49] Both young men, the report concluded, suffered from mental illness but were not technically insane.

The evidence supporting these findings, as historian Paula Fass wrote, was based on a random collection of contradictory factors: they were too intelligent or spent too much time alone with their varied fantasies; they drank too much; they read too much (in Nathan's case), or not enough (in Richard's case); and they indulged in a sexual relationship. "These were generous definitions of abnormality indeed," Fass noted, "and so broad and flexible as to be extremely frightening. If applied generally, any special trait or eccentricity became a source of concern, every character flaw a mark of emotional disease."[50]

But suppressed reports and opinions that four of the defense psychiatrists made for Darrow shed a different light on the case. White, Gleuck, Healy, and Hulbert were unanimous in declaring that both Leopold and Loeb were insane. White insisted that Nathan lacked the ability to determine right from wrong. Healy found that Richard had "an abnormal split personality" and that Nathan was "mentally diseased" and "suffering from psychosis." And Hulbert flatly declared that Richard was "insane, in my opinion" and that both he and Nathan were suffering from schizophrenia.[51]

These opinions armed Darrow with the ammunition needed to present a defense: his own psychiatrists had declared that both Nathan and Richard were insane. But if he put the doctors on the stand and they testified to this, the law was clear: the judge would have no choice but to call a jury to hear the case, something Darrow meant to avoid at all costs. And so he suppressed the damning diagnoses. As case historian Nina Barrett notes, this confirms "the extent to which Darrow was willing to manipulate the definition of legal insanity in the service of his clients, and how the hired alienists were willing to manipulate their own professional diagnoses to suit the terms of their employment."[52]

Darrow decided to plead the pair guilty. If Nathan and Richard entered pleas of guilty, no jury would be called: it would be up to the presiding trial judge to hear the evidence and decide their sentences—and Darrow knew he had a better chance of persuading one man to spare their lives than he did with a jury of twelve. Both Leopold and Loeb were nineteen, minors according to the law. Darrow thought that he could use this to ease their punishment. Then, too, there was a statute in the Illinois State Criminal Code which obligated any judge, if called upon to determine punishment, to examine witnesses who offered either aggravating or mitigating evidence. Darrow gambled that this psychiatric testimony would work in his favor.

Unable to ask his own psychiatrists to testify truthfully about their findings, Darrow resorted to some chicanery. He would use their findings to show that the defendants were unbalanced and suffered from some vague mental illness that he would carefully prevent his own witnesses from naming. It was a dangerous gamble: if one of them accidentally mentioned insanity, it would result in a jury trial. As one legal journal noted, the tactic was "probably the first instance of the offer of elaborate psychiatric analyses as the basis for remitting the law's penalty for a calculated, cold-blooded murder, committed by persons not claimed to be insane or defective in any degree recognized by the law as making them not legally responsible."[53]

Darrow's strategy relied on secrecy. "What we most feared," he recalled, "was that if the State had any conception of our plan, they would bring up only one case at a time, saving a chance, if given a life sentence, to bring up the second case and, as it were, catch us on the rebound. We were conscious of the risk we were taking and determined to take one chance instead of facing two."[54] He kept word of his decision from nearly everyone, including the two loquacious defendants. Assuming that Darrow planned to offer insanity pleas, Nathan erupted in anger. "I'm not insane," he told a reporter, "and I'm not going to be made to appear insane. I'm sane—as sane as you are. . . . Loeb and I are being trained like fleas to jump through hoops."[55] He and Richard would only be told of Darrow's decision to plead them guilty on their first day in court.

PSYCHIATRY WAS STILL IN ITS infancy in 1924. A century later, neurological developments, previously unknown disorders, and advances in behavioral studies suggest new possibilities when it comes to assessing Leopold and Loeb. In a 2018 reexamination of the psychiatric evidence in the case, authors David L. Shapiro, Charles Golden, and Sara Ferguson speculate that Richard may have been unable to control his actions because of a "deficient frontal lobe."[56] As for Nathan, they suggested he was possibly delusional and may have suffered from "impaired connections between frontal lobes and structures of the limbic system."[57] There is, they note, no way to prove any of this.

Modern diagnostic approaches, though, allow for interesting, if speculative, analyses of Richard and Nathan. Richard may have suffered from bipolar II disorder. He had many of the symptoms associated with the condition: erratic, often reckless behavior; rapid speech and inability to focus; and bursts of unexpected energy followed by depressive periods marked with feelings of worthlessness and thoughts of suicide. Nathan, for his part, may have had borderline personality disorder. His varying moods; inflated sense of self; heightened sensitivity to criticism; tendency to view people and questions in terms of absolutes; reckless behavior; and disproportionate reactions to situations, all suggest that he likely suffered from the condition. And, almost certainly, Nathan also had narcissistic personality disorder. He had nearly all of the typical symptoms: grandiose sense of self; deep insecurity; arrogance; lack of empathy; manipulation; and aversion to criticism were hallmarks of his behavior.

It's impossible, of course, to know for certain what disorders may have afflicted Richard and Nathan. The opinions of the defense experts were informed by the era in which they operated, and progress in psychiatry renders much of what was claimed suspect. Richard and Nathan likely suffered from some form of personality disorders, but none would be sufficient to render a verdict of insanity. And none of them, either singularly or together, deprived them of free will or constituted a compulsion to murder. Individually, Richard and Nathan were damaged but probably not dangerous. It was their coming together that proved deadly.

CHAPTER THIRTEEN

DURING INTERVIEWS WITH DEFENSE PSYCHIATRISTS, RICHARD ADMIT-
ted that he—and likely Nathan, too—had committed at least four
additional, unknown crimes, which the doctors designated as "A, B,
C, and D." These had occurred before Bobby's murder. Richard refused, on the advice of counsel, to reveal what they were. Psychiatrists
never pressed him, finding it "forensically inadvisable" to pursue details. "There is a certain legal advantage," they noted, "in minimizing
the broadcasting of these episodes, even keeping them secret from his
attorneys, examiners, or relatives."[1]

What were these four additional crimes? Author Hal Higdon suggested that several University of Chicago fraternity robberies offered
a likely answer. On November 26, 1923, two men broke into Sigma
Nu, stealing $150 in cash and three watches before being confronted
by a pledge. They waved revolvers at the startled man and fled into the
night. Then, on the night of February 3, 1924, someone robbed Delta
Sigma Phi, taking two new tuxedos, a dress coat, some suits, dressing
gowns, and a few suitcases. A week later, members noticed a car idling
across the street from their house; two men were visible inside. When
one member stepped out to investigate, the car sped away.[2]

These fraternity thefts sound like something Leopold and Loeb might have done, but they don't fit the description of crimes that the defense found "forensically inadvisable" to investigate. The pair had already admitted to robbing two fraternities in Ann Arbor; why, then, should they fear mentioning similar crimes in Chicago? Higdon speculates that the defense didn't pursue details because "these were crimes for which restitution might have been expected had they been identified."[3]

But this isn't convincing. These fraternity thefts were minor offenses. Why would it be inadvisable to question them about petty thefts at a time when they were on trial for kidnapping and murder? There must have been something far more damaging than a potential (and minimal) financial payout that lay behind the decision not to pursue the information.

After their arrests the press speculated that Leopold and Loeb might have assaulted middle-aged Chicago housewife Louise Hohley in May 1924. Hohey had been abducted and raped with iron bars before being tossed from the car.[4] Hohey filed a $100,000 lawsuit against the pair, but there was little evidence and police doubted that Leopold and Loeb were involved.[5] Then there were allegations that Richard and Nathan killed a man whose mutilated, unidentified body was found in Geneva, Illinois, in 1922. Richard denied any knowledge, and the state attorney's office said it didn't believe that they had been responsible.[6]

Perhaps one of the "A, B, C, and D" designations referred collectively to the "Chisel Bandit" crimes that had apparently taken place in 1921, in Chicago's Hyde Park and Woodlawn neighborhoods. One man brandishing a revolver, it was said, confronted late-night pedestrians as his partner crept up from behind and knocked the victim out with the end of a chisel. The pair then robbed their victim and disappeared. The thefts were all minor—wallets, cigarette cases, watches, and the like—and none of the victims were seriously injured. Because these crimes occurred near Kenwood; involved petty thefts; and were undertaken by a pair of men, suspicions against Richard and Nathan made a certain amount of sense. There weren't many crimes committed using a chisel, a tool favored by Leopold and Loeb: after their arrests, the *Daily Tribune,* citing an unnamed psychiatrist Robert Crowe had brought in to the case, reported that Loeb had confessed that he and Leopold had been the Chisel Bandits—and Crowe never issued a correction.[7]

But what of the three other crimes? It has been suggested that the answer lay in a sexual assault, a murder, and a mysterious death. Early on the morning of Tuesday, November 20, 1923, twenty-one-year-old Yellow Cab driver Charles Ream was walking home after his shift. He boarded a streetcar at 59th Street, exiting at Dorchester Avenue and began walking north, toward the apartment of his cousin Earl English, at 5217 Dorchester near Kenwood, where he was living.[8] He remembered being somewhere between 53rd and Dorchester when, about 2:00 a.m., a car drew up alongside him. "Hands up!" a young man shouted while aiming a revolver. "Get in the car!" "I obeyed," Ream said. "I was scared."[9]

One man was driving; the one with the gun was in the back seat, and both wore handkerchiefs over their lower faces.[10] "I was ordered to turn around in the seat, to put my head in the corner of the car and to put my hands behind my back," Ream said. "Instantly the coils of a small rope went around my wrists. Then a gag was pushed into my mouth and a rope was tied around my head, holding the gag firmly. In another moment a bandage was slapped over my eyes. It was made secure. Then the beams of a flashlight fell upon my cheeks as they made sure the blindfold was secure. I was flopped into the bottom part of the car and a blanket or some heavy piece of clothing was spread out." The last thing Ream recalled was the smell of ether as a rag was pressed to his face.[11]

Ream awoke about six that morning at 92nd Street: his abductors had thrown him from the car and left him along an isolated stretch of road at the edge of the prairie a few miles from Wolf Lake.[12] Ream was in great pain. "My clothes were half-removed," he said, and his waist and legs were covered in blood.[13] He stumbled some five blocks before reaching a house and calling the Yellow Cab Company, which sent a taxi that took him to the Chicago Memorial Hospital.[14]

Ream had been castrated—accounts were never more definitive as to whether his penis, or testicles, or all three, had been removed. Dr. Orlando F. Scott believed that some level of skill had been involved. "The operation was performed by someone who knew what he was about," Scott asserted. "It could not have been done under a flashlight out there in the prairies, for it is a delicate operation and one that is likely to result in death from loss of blood if crudely preformed. Ream had been expertly bandaged."[15] But he later confusingly described the castration as "skillful, not surgical."[16] Dr. Joseph Springer, the same police physician who conducted the autopsy on Bobby Franks, examined Ream after the wound had swollen. He called it "a bungling job," adding that in his opinion the castration hadn't been the work of a professional.[17]

Ream didn't think he could recognize both his attackers but told police that he might be able to identify the man with the gun, as his handkerchief had slipped during the struggle. He thought that the assailant in the rear had been about five feet, nine inches, perhaps twenty-five-years old, and around 180 pounds.[18]

"Find R. C.," Ream told police. "He threatened that he'd get me and I'm sure he knows a lot about this business."[19] "R. C." was James "Red" Carrigan, a fellow driver at the Yellow Cab Company. Police questioned him but soon let him go: there was no evidence against him and Ream hadn't identified him as his assailant, merely suggested that he might know something about it. Next, police focused on Ream's cousin Earl English, with whom he lived. There were stories that English had caught Ream in his sister's bedroom a few days earlier, and suspicions that this might have led to the assault.[20] But as with Carrigan, there was no evidence to support the idea, and the case went cold.

Early on the morning of Sunday, November 25, 1923, twenty-three-year-old part-time University of Chicago student Freeman Louis Tracy was murdered after attending a dance. Popularly known as "the handsomest man in the university," Tracy had lost his lower left leg in a June 1917 accident while operating a crane.[21] He called it "the most exciting thing in my life."[22] Tracy got some $1,900 in compensation and was fitted with an artificial lower left leg; despite this, he was known to be an "excellent dancer." Four or five years after the accident, he started attending the University of Chicago, studying political economics and electrical engineering.[23] But in March 1923 he temporarily dropped out and got a job with the Commonwealth Edison Company. He still had friends on campus: "Girls regarded him as serious, though pleasant," the *Daily Tribune* reported, "intelligent and an interesting chap, and because of his winning personality he was a social favorite."[24]

Tracy left the dance shortly after midnight; a friend gave him a ride to the corner of Cottage Grove Avenue and 63rd Street, near the Midway Gardens, a popular nightspot. At half past two a man wearing a buttoned overcoat and a fedora, and who resembled Tracy, was seen leaving the area, walking west on 55th Street, possibly to catch the streetcar at Kenwood Avenue.[25] At 2:41 that morning, police received an anonymous telephone call from the 5th Ward Republican Club at East 55th Street. "There is a big fight at 55th and Kenwood Avenue" the caller said before hanging up.[26] Police found nothing but twenty minutes later came upon Tracy's body in the middle of 58th Street near Woodlawn Avenue; a two-block-long trail of blood led them to his fedora in front of 5766 Kenwood Avenue. Tracy had been shot in the temple, probably in a car; his bleeding head had hung out of the car for two blocks before he was dumped into the street.[27]

Shortly after Tracy's murder police found a stolen Cadillac abandoned in southwest Chicago, whose interior was spattered with blood. They suspected it had been used in the murder but found no definitive evidence. It seemed to be a motiveless crime: Tracy's wallet and forty-one dolllars in cash had been left untouched. Police believed that the same pair who had attacked Charles Ream might have killed Tracy in a botched kidnapping attempt in which they had hoped to "obtain the glands of a good looking, healthy, virile young man."[28]

Investigation found a few drops of blood in the bathroom of the 5th Ward Republican Club. Tracy knew the club but police found no evidence to link him to the blood.[29] Elmer Peddy, a driver for the Yellow Cab Company, said that around three that Sunday morning he had spotted a wounded man being led along Kenwood Avenue, some five blocks from the 5th Ward Republican Club. Police suspected that Tracy had been attacked in the club's washroom by political enemies or by members of the so-called Kenwood Gang, which supposedly had a habit of breaking into deserted clubs. According to this theory, after the initial attack inside, Tracy had left the club; there had been a second altercation on the street outside, as mentioned by the anonymous caller, in which Tracy was wounded. His assailants then walked with him some five blocks before shooting him in the head.[30]

But this contradicted all of the physical evidence. Tracy had been shot in the head and bled copiously—so much blood that it had left a two-block-long trail in the street connecting his body to his hat. He had no other wounds that could account for the blood in the club bathroom. If he been shot there, there should have been a significant amount found. Criminals would certainly have robbed him. After being shot in the head, Tracy would not have been upright and walking, nor did this theory explain the two-block-long trail of blood. He cannot have been the wounded, bleeding man led along Kenwood Avenue—the bullet was instantly fatal.

Then there was the mysterious death of handsome, twenty-three-year-old Melvin L. Wolf, who lived with his grandfather Henry Lindenthal at 4553 Ellis Avenue.[31] The scion of Russian and Polish Jewish immigrants, Wolf worked in the advertising department of his grandfather's successful clothing store, H. M. Lindenthal and Sons. Money was plentiful: in 1922 Melvin had gone on a lavish trip to Europe, traveling first class on the ocean liners *Mauretania* and *Berengaria*. He earned an annual salary of $3,000, and had a similar amount in the bank—so much disposable income that he generously supported numerous charities. Shortly before ten on the evening of April 7, 1924, Wolf left his house to mail a letter and simply disappeared. On May 7, his body (fully clothed, not nude as has been previously reported) was spotted floating facedown in Lake Michigan just off the Jackson

Park Beach at 64th Street, about a mile away from his house. He hadn't been robbed: when he went into the water, he still had his wallet, with cash, and he wore a gold signet ring, gold pocket watch, and gold tie clasp. There was no indication of how he had died—no physical evidence suggested he had suffered any injuries before death. At the inquest, relatives testified that he had never shown any signs of depression and had no motive to kill himself. Police investigated and concurred: "I can't see anything connected with that," said Detective Michael Neary. "I don't think there was any motive of self-destruction. . . . He was a good athlete and a good swimmer."[32] His death remains a mystery.

In June 1924 the arrests of Leopold and Loeb were on the front page of every Chicago newspaper. "When I read that the Franks boy was missing, and of the manner in which he had disappeared," Ream said, "I started to take a keen interest in the case. I read every paper and the longer the thing went on the more positive I became that these kidnappers had robbed me. Then one day I saw the pictures of Leopold and Loeb in the paper. At once I was sure." Ream took his story to the *Daily Tribune,* which arranged for him to see the two. The confrontation happened on June 2, as Ream stood in a hallway in the Criminal Courts Building as the pair walked by. "The recognition of the confessed slayers by Ream sent an electric thrill through the Criminal Court Building," the *Tribune* reported. "It was a tense bit of drama, quite as much because of the importance it had in the sensational case as because of the terrifying effect it had on the accuser . . . He trembled, sobbed, gasped for breath. He could not speak and would have fallen had not a reporter grasped his arm. All because he had looked into and recognized the face of the man who blighted his life in young manhood. . . . Anyone who saw the look of horror come into Ream's eyes as he swept into his victim would feel his identification was true."[33]

"Do you think I could forget the face of the men who have taken so much out of my life?" Ream asked. "I knew them when I first saw their pictures in the paper. Loeb drove the car on the night I was kidnapped. Leopold is the man who prepared the ether bandage." He added that he had decided that Loeb "was soft, not a tough. But the fellow who pulled me into the car, Leopold, had a hard face. He looked like a thug from the west side. I think Leopold is one of the toughest men I have ever seen. . . . There was murder in his eyes that night. It scared me."[34]

Richard denied any involvement in what authorities euphemistically termed the "gland robbery."[35] Nathan refused to discuss the matter on the advice of his attorneys. But a few days after Ream's identification, Robert Crowe launched an investigation into whether Leopold and Loeb had attacked Ream and Tracy.[36] Melvin Wolf's grandfather apparently supported the investigation but said he didn't want to talk about Leopold and Loeb, perhaps fearing that his grandson would be tarred with the sexual rumors surrounding the murderous pair: "It would not bring back the boy if we find out."[37]

In August 1924 Tracy's father met with Crowe, apparently handing over evidence he believed tied Leopold and Loeb to his son's murder. As late as October, Crowe was said to be seriously considering charging Richard and Nathan with Tracy's death.[38] Ultimately he did not: he later said that while evidence pointed to Leopold and Loeb as definite suspects in other crimes, particularly the Ream case, he omitted any additional charges from the trial so as not to muddy the Franks case.[39]

CRIMINAL PSYCHOLOGICAL PROFILING WAS UNKNOWN in 1924. Today, it has become a standard part of investigations, its techniques developed and refined in the United States by the FBI's Behavioral Analysis Units and the Violent Criminal Apprehension Program. Utilizing diagnostic tools, criminal profiling can help sharpen inquiries and suggest the kinds of suspects authorities should be seeking.

In a modern reassessment, Nathan would score exceptionally high on the FBI's list of behavioral indicators displayed by serial killers. As a child, he was aggressive; had a taste for killing animals; was sexually abused; had a distant relationship with his family; harbored sadistic fantasies; was bullied by other children; engaged in forced sexual activity; and humiliated others. As a young adult, he lacked empathy and remorse; exhibited a need for control; engaged in violent sexual encounters in pretending to rape Richard; fantasized about rape and torture; suffered from social isolation; and believed himself superior to others. Richard, in contrast, had few of these signs.

With multiple murders, authorities search for commonalities: similarities in the type of victim; weapons used; and the locations where the crimes were committed. There is no known connection between Ream and Leopold and Loeb; they are said to have known Tracy, and it is likely that they knew Wolf. All may simply have been victims of opportunity, but they do fit the same demographic profile: young white males in their early twenties.

Ream was castrated, Tracy was shot, and no one knows how Wolf died. This disparity, though, is not uncommon. Killers often experiment with different methods and weapons as they refine their techniques. It may be significant that Ream's attackers used ether to render him unconscious: Nathan certainly had a supply, and he and Richard discussed using this method to subdue their eventual kidnapping victim. A test of this method on Ream makes a certain amount of sense; his castration also suggests the fantasies of overpowering someone and causing pain through sexual violence that were never far from Nathan's mind.

Profiling has revealed the importance of location in solving criminal cases. Criminals tend to begin in areas familiar to them. Ream, Tracy, and Wolf were all attacked within a mile of Kenwood. Then, too, Ream was dumped at the edge of the prairie, in an area Nathan knew and a few miles from the spot where they later attempted to conceal Bobby's body.

These episodes also fit patterns of criminal escalation. Nathan and Richard went from cheating at cards to stealing cars, calling in false fire alarms to arson, from robberies to kidnap and murder. There is nothing to suggest that the same pair who had tried to kill Hamlin Buchman in 1921 was incapable of murder in 1923; this was a mere seven months before they killed Bobby. If they were indeed the Chisel Bandits, they were gradually accelerating, honing their skills and moving from attacking objects to personal attacks on people, perhaps testing themselves and each other, seeing just how far they could or would go.

The timeline may also be pertinent. Ream was assaulted a few hours after Nathan celebrated his birthday, and two weeks after Leopold and Loeb made their infamous pact. Nathan was desperate to cement that pact, to ensure that Richard remained committed to him. It is not a stretch to envision the attack on Ream as a kind of perverse "birthday celebration," a cementing of their criminal agreement, and as a trial run for further assaults. Five days later Tracy was shot. In March Leopold and Loeb had a serious fight and Richard wanted to replace Nathan with another partner and pursue financial crimes. A few weeks later, Melvin Wolf was killed.

If Leopold and Loeb were responsible for any of these crimes, they would fit the definition of hedonistic killers, falling into the subcategory of thrill killers. Such killers focus on the planning and execution of the crime; the actual murders are usually quick. They strike against strangers or victims of opportunity. Time passes between crimes, and perpetrators experiment with and refine their methods. The crimes occur simply for the thrill of the experience.

DID LEOPOLD AND LOEB COMMIT any of these crimes? Evidence is sketchy, but they do fit the parameters delineated by the designations "A, B, C, and D," if one gathers the Chisel Bandit assaults under a single umbrella. Robert Crowe characterized "A, B, C, and D" as "major crimes," seemingly eliminating any fraternity robberies from the list.[40]

The Ream case rests on his identification and on circumstantial evidence. Ream's description of the man in the rear of the car, who he claimed was Nathan, differed from Leopold in several respects.

Eyewitness accounts, though, are notoriously unreliable. Ream was, after all, traumatized and got only a brief glimpse by flashlight. Understandably his recall might well be off. It is harder to explain his identification of Richard as the driver; in 1923 Ream said that he never got a good look at the second man.

This wasn't the only change Ream made to his story. In 1924 he said that an ambulance, not a taxi, had taken him to Chicago Memorial Hospital—though perhaps this, too, could be dismissed as an innocent error by a barely conscious young man. The most significant change, though, involved where Ream said he had been attacked. In 1923 he said he had awoke around 92nd Street, on the edge of the prairie. In 1924, he moved the location to 109th Street and Avenue G, still on the edge of the prairie but much closer to Wolf Lake, where Bobby's body had been found, and presumably in an effort to provide a link between the crimes.[41] Perhaps Leopold and Loeb were indeed behind the attack on Ream, though the evidence is conflicted.

The case that Leopold and Loeb may have killed Tracy seems more solid. There were reports that either Nathan or Richard or both had some passing acquaintance with him.[42] They may have known of his reputation as the "handsomest man on campus," but it seems more likely that if they did abduct him, it was simply an accidental encounter. They were in the habit of cruising the same neighborhood in the early morning hours, looking to commit crimes.

It would all be speculative except for one thing. After Nathan was taken in for questioning, police searched his home and took two revolvers, one belonging to him and the other belonging to his brother. Police did a ballistic comparison between a test bullet fired from one of these guns and the bullet retrieved from Tracy's head. Word of a ballistic match was first reported on June 4, but without any attribution.[43] Then, as part of the grand jury presentation that Leopold and Loeb killed Bobby, coroner's physician Joseph Springer gave evidence. Grand jury foreman F. D. Hoffman told the *Daily Tribune* that Springer testified that "the bullet which killed Freeman Louis Tracy fit one of the pistols found in the room of Nathan Leopold."[44]

The case of Melvin Wolf is more enigmatic; we don't even know how he died. But he did live in Kenwood, five blocks down Ellis Avenue from Richard. Both Leopold and Loeb were said to have known him, making it possible that they could have easily approached Wolf and, as they did with Bobby, lured him into an automobile and to his death.

Tracy and Wolf seem more likely to have fallen victim to Richard and Nathan than Ream. But it's also possible that Loeb was thinking of their attempted murder of Hamlin Buchman, or some other serious crime we know nothing about. A dearth of evidence in these cases seemingly condemns them to the realm of permanent enigmas.

We can't be sure when, precisely, Nathan and Richard crossed the line into murder. Whether they first did so in November 1923 rather than May 1924 cannot be established. That difference of seven months, though, matters little in their shared pathology. Both were ready and willing to kill.

PART IV

BEFORE THE BAR
OF JUSTICE

CHAPTER FOURTEEN

CHICAGO WAITED WITH BATED BREATH FOR THE TRIAL OF LEOPOLD and Loeb. The day after the pair had confessed, the *Chicago Herald and Examiner* declared Bobby's kidnap and murder "the crime of the century."[1] Papers devoted special sections to exploring the crime and the killers. "Newspaper sales shot up beyond belief," Clarence Darrow recalled, noting the "wide discussion and publicity, not only in America but anywhere in the world."[2]

"For some reason," Nathan later said disingenuously, "back in 1924, the newspapers found in my particular case apparently something that would sell, something that would interest the public, whether it was youth, the position of our families, the fact that we were college students, a combination of these things, I really don't know."[3] It was, of course, all of these things, coupled with the apparent randomness of the crime; its brutality; the inexplicable relationship between Leopold and Loeb; and a belief that it was America's first thrill killing. "The murder was a superlative crime," the *Chicago Daily Tribune* announced. "It will be a superlative trial."[4]

The *Tribune,* in fact, hoped to take the trial to new heights, suggesting that radio station WGN should broadcast the proceedings live from the courtroom. They asked readers to clip and return a coupon, voting either for or against airing the trial. It was an intriguing idea, but in the end public opinion went against a live broadcast: there was always the danger, some people worried, that impressionable children might tune in and overhear the sordid details of the crime.[5]

Recognizing the publicity that would surround the trial, William Randolph Hearst, publisher of the *Herald and Examiner,* attempted to lure Sigmund Freud to Chicago to sit in on the trial and offer his analysis. When Freud rejected the initial offer, Hearst upped the ante: he would pay Freud $500,000 and charter a small ocean liner on which the psychoanalyst would be the only passenger. Robert McCormick, coeditor of the rival *Daily Tribune,* also contacted Freud and offered to pay "anything he names" if he would come to Chicago and opine on the trial. But Freud, ill from cancer, refused the overtures: "I cannot be supposed to be prepared to provide an expert opinion," he said, "about persons and a deed when I have only newspaper reports to go on and have no opportunity to make a personal examination."[6]

And so Monday, July 21, 1924, arrived. A police cordon ringed the Criminal Courts Building on the northwestern corner of Dearborn and Hubbard Streets, where the trial was set to begin. The crowd of curious spectators was enormous, and throughout the morning they pushed to gain entrance to the sixth-floor courtroom. Police were stationed in the building corridors, at stairwells, and at elevators to turn back the constant waves.[7] Fewer than a hundred seats were available to the public, who had to show special pink admittance tickets; by contrast, the court issued press passes to some two hundred reporters.[8]

Shortly after nine, deputies escorted the two defendants from their cells in the Cook County Jail, along an upper corridor, nicknamed "the Bridge of Sighs," connecting to the Criminal Courts Building and into the sixth-floor courtroom. Both wore dark suits and white shirts, with their hair slicked back; Nathan seemed interested in everything, but Richard looked pale.[9] The deputies removed their handcuffs and Nathan and Richard took their seats between Darrow and the two Bachrach brothers who would share duties in defending them. Behind them, a seat was reserved for Jacob Franks, who usually attended court each day; he was barely separated from Richard's brother Allan and his uncle Jacob Loeb, who sat near Nathan's father and his brother Mike.[10]

Richard's parents were absent. Although his brother Allan had visited him in the Cook County Jail, neither of Richard's parents did so in the four weeks following his arrest. His father was still recovering from his heart attack, but a reporter did manage to ask about the charges against his son. "I tried," Albert said, "to bring Dick up to be a good boy and a good man. I always hoped he would become a model citizen. I am sorry that he has not been." And then, as if washing his hands of any responsibility, he added, "I cannot believe that it has been my fault."[11]

Anna Loeb, though, apparently made no effort to see her son, at least until Clarence Darrow intervened. "If you don't show mercy to your own son by at least visiting him in jail," he supposedly told her during a visit to her Ellis Avenue mansion, "how can you expect the judge to show mercy?"[12] And so on Saturday, June 28, Anna had gone with Allan and her brother-in-law Jacob to finally see Richard.[13] "My boy, Dickie!" Anna allegedly shouted as Richard walked in. Authorities apparently let her hug Richard and speak to him for some ten minutes; her son "was sobbing hysterically" at the reunion.[14] On returning home, she collected her ill husband and left Chicago for their estate at Charlevoix, where they would both remain throughout the trial. Richard, faced with this parental abandonment, agreed it was for the best. "In regard to coming down for the trial," he wrote to his mother, "it could not possibly do any good and altho' I should love to see you, I feel that it would only bring more sorrow to you and that we must all think of dad first and foremost."[15]

At half past nine, Chief Justice John R. Caverly entered, took his place on the bench, and with his gavel rapped the Case of the People of the State of Illinois vs. Nathan Leopold Jr. and Richard Loeb on charges of kidnapping and murder into session. Born in London, Caverly had come to America with his family at the age of six. He'd worked his way through law school, obtaining his degree from Lake Forest University in 1897 and taken a position as assistant city attorney in Chicago. In 1903 he was appointed a justice of the peace and police magistrate before returning to the job of city attorney in 1906.[16] After rising to municipal court judge, Caverly became Chief Justice of the Cook County Criminal Court in 1923.[17]

An official publication praised Caverly as "a strong and successful man, popular, clear of head and practical of purpose, charitable and yet a keen judge of human nature."[18] But Ernst Puttkammer, Nathan's law professor at the University of Chicago, remembered, that he "did not enjoy the highest of reputations, frankly, for his legal acumen and ability."[19] Caverly had something of a mixed record in court. He had never condemned a prisoner to death and was thought to be liberal in sentiment and loath to engage in controversy.[20] This latter characteristic would come into play in the Leopold and Loeb trial, as Darrow overwhelmed him with rhetoric and insistent motions.

The trial opened as Caverly asked the two defendants to enter their pleas. Darrow, clad in a rumpled, baggy gray suit and wiping sweat from his brow, rose from his chair and faced the judge.[21] "It is," he began, "unnecessary to say that this case has given us many perplexities and sleepless nights. Nobody is more aware than we are of what this means and the responsibility that is upon us. We have sought to consider it from every standpoint. First, of course, from the interests of our clients. . . . No one . . . will doubt for a moment that we have deepest sympathy for the three families involved. Of course, this case has attracted very unusual attention on account of the weird, uncanny and terrible nature of the homicide. . . . We want to state frankly here that no one in this case believes that these defendants should be released. We believe they should be permanently isolated from society and, if we as lawyers thought differently, their families would not permit us to do otherwise. We know, your honor, the facts in this case are substantially as have been published in the newspapers and what purports to be their confession, and we can see we have no duty to the defendants, or their families, or society, except to see that they

Bobby Franks, 1924. He is wearing his Harvard School uniform. *Chicago History Museum, ICHi-031773.*

Jacob Franks (left), Bobby's father, standing with his brother-in-law, Edwin Gresham, who identified the boy's body in the morgue. *DN-0077049, Chicago Daily News collection, Chicago History Museum.*

The Franks mansion on Ellis Avenue in Chicago's Kenwood neighborhood. *Courtesy of Erik Rebain.*

Flora Franks, Bobby's mother, testifying at the sentencing hearing. *DN-0077520, Chicago Daily News collection, Chicago History Museum.*

Dear Sir:

Proceed immediately to the back platform of the train. Watch the east side of the track. Have your package ready. Look for the first LARGE, RED, BRICK factory situated immediately adjoining the tracks on the east. On top of this factory is a large, black watertower with the word CHAMPION written on it. Wait until you have COMPLETELY passed the south end of the factory - count five very rapidly and then IMMEDIATELY throw the package as far east as you can.

Remember that this is your only chance to recover your son.

Yours truly,

GEORGE JOHNSON

MR JACOB FRANKS

Should anyone else find this note, please leave it alone. The letter is very important.

The ransom letter sent to Jacob Franks. *DN-0077257, Chicago Daily News Collection, Chicago History Museum.*

Police investigating the culvert where Bobby's body was discovered. *DN-0077260, Chicago Daily News Collection, Chicago History Museum.*

The glasses found near the body at Wolf Lake. *Chicago History Museum, ICHi-073838.*

The Franks mausoleum at Rosehill Cemetery in Chicago. *Courtesy of Erik Rebain.*

Richard Loeb, 1924. *DN-0077052, Chicago Daily News Collection, Chicago History Museum.*

Nathan Leopold, Jr., 1924.
*DN-0077057, Chicago Daily News
Collection, Chicago History Museum.*

Chicago Daily News reporters James
Mulroy (sitting) and Alvin Goldstein,
who helped break the Franks case.
*DN-0077128, Chicago Daily News
Collection, Chicago History Museum*

Sven Englund,
the Leopold
family chauffeur,
who unwittingly
destroyed the alibi
given by the two
killers. *DN-0077629,
Chicago Daily News
Collection, Chicago
History Museum.*

The Leopold family home at 4754 South Greenwood Avenue in Chicago's Kenwood neighborhood. *DN-0077059, Chicago Daily News Collection, Chicago History Museum.*

Nathan Leopold, Sr., sitting, during the sentencing hearing. *DN-0078049, Chicago Daily News Collection, Chicago History Museum.*

The Loeb mansion on Ellis Avenue in Chicago's Kenwood neighborhood. *DN-0077054, Chicago Daily News Collection, Chicago History Museum.*

Richard Loeb in cowboy costume as a child. *DN-0077990, Chicago Daily News Collection, Chicago History Museum.*

Clarence Darrow, the attorney who represented Leopold and Loeb throughout their trial. *Library of Congress.*

State's Attorney Robert E. Crowe during the sentencing hearing. *DN-0077491, Chicago Daily News Collection, Chicago History Museum.*

Dr. William White, president of the American Psychiatric Association, testifying for the defense during the sentencing hearing. *DN-0077454, Chicago Daily News Collection, Chicago History Museum.*

The crowd gathered outside Chicago's Criminal Courts Building during the sentencing hearing. *DN-0078046, Chicago Daily News Collection, Chicago History Museum.*

Richard Loeb, far left, listening to testimony during the sentencing hearing. *DN-0077987, Chicago Daily News Collection, Chicago History Museum.*

Judge John R. Caverly during the sentencing hearing. *DN-0077503, Chicago Daily News Collection, Chicago History Museum.*

Nathan Leopold, Jr., as an inmate at Illinois State Penitentiary at Joliet, October 1924. *DN-0078243, Chicago Daily News Collection, Chicago History Museum.*

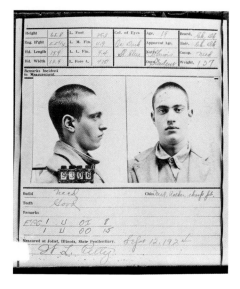

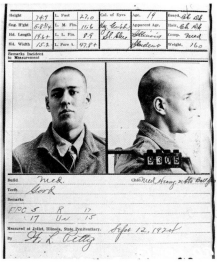

Richard Loeb as an inmate at Illinois State Penitentiary at Joliet, October 1924. *DN-0078242, Chicago Daily News Collection, Chicago History Museum.*

are safely and permanently excluded from the public. . . . After long reflection and thorough discussion . . . we have determined to make a motion in this court for each of the defendants in each of the cases to withdraw our plea of not guilty and enter a plea of guilty."[22]

Gasps filled the courtroom: everyone had expected pleas of not guilty by reason of insanity. Darrow continued: "We dislike to throw this burden upon this court or any court. We know its seriousness and its gravity. And while we wish it could be otherwise we feel that it must be as we have chosen. The statute provides, your Honor, that evidence may be offered in mitigation of the punishment, and we shall ask as such time as the court may direct that we be permitted to offer evidence as to the mental condition of these young men, to show the degree of responsibility they had, and also to offer evidence as to the youth of these defendants, and the fact of a plea of guilty as a further mitigation of the penalty in this case. With that we throw ourselves upon the mercy of this court and this court alone."[23]

Guilty pleas meant that there would be no trial: instead, Leopold and Loeb's fate would be decided solely by Judge Caverly. "We believed," Darrow recalled, "that he was kindly and discerning in his views of life."[24] Darrow had known that it would be easier for a jury of twelve to impose the death penalty than it would be for one judge, who would have to wrestle with his conscience, knowing that he alone would decide their fate. As he later admitted, he also thought that, as a Catholic, Caverly would be less likely to sentence the pair to death.[25]

Caverly was startled by this announcement. Addressing the defendants, he warned them, "As a consequence of the plea of guilty in the murder of Robert Franks, the Court has the power to fix your punishment at death, or imprisonment in the penitentiary for your natural life, or imprisonment in the penitentiary for a term of years not less than fourteen years, and that such plea of guilty will make no alteration in the punishment. And the Court desires to know whether, with the consequences of entering your plea of guilty before you, you now persist here in pleading guilty?" Both Richard and Nathan stood and agreed that they wished to plead guilty. Still stunned, Caverly looked at Darrow. "You have unloaded a big responsibility upon me," he said. "It was totally unexpected."[26] Before leaving the bench, Caverly announced that the sentencing hearing would begin on Wednesday, July 23.

The pleas also came as a surprise to state's attorney Robert Crowe. "There was nothing left for Leopold and Loeb to do but plead guilty," he announced. "The proof was so overwhelming that no jury could return any verdict except one of guilty. The crime was so cold blooded, premeditated and atrocious that no jury could fix any punishment except death. The fact that the two murderers have thrown themselves on the mercy of the court does not in any way alleviate the enormity of the crime they committed. As I informed the court this morning, the state is going to prove not only that these boys are guilty but that they are absolutely sane and should be hanged. Every exhibit . . . will be laid before Judge Caverly. . . . The defense is not permitted to introduce any insanity testimony because the law states that a plea of guilty to a fact automatically presumes the defendant to be sane. An insane man is not allowed to plead guilty to a fact. The defense may show certain circumstances which might have been a motive for the murder. But for the defense to say they attempt to introduce alienists to testify regarding the mental condition of the two slayers would be going clearly outside the rules of evidence. There can be no insanity for a person who pleads guilty. . . . There is but one punishment that will satisfy the prosecution. All our efforts will tend toward that one goal. They have thrown themselves upon the mercy of the court and we demand they be hanged."[27]

Wednesday, July 23 dawned exceptionally warm in Chicago. A miasma of unrelenting heat hovered over the city. Once again crowds rimmed the Criminal Courts Building, hoping to win one of the few public seats in the courtroom. Even though there would be no trial, the sentencing hearing promised drama previously unseen in the city. Everyone wondered if Leopold and Loeb would escape the death penalty.

The proceedings were scheduled to begin at 10:00 a.m. The two defendants seemed at ease as they spoke to reporters who crowded around their cells. Richard announced that he had an important statement to make: this turned out to be a joke, as he expressed the hope that the courtroom would be "a damned sight cooler" than it had been the day before.[28] But if he enjoyed toying with the reporters, he also had short fuse, at least when it came to Nathan's jocularity. "I heard you had a hard time describing our clothes," Nathan told reporters before launching into a recitation of their wardrobes: Richard in a black worsted suit, powder blue shirt and gray bow tie, and himself in a tweed coat, button-down shirt, and black tie.[29] Hearing this, Richard shot him a look and said, "Oh, shut up Babe!" as he turned his back on his fellow defendant.[30]

Crowe, accompanied by his assistants John Sbarbaro, Joseph Savage, and Milton Smith, walked into the courtroom and took seats on the left side of the main aisle. Because there was no jury, their box was now filled with reporters hunched over telegraph machines, ready to record every word.[31] Police escorted Richard and Nathan into the room. "Leopold seemed unconcerned," a reporter noted. But Richard "was pale, and an almost startled expression widened his eyes and dropped his jaw" as he passed the table where the physical evidence—the chisel, one of Bobby's socks, his belt buckle, and bloodstained floorboards taken from the rental car—waited to be introduced.[32]

As soon as Caverly called the proceedings to order, Robert Crowe rose and began his opening statement: "The evidence in this case will show that Nathan Leopold, Jr., is a young man nineteen years past, that the other defendant, Richard Loeb, is a young man of nineteen years; that they are both the sons of highly respected and prominent citizens of this community; that their parents gave them every advantage that wealth and indulgence could give to boys. They attended the best schools, from time to time had private tutors.

"The evidence will further show that long in October or November of last year these two defendants entered into a conspiracy, the purpose of which was to gain money, and in order to gain it they were ready and willing to commit a cold-blooded murder.

"The state will show, un-argued to your honor, that the motive which prompted Richard Loeb to so suddenly and unexpectedly confess was another evidence of his cautiousness and his craftiness and his desire to protect his own hide. He knew that the man who had beaten the life out of this little boy was his confederate Leopold." With this last statement, Crowe thus declared the state's position: Leopold had struck the blows, and Loeb had driven the car. Privy to all of the collected evidence as well as interviews with the pair, the state's attorney clearly believed Richard's version of events.

"The state will show to your honor by facts and circumstances, by witnesses, by exhibits, by documents, that these men are guilty of the most cruel, cowardly, dastardly murder ever committed in the annals of American jurisprudence. The state will demonstrate their guilt here so conclusively that there is not an avenue for them to escape. And making a virtue of necessity, when they have no escape, they throw themselves on the mercy of this court. . . . In the name of the people of the state of Illinois, in the name of womanhood and the fatherhood, and in the name of the children of the state of Illinois, we are going to demand the death penalty for both of these cold-blooded, cruel and vicious murderers."[33]

Throughout this oration, Richard and Nathan sat "apparently unmoved." Richard "frequently adjusted his stylish bow tie, moistened his lips with his tongue, and picked at specks on his sleeve." Nathan sat "virtually motionless" throughout Crowe's opening. Behind them, Jacob Franks looked on quietly, "chewing gum with apparent determination but wholly without outward feeling of show."[34]

As Crowe sat, Darrow rose to begin his opening statement. "A death in any situation," he declared, "is horrible but when it comes to the question of murder, it is doubly horrible. But there are degrees perhaps of atrocity, and as I say, instead of this being one of the worst of the atrocious character, it is perhaps one of the least painful and of the smallest inducement."[35]

Crowe objected to these incendiary words, which minimized Bobby's death, and which seemed designed to inflame passions. Caverly agreed that Darrow should confine his opening to a statement of what he intended to present as the defense case.

Darrow appeared duly chastised, saying, "Very well, your honor. I am aware at this time it isn't a proper statement, but I felt outraged at the whole statement that has been made in this case. That accounts for it. All this evidence that is sought to be introduced in this case is utterly incompetent. All of this is added to statements already made publicly and have no bearing on this case whatever with pleas of guilty in it. No one part of the defense claims that there was not a conspiracy, that there was not a murder, that it was not done by these two boys, that it was not done in a way that they have already given to the press. We shall insist in this case, your honor, that terrible as this is, terrible as any killing is, it would be without precedent if two boys of this age should be hanged by the neck until dead, and it would in no way bring back Robert Franks or add to the peace and serenity of this community. I insist that it would be without precedent. . . . I know this court will take it, take it calmly and honestly, in consideration of the community and in consideration of the lives of these two boys and that any echo that may come back from this extravagant and unlawful statement and from the lurid painting in this courtroom which was made for nothing excepting that a hoarse cry of angry people may somehow reach these chambers—we know your honor would disregard that and do in this case what is just, fair and merciful and a court must always interpret justice and mercy together."[36]

Once Darrow finished, Crowe began presenting his case. Because the two defendants had entered guilty pleas, this was not necessary, but Crowe wanted to show how the crime had been meticulously planned, rehearsed, and carried out in an effort to undermine any defense contention that Leopold and Loeb were suffering from mental illness. He also hoped to underscore a point he had made earlier to the press—that the evidence against them was so overwhelming that Darrow had no choice but to plead them guilty.

An emotional high point came that first day, when Bobby's parents took the witness stand. Jacob Franks told how he had last seen Bobby alive when he'd returned home for lunch on Wednesday, May 21, and related how the ransom call and letter had come. When Crowe placed Bobby's class pin and shoes before him for identification, Jacob looked shattered.[37]

Bobby's mother, Flora, came next, wearing a black cloche hat and a black coat piped in white. She seemed, the *Daily Tribune* told its readers, to be "a figure of listless sorrow, reticent in her grief, terrible in her voice, and hopelessly unmindful of the future." There was a kind of "primitive torture chiseled so carefully in her face," but she shed no tears as she gave her testimony. "When they put the crumpled shoes and the one brown stocking into her lap, she fingered them and identified them. But from out of a mosaic of the most brilliant colors, perhaps that have been painted into a sensational murder trial, an obscure, subdued and broken segment of the pattern was suddenly lifted to the key position. For with her testimony Mrs. Franks became the real victim of the murder for which Nathan Leopold, Jr., and Richard Loeb, the confessed killers of fourteen-year-old Bobby Franks, are now awaiting sentence."[38] In a soft voice, Flora, too, identified Bobby's shoes, socks, and belt before stepping from the witness box and exiting the courtroom.[39]

Crowe asked coroner's physician Dr. Joseph Springer to describe Bobby's injuries and read the autopsy report into the record. As Jacob Franks listened in silence, Springer detailed each of the four wounds to Bobby's head, the scratches on his body, and the face discolored by acid. Bobby had fought hard for his life, and after the rag soaked in ether was shoved down his throat, he continued to struggle for breath, drawing the fumes down into his lungs and into his kidneys and liver.[40]

Other witnesses, from the Hyde Park State Bank, the Rent-A-Car company, the Morrison Hotel, and Barish's Delicatessen, all easily identified either Leopold or Loeb as the men who had opened accounts, rented rooms, arranged for a car, or waited by the telephone to give fake references to "Morton Ballard." The defense objected to this recitation of evidence. "It is not necessary to question an unending line of witnesses to prove the thing that has been admitted," Darrow said. "There is a plea of guilty here. . . . We think the court should not permit, for the pure purpose of rehearing again to this community to stir up anger and hatred."[41]

"A plea of guilty, yes," Crowe shot back, "making a virtue of necessity. It was done because there was no escape. . . . I prefer if your honor pleases, to present my case. Of course, the plea of guilty admits everything. Your honor is going to be asked to fix the punishment here and I want to show by the mountain of evidence we have piled up that when they pleaded guilty there was not anything else they could do but plead guilty. I want to show their guilt clearly and conclusively and the details of it and ask that they be hanged. I don't think I ought to be limited."[42] Caverly agreed, and Crowe continued his presentation.

The next day brought more witnesses: Emil Deutsch, who had prescribed Nathan's glasses; members of Nathan's law study group and maid Elizabeth Sattler, who all recalled seeing the portable typewriter in the Leopold house before the crime; and Leopold family chauffeur Sven Englund, who had unwittingly demolished Nathan's alibi. Tony Minke spoke about discovering Bobby's body, and Cook County coroner toxicologist Dr. William McNally testified about the bloodstains he had found in the rental car and on the clothing Leopold and Loeb had worn on May 21 and rather stupidly kept after the crime.[43]

Crowe went through quick examinations with Nathan's law professor; handwriting experts who matched Nathan's writings to the address written on the ransom envelope; several reporters who had interacted with Leopold and Loeb before and immediately after their arrests; and with members of the police, who gradually related how the evidence against the defendants had accumulated during their investigation. Throughout the proceedings, both Nathan and Richard alternated between open boredom and sneering contempt. Newspapers were quick to comment on the demeanor of these two young men. The smiles, the laughter, and the constant whispers seemed beyond understanding; it was even more curious that Darrow apparently never cautioned them to act differently, but then their antics played into his position that both were mentally ill and may have served his purpose. They continued to chortle and make faces throughout the hearing, as if it was a lark. Confronted with questions over his behavior, Richard asked a reporter, "What do they want me to do? I sit in the courtroom and watch the play as it progresses. When the crowd laughs, I laugh. When it is time to be serious, I am that way. I am a spectator, you know, and I feel myself as one. You can tell the people on the outside there is no faking or pretending. I have watched you reporters across the table: you laugh, smile, yawn, look bored, and all the other things. Why should I be different?"[44]

Privately, though, Richard was more contemplative. In a letter to his parents, he wrote:

Of course dear Mompsie and Popsie, this thing is all too terrible. I have thought and thought about it and even now I do not seem to be able to understand it. I just cannot seem to figure out how it all came about. Of one thing I am certain tho—and that is that I have no one to blame but myself. . . . I am afraid that you two may try and put the blame upon your own shoulders and I know that I alone am to blame. I was never frank with you—Mompsie and Popsie dear—and had you suspected anything and came and talked to me I would undoubtedly have denied everything and gone on just the same. Dr. Glueck says that I was bent on destroying myself, and I believe he was right. I seem to have discarded all the finer things out of my life, Mompsie and Popsie, dear, it may seem terrible, but in one way it is almost providential that I was caught going on that way, confiding in no one—there is no telling how far I might have gone. This way at best I have a long prison sentence staring at me, but I am hopeful that someday I shall be free again and I really and truly think that I shall be able to do some good and at least live a much better life than I would have been able to otherwise. I realize that there is always a chance of the death penalty. However I am not worried and I assure you that although I know I never lived the part I do know that should I have to pay the penalty that I will at least die as becomes the son of such a wonderful father and mother as I know now more than ever that I have. What I wanted to tell you is that I am not really so hardhearted as I am appearing. Of course, dearest ones, I am afraid that my heart is not what it should be, else how could I have done what I did? . . . I intend to be very brave all the way thru and I want you both to know that I will do everything in my power to try and rectify a little the awful thing that I have done.[45]

Nathan remained as cold as ever. Although he told a reporter that he was sorry for his family, he insisted, "I don't want you to feel sorry for me, and if you do I wish you'd change your mind. I don't feel sorry for myself for what I did. I don't feel sorry for what I did. I did it, and that's all. . . . As far as being remorseful, I can't see it."[46]

The behavior and the comments were too much for Jacob Franks to comprehend as he sat in the courtroom. "I have been watching these two boys for the last three days and they had got me utterly baffled," he said. "I thought I was a pretty good judge of human nature during my long experience, but I find I have encountered an unsolvable problem. It is impossible for me to believe, as I sit here and watch these boys, that they're the ones who killed my child. They are so gentle mannered and refined looking."[47]

Although generally bored, Nathan took exception when Crowe offered up two of his most damning witnesses. The first was Carl Ulving, chauffeur for the Spiegel family. Ulving was adamant that he'd seen Loeb driving a dark-colored touring car, whose side curtains had been put up, on Ellis Avenue just before Bobby was kidnapped on the afternoon of May 21.[48]

Hearing this, Nathan grabbed Darrow: "That man is not telling the truth, he is badly mistaken." He falsely insisted "the car did not have the curtains up," something that both he and Richard had already described doing.[49] Nathan demanded that Ulving be harshly cross-examined. Benjamin Bachrach did so, but he was unable to shake Ulving's story: the chauffeur insisted that Richard "was sitting behind the wheel" and recalled how he had waved to him. A minor detail bolstered his credibility. On May 31, Spiegel told Ulving that Richard and Nathan were being questioned by police. At the time, and going by the account of Irvin Hartman Jr., newspapers assumed that the killers had been driving a Winton. But Ulving told Spiegel, "I saw Dick Loeb driving a car that Wednesday, but it was no Winton."[50]

Nathan realized how damaging the statement was: it was the piece of trial testimony that he discussed at greatest length in his later memoirs. Yet he did so in his typically erroneous fashion, distorting what Ulving had said. Nathan claimed that the chauffeur said he had seen Richard driving "about four o'clock" when Ulving clearly placed it sometime after 4:30 p.m. He also insisted that Ulving had first heard of Richard's arrest from his employer's son, when in fact it had been his employer. Although he speculated that the testimony might have been an "honest mistake," Nathan went out of his way to claim that Ulving disliked him and had fabricated the story as a result.[51]

The second witness was more controversial. Detective James Gortland recounted his conversations with Nathan on the evening of June 1 while Leopold was in custody. He spoke of Nathan's callous dismissal of Bobby's death and of his family's grief, but this was nothing new. Rather, it was his claim that Nathan had spoken of pleading guilty "before a friendly judge" to escape the death penalty that rocked the courtroom.[52]

Darrow asked Nathan if he had said this. "Hell, no!" Nathan replied.[53] When Darrow cross-examined the detective, Gortland admitted that, although he had written some vague shorthand comments in a notebook about the conversation and said that he had told his fellow officer Frank Johnson of the remarks that night, he had not made an official report. He had first mentioned the damning comment to Crowe only a week earlier, as he was preparing his testimony.[54] None of this particularly undermined Gortland's story: indeed, Nathan had said the exact same thing to Crowe the day before this conversation with Gortland took place, which only supported the detective's story.

On Wednesday, July 30, after the confessions and transcripts of police interviews and questioning of Leopold and Loeb were read into the court record, Crowe finished his case. He had called eighty-one witnesses and laid out, step by step, how Leopold and Loeb had planned their scheme and carried it through. Crowe's presentation cemented beliefs that the crime had been an experiment, a murder enacted for the thrill and carried out by two cold-blooded young men. Indulgence, precocity, and parental failure had led them down this dangerous and ultimately lethal path. The defense would soon upend these ideas, leaving Chicago and the nation stunned as a darker tale unraveled in that sixth-floor courtroom.

CHAPTER FIFTEEN

CLARENCE DARROW WAS FULL OF TRICKS. IT WASN'T JUST HIS SUPPRES-
sion of the psychiatric opinions or his legal maneuvers to save Leopold
and Loeb from the uncertainties of a jury trial. The weekend before he
was to begin his case, portions of the Bowman-Hulbert report were
deliberately leaked to the press. Darrow disclaimed all knowledge—"I
do not know how the report got out," he insisted.[1] A reporter, he said,
must have stolen it from his secretary's desk. But it seems that Darrow
arranged to have the report "stolen," knowing it would be reprinted in
newspapers, in an effort to soften perceptions and portray the killers
as mentally ill.[2]

Robert Crowe was furious about this development. It was, he
thought, a blatant attempt to influence public opinion and muddy the
question of sanity. He let his anger fly when the defense called their first
witness, Dr. William White, on July 30. Crowe immediately objected to
White's testimony, calling it "incompetent, irrelevant, and immaterial.
The only purpose of it would be to lay a foundation for him to testify
as an expert on the question of the sanity or insanity of the defendants.
On a plea of guilty your honor has no right to go into that question. As
soon as it appears in the trial, it is your Honor's duty to call a jury. . . .
Insanity, if your honor pleases, is a defense the same as an alibi would

be. Would your honor tolerate or permit these defendants to enter a plea of guilty in this case and then put witnesses on the stand to show that when the crime was committed, they were in California? . . . What is the defense trying to do here? Are they attempting to avoid a trial upon a plea of not guilty with the defendants before twelve men that would hang them and trying to produce a situation where they can get a trial before one man that they think won't hang them?"[3]

"I have a right to know," Judge Caverly replied, "whether those boys are competent to plead guilty or not guilty. When the defense arrives at such a point that this court, if this court was satisfied that the boys were insane, the court could, and very likely would, direct the plea of guilty to be withdrawn and a plea of not guilty entered and let the defendants plead their insanity as a defense. . . . The defense hasn't said they are going to put on alienists to show that these man are insane and I don't think they are going to attempt to show that they are insane."

"Well then," Crowe interjected, "what is the evidence for, what are they going to show?"

"You will have to listen to it," Caverly replied.

A guilty plea, Crowe tried to explain, meant that "the only place your honor can find evidence of mitigation is in the things surrounding the commission of the crime. You do not take a microscope and look into his head to see what state of mind he was in because if he is insane he is not responsible, and if he is sane he is responsible. . . . Did he kill the man because the man had spread slanderous stories about him? Then there is mitigation. Did he kill the man in the heat of passion during a drunken fight? That is mitigation."[4]

Walter Bachrach insisted that the defense was differentiating between "a mental condition, a mental disease" and "an organic brain disorder . . . that would affect the capacity of the defendants to choose between right and wrong." He said that both defendants suffered from "a functional mental disease" that, while not sufficient to prove insanity, would nonetheless provide mitigation when it came time for the court to determine punishment.[5]

This was a dangerous argument to advance. Precedent for introducing psychiatric testimony to mitigate a criminal sentence was practically nonexistent.[6] Crowe was technically correct in insisting that the law didn't allow evidence on sanity if the defendants pleaded guilty. While the state of Illinois allowed mitigating evidence in a criminal case, it didn't yet recognize the concept of diminished capacity, which is what Bachrach was essentially arguing, and arguing contrary to the suppressed reports of the defense's own experts.[7]

Darrow, for his part, railed against the state's arguments: "I cannot understand the glib, lighthearted carelessness of lawyers who talk of hanging two young boys as if they were talking of a holiday or visiting the races. . . . I have never seen a more deliberate effort to turn the human beings of a community into ravening wolves as has been made in this case, and to take advantage of anything that might get every mind that has to do with it into a state of hatred against these boys. . . . I don't believe there is a judge in Cook county that would not take into consideration the mental status of any man before they sentence him to death."[8]

The continuous references to "two young boys" got to Crowe. He sarcastically shot back: "These two men are not men of intellect and men of education, they are not graduates of the universities here that should be held to strict accountability, they are mere infants wandering around in a boyish dreamland. The state's attorney ought not to be permitted to discuss the gruesome details of the horrible murder in their presence. A kindly old nurse ought to tell them a bedtime story. They did not commit a murder. They broke a jar of jam in the pantry. That is not blood on their hands, that is jam. If your honor pleases they are not the cold blooded murderers, egotistical and secure in their conceit that they are above and beyond the law on account of their wealth and their influence. They have not sat here day after day and mocked the law, and as the details of this murder went in, sneered and smiled and laughed at the representatives of the law. No, they merely committed some little boyish prank and they are sitting here sobbing for mercy, crying their very heart out. . . . Mr. Darrow says put away the judicial slaughter and do not spank these naughty boys, but let their nurse take them out to play. They are not the intellectuals who assume a superiority and say there is no God. No, they both believe in Santa Claus."[9]

After three days of arguments, Caverly shut Crowe down: "Under that section of the statute which gives the court the right, and says it is his duty to hear evidence in mitigation, as well as evidence in aggravation, the Court is of the opinion that it is his duty to hear any evidence that the defense may present, and it is not for the court, to determine in advance what it may be. The Court will hear it and give it such weight as he thinks it is entitled to. The objection to the witness is overruled, and the witness may proceed."[10]

And so William White returned to the witness stand. Throughout his testimony, he—along with the other defense psychiatrists—referred to the defendants as "Babe" and "Dickie," childish references that grated on Crowe's nerves and even more ominously infected the judge—at one point in White's testimony Caverly clarified, "He says Dickie told him these things."[11] John Wigmore, dean of the Northwestern University School of Law, attacked "this voluntary adoption of the endearing, attenuating epithets 'Dickie' and 'Babe,'" which he said "reflects seriously on the medical profession." It was a "sad spectacle . . . calculated to emphasize the childlike ingenuousness and infantile naivete of the cruel, unscrupulous wretches" on trial to a "partisan end."[12]

"We can only understand this homicide," White declared, "by understanding the back and forth play of these two personalities as they are related to each other. Now, Dickie Loeb, with his feeling of inferiority, developed certain anti-social tendencies which are characterized to a certain extent to compensate him personally, but which are disintegrating and socially destructive, namely, his criminalistic tendencies. He develops these tendencies as being the head of a gang because, obviously, it is not half as satisfying to an individual to be a great man in secret. Dickie needed an audience. In his fantasies, the criminalistic gang was his audience. In reality, Babe was his audience."

The crime, he thought, was due to this interplay. "I do not believe that the Franks homicide can be explained without an understanding of this relationship," White declared. "I cannot see how Babe would have entered it alone, because he had no criminalistic tendencies in any sense, as Dickie did, and I don't believe Dickie would ever have functioned to this extent all by himself."

Richard, White said, "was continually building up all sorts of artificial situations, until he himself says that he found it difficult to distinguish between what was true and what was not true."[13]

Hearing this, Crowe shot from his seat and objected. "If he could not distinguish between right and wrong," he said, "I submit we are getting now clearly into an insanity hearing and I suggest that a jury be impaneled."[14] Caverly, though, denied the objection.

Like most of his colleagues, White was more nuanced in describing Nathan's king/slave fantasies than newspapers of the day reported. "It was an elaborate fantasy," White testified, "played out in innumerable ways, yet it always allowed Nathan to imagine himself as superior. . . . Dickie sometimes plays the part of the superior and sometimes the inferior; Babe plays the part of the superior and some times the inferior. Babe is the slave but he is a very powerful slave . . . he is the slave who makes Dickie the king, maintains him in his kingdom like the premier who occupies the principal state office over the weakly king. He maintains the kingdom for the king and is really the strong man, so in the position he occupies either as king or slave he gets the expression of both components of his makeup, with a desire for subjugation on the one part, and his desire for supremacy on the other."

White rebutted the idea of Nathan as a reluctant partner. "In several of their joint experiences," he said, "whenever Dickie intended to fall down in his role of leader, Babe always stepped into the breach and picked up the direction of the situation. . . . He comes in and takes the reins whenever the other boy falls down."[15]

But White dipped into absurdities when analyzing a photograph of a four-year-old Richard, dressed up as a cowboy complete with a revolver. White suggested that the "exceedingly tense" look on his face indicated dangerous, pathological aggression.[16] This was too much for the press. "An idea strikes me," opined a columnist in the *Herald and Examiner,* "a great idea, and one that may eliminate murder forever. If childhood pictures are indications of our future deeds, there need never be another murder. A law should be passed at once compelling parents to have photographs taken of their children annually between the age of three and nine, and then if a child should pose in the costume of an Indian or is snapped while aiming a pop gun at any object whatever, hang the child at once and thus prevent murder for all time."[17]

On cross-examination, Crowe vigorously attacked White and his questionable conclusions. He asked the psychiatrist who had wielded the chisel. "I think it was Dickie," White said. But when Crowe pressed him, White admitted that he hadn't even asked the central question in the murder case—"I was interested, but I wasn't curious," White said.

During his direct testimony White implied that Leopold and Loeb's drinking and petty vandalism signified deep psychological problems. Crowe was having none of it. "That is rather common for people who are drunk to break things, isn't it?" he asked White. The doctor agreed. Crowe then asked if throwing a brick through a window suggested that the perpetrator would commit murder; once again, White was forced to agree that it did not.

Did the defendants, Crowe asked, know right from wrong when they kidnapped and killed Bobby? White thought that Richard "knew intellectually that murder was proscribed by law," but that he hadn't possessed "adequate feeling toward its moral wrongness" to avoid committing the murder. Nathan, too, had known "intellectually" that murder was wrong, but lacked the moral sense to avoid it. Instead, White said, Nathan considered the murder only in terms of "the pleasure it brought" to him. White insisted that responsibility "is a legal fiction, which is pinned on the defendant for the purpose of justifying a verdict either of guilty or not guilty as the case may be."

Crowe probed the issue of dominance. "The character of the act," White said, "was the outgrowth much more of Dickie's way of thinking and feeling than of Babe's. But the relationship that was maintained between them was largely maintained as the result of Babe's intellectual agility."

"Which one, in your judgment, has the stronger mind?" Crowe asked.

"I should say Babe had the most definite objectives."

Crowe also scored points by calling White's conclusions into doubt. The doctor admitted that he had formed them based either on what the defendants had told him, or what the Bowman-Hulbert report commissioned to help the defense had found. As such, his testimony was entirely one-sided and far from being the neutral data that objective science demanded.

"Do you think that Nathan Leopold would attempt to mislead you?" Crowe pressed.

"I don't think he did," White answered.

"He has not lied to you at all?" Crowe pressed.

"I don't remember any particular instance at this moment where I believe Nathan lied to me. I think he was frank, as frank as he could be."

"The fact that Nathan Leopold has lied to every other person that he has talked to except you, doesn't make any impression on your mind at all?" White, though, insisted that he had not been deceived.

And then, Crowe unknowingly homed in on an issue that could have blown apart the entire defense case: he asked to see White's original psychiatric report. Under the rules of trial discovery, Crowe was entitled to read reports made by defense witnesses. Not surprisingly Walter Bachrach immediately objected—White, after all, had originally declared that the defendants were insane, only for Darrow to suppress this opinion. Crowe must have had some inkling of this. The issue, he told Judge Caverly, was "whether or not in his original report he didn't find them both insane and then after finding out what the defendants' position was. . . ."

"Well," Judge Caverly interjected, "I don't care."

"I understand your honor's position," Crowe replied, "but your honor does not understand mine. You are asked to believe what this doctor tells you. I have asked him whether in his original report he did not make a different finding than he is now testifying to and that he changed it in order to suit the purposes and needs of the lawyers."

Caverly finally asked White to hand over his original report; White hedged, said that he'd given it to Walter Bachrach. And Bachrach steadfastly refused to let Crowe see it. If Crowe or Caverly learned that Darrow's psychiatrists had originally found the defendants insane, and were now refusing to say so on the stand, the judge would have no choice but to immediately end the sentencing hearing and call a jury to hear the case—the one thing Darrow was determined to avoid.

Crowe tried one last time: "If your honor please, if I can prove that this man has changed his conclusions, that at one time he was willing to swear for $250 to one thing and on another occasion he is willing to swear to a different set of facts for $250, I think I have destroyed the value of his testimony." And then, amazingly, inexplicably, Crowe simply gave up the point. "If he is not willing to produce the report I will let it rest with that."[18] Had he insisted, the fates of Leopold and Loeb would have been very different.

The next defense witness was Dr. William Healy. "To my mind," he said, "this crime is the result of diseased motivation, that is, in its planning and commission. It was possible only because he [Leopold] had these abnormal mental trends with the typical feelings and ideas of a paranoiac personality. He needed these feelings and ideas supplemented by what Loeb could give him. There is no reason why he should not commit the crime with his diseased notion. Anything he wanted to do was right, even kidnapping and murder. There was no place for sympathy and feeling to play any normal part. In other words, he had an established pathological personality before he met Loeb."

Richard, Healy said, "is very friendly, pleasant, well-mannered; a very charming boy, having many nice qualities on one side, and yet on the other hand, having carried out for many years a dual personality, having been an extensive liar and a most unscrupulous individual, in a manner and to an extent that is quite beyond any in my experience. He has shown a curious desire for sympathy in pathological ways; a desire to get along socially. Contrasted with this is the fact that he is most remarkably unscrupulous, untruthful, unfair, ungrateful, and disloyal in many social relationships, disloyal even to his comrade when he cheated him, and to his fraternity when he robbed them." Richard's "secret abnormal mental life," Healy insisted, revealed "a disparity and a contradiction that to my thinking is certainly abnormal. The ability to carry on for many years this tremendously contradictory dual life is certainly pathological."

As for Nathan, Healy noted that he "showed himself to be self-centered and egotistical beyond any normal limits. He is extremely critical of other people and decidedly supercilious about his own mental attainments. Very stubborn in his opinions. He is right, the world is wrong." Nathan coldly told Healy, "Making up my mind to commit murder was practically the same as making up my mind whether or not I should eat pie for supper, whether it would give me pleasure or not."

But Healy's most important testimony concerned the relationship between Richard and Nathan. "In the matter of the association I have the boys' story, told separately, about an incredibly absurd childish compact that bound them, which bears out in Leopold's case particularly the thread and idea of his fantasy life. Loeb says the association gave him the opportunity of getting some one to carry out his criminalistic imaginings and conscious ideas. In the case of Leopold, the direct cause of his entering into criminalistic acts was this particularly childish compact."

The defense team was willing to let the matter rest there, but not so Robert Crowe. "You are talking about a compact that you characterize as childish," he said on cross-examination. "Kindly tell us what that compact was."

"I am perfectly willing to tell it in chambers," Healy replied delicately, "but it is not a matter that I think should be told here."

"I insist that we know what that compact is," Crowe replied, "so that we can form some opinion about it. . . . Tell it in court. The trial must be public, your honor. I am not insisting that he talk loud enough for everybody to hear, but it ought to be told in the same way that we put the other evidence in."

Caverly called both sides to the bench; Darrow didn't want the information made public, while Crowe again argued that it must be heard. Caverly finally agreed that Healy must openly testify about the compact. Healy complied, speaking barely above a whisper. "This compact, as was told to me separately by each of the boys, consisted in an agreement between them that Leopold, who has very definite homosexual tendencies was to have the privilege of . . . do you want me to be very specific?"

"Absolutely," Crowe answered, "because this is important."

Leopold, Healy continued, "was to have the privilege of inserting his penis between Loeb's legs at special rates; at one time it was to be three times in two months, if they continued their criminalistic activities together . . . then they had some of their quarrels, and then it was once for each criminalistic deed."

Newspaper reporters strained to hear the words. Seeing this, Caverly bristled and warned, "Gentlemen, will you go and sit down, you newspapermen! Take your seats. This should not be published!"

Crowe pressed for details: "What other acts, if any, did they tell you about?"

Darrow again objected to this, but Caverly allowed Healy to continue. "They were just experimenting once or twice with each other. They experimented with mouth perversions," which Healy summarized as Nathan performing oral sex on Richard. "Leopold has had for many years a great deal of fantasy life surrounding sex activity. . . . He has fantasies of being with a man, and usually with Loeb himself. . . . He says he gets a thrill out of anticipating it. . . . Loeb would pretend to be drunk, then this fellow would undress him and he would almost rape him and would be furiously passionate. . . . With women he does not get that same thrill and passion. That is what he tells me. Loeb tells me himself . . . how he feigns sometimes to be drunk, in order that he should have his aid in carrying out his criminalistic ideas. That is what Leopold gets out of it, and that is what Loeb gets out of it."[19]

Healy spent two more days on the witness stand, during which he offered up some important observations. Both Richard and Nathan, he said, had taken an interest in planning the kidnapping and murder.[20] But he believed that Richard had "been in it mostly, most completely, with respect to the preliminary planning of the details, and picturing himself carrying out the efforts."[21] It was the preparation, and anticipation, not the actual crime, that had buoyed Richard's interest.

There was also talk of Nathan's king/slave fantasies. Nathan, Healy said, had "told me of his attitude toward Loeb, and of how completely he had put himself in the role of slave in connection with him," insisting, "I felt myself less than the dust beneath his feet." Yet like the other defense psychiatrists, Healy was careful to point out that, in Nathan's mind, the positions were interchangeable, and that he was struck by "how readily he identified with either role."

Healy summed up that "the Franks case was perhaps the inevitable outcome of the curious coming together of two pathologically, disordered personalities." Richard, he declared, suffered from "a profound pathological discord between his intellectual and emotional life." And Nathan, who told the doctor that his ambition was "to become a perfect Nietzschean and to follow Nietzsche's philosophy all the way through," was, Healy thought, "a definitely paranoid personality, perhaps developing a definite paranoid psychosis."[22]

After these first two witnesses, the public narrative on the case shifted. In 1924 discussions about homosexuality were taboo; both Richard and Nathan admitted to aspects of their sexual relationship in interviews with the defense psychiatrists, though they tried to minimize their activities. It was the one subject that really bothered Nathan. He told Healy that "preservation of his dignity" was more important than saving his life, and that he "would rather hang" than have people hear his sexual history in court.[23]

From the start of the case there had been a lot of talk—insinuations, whispers, veiled language—hinting that there was something peculiar about the relationship between Leopold and Loeb. Early on, the *Daily Tribune*—without printing the phrase—took note of the "pair of cocksuckers" letter that Nathan had written to Richard. This, the *Tribune* declared, "resulted in embarrassment to both youths," and contained "a sentence that was regarded as at least peculiar." But, the paper said, Leopold and Loeb's "manly appearance" helped counter the mysterious phrase.[24]

The *Herald and Examiner* was less cautious. It noted that, among their classmates, "there was the suspicion that the murderers were perverts."[25] This use of the word "pervert" became commonplace in news accounts of the case; everyone understood that "pervert" really meant "homosexual." As Meyer Levin later wrote, "all were ready to use the horror word as a stamp to explain everything . . . there was a blanketing of homosexuality with every form of depravity."[26] And newspapers dropped enough hints that careful readers got the message. "Loeb 'Master' of Leopold Under Solemn Pact Made; Sex Inferiority Is Factor," the *Daily Tribune* declared in one headline.[27] By the second week of August, the *Tribune* stopped being coy. Richard, the paper declared, had found his "sex life" with Nathan "disgusting."[28]

During the trial, Darrow and his psychiatrists, as Paul Franklin notes, deliberately infantilized the pair not only to emphasize their youth but also because it "resonated with the homophobic psychoanalytic conception of male homosexuality as arrested development." The fact that Nathan was gay, and that Richard had joined him in a sexual relationship, thus was deployed as more "evidence" that they were mentally ill.[29]

At first Leopold and Loeb had been presented as cautionary figures, living warnings of the dangers of precocity, too much money, too few restrictions, and too many dangerous "modern" influences. But increasingly, certain elements blamed the crime on their sexuality itself, as if their relationship had somehow driven them to kill. This in turn reinforced perceptions that linked queerness with murder and, even worse, suspected pedophilia. It was nonsense, of course: sexuality had nothing to do with the crime. The motives that drove Leopold and Loeb to murder Bobby Franks were numerous, conflicted, even sometimes contradictory, but his death didn't come as the result of their sexual affair.

CHAPTER SIXTEEN

INTEREST IN THE SENTENCING HEARING CONTINUED UNABATED AS THE August sun turned the courtroom into a steam bath. The tall windows were thrown open and electric fans buzzed in a futile effort to provide ventilation. Hundreds of people continued to line up outside the Criminal Courts Building, hoping to witness the proceedings. "Pretty girls by the dozen," one witness recalled, "pouted and rolled their eyes at the doormen. They were either sweethearts of Dick or Babe or they 'just once wanted to see those dear boys,' they said. The gruesomeness of the crime seemed to have no effect upon the feelings of the giddy little flappers who begged to get in."[1]

Darrow waged a systematic campaign to win the press over to the side of the defendants. He encouraged his clients to speak daily to reporters in an attempt to humanize them—a strategy that backfired as much as it succeeded as the pair joked and complained about the weather.[2] The defendants, too, developed their own approach: as Nathan admitted, they gave interviews only to reporters who wrote favorable stories. "Public opinion is an important factor in our particular predicament," he explained.[3]

After the shocking testimony of Healy, the remaining two defense psychiatrists were something of a letdown. "I was amazed," Dr. Bernard

Glueck said of Richard, "at the absolute absence of any signs of normal feeling, such as one would expect under the circumstances. He showed no remorse, no regret, no compassion for the people involved in this situation, and as he kept talking on, it became very evident to me that there was a profound disparity between the things that he was talking about, the things he was thinking about, and the things that he claimed he had carried out." Nathan, Glueck declared, was "a definitely paranoid personality, perhaps developing a definite paranoid psychosis." Glueck believed that the crime "was perhaps the inevitable outcome of this curious coming together of two pathologically disordered personalities, each one of whom brought into the relationship a phase of their personality which made their contemplation and the execution of this crime possible."

Glueck offered up one last bit of damning testimony. "Did Loeb say who it was that struck the blow on the head of Robert Franks with the chisel?" asked Benjamin Bachrach on direct examination.

"He told me all the details of the crime," Glueck said, "including the fact that he struck the blow."[4]

Crowe, believing Nathan had struck the blow, went straight to this last point on cross-examination, asking Glueck where he had noted this admission in his report. Glueck pointed to a brief comment, "The Franks murder, profound lack of adequate emotional response in presence of intact intelligence." Glueck added, "That was sufficient notation for me."[5] This wasn't terribly convincing, but Crowe let the matter drop.

Harold Hulbert, who with Karl Bowman had authored the psychiatric report for the defense, was next on the stand. According to Hulbert, Richard was "not normal physically or mentally. . . . Intellectually, he far excels the average boy of his age. But his emotional reactions are those, I estimate because I cannot measure, of a boy of about nine or ten, certainly less than a boy of puberty. And in matters of judgment he is childish." In interviews, Hulbert noted, Richard was "quite interested in describing the planning of this crime. In the description of the crime itself he was extremely indifferent."[6] This

Hulbert took as evidence that Richard "prefers greater to the thinking than the doing"—in other words, it was the plotting and buildup to the crime that had appealed to him, not the actual kidnapping and murder.[7]

Nathan, Hulbert said, "preferred to live a non-emotional life." He held that "the rules and customs and laws and criticisms which hold ordinary men did not apply to him, because he was superior to the average person. The only serious mistake he could make would be a mistake of intellect." In discussing the crime, Hulbert said, Nathan "took particular pains to be accurate. There was no other emotion. He denied any feelings of remorse. He had no feeling of having done anything morally wrong because he does not feel there is such a thing as morality in the normal sense." Nathan "appears to have the intellect of a man thirty years of age," Hulbert said, but added that he was emotionally immature, and that his judgments were childish.

"The psychiatric cause for this," Hulbert declared, "is not to be found in either boy alone, but in the interplay of their two personalities, caused by their two constitutions and experiences. This friendship between the two boys was not altogether a pleasant one to either of them. The ideas that each proposed to the other were repulsive. Their friendship was not based so much on desire as on need, they being what they were. Loeb did not crave the companionship of Leopold, nor did he respect him thoroughly. But he did feel the need of someone else in his life. Leopold did not like the faults, the criminalism of Loeb, but he did need someone in his life to carry out this king-slave compulsion."[8]

Hulbert testified that Richard and Nathan suffered from a host of physical ailments that had led to their crime. All that he could offer with Richard was a litany of trivialities: that he still has several of his baby teeth, didn't need to shave every day, and had a low metabolic rate.[9] But with Nathan, Hulbert found "considerable pathology." He cataloged a long list of asserted physical peculiarities: too much hair; low blood pressure; flat feet . . . and on and on it went. X-rays revealed that Nathan's pineal gland had prematurely calcified, and he had circulatory problems. Hulbert claimed that Nathan's "endocrine disorder" had caused his exaggerated sexual urges, his "unmoral" thinking, and his neurotic attitudes toward life.[10]

Both defendants, Hulbert insisted, were suffering from some mental disease—a disease he couldn't or wouldn't define—that had led to the crime. With Nathan, this "caused him to ignore the ordinary restraint which individuals impose upon themselves" and to "justify his own actions to himself." But for this "mental disease," Nathan would not have committed the crime. So, too, Hulbert said, did Richard's "mental disease," which the psychiatrist classified as emotional immaturity and "only an academic realization of what he owed to society," impel him to kidnap and murder Bobby Franks. For Hulbert, the "greatest illustration" of Richard's alleged mental illness was the fact that he had participated in the crime at all.[11]

With the psychiatric testimony for the defense at an end, Darrow and his team wrapped up their case with a host of witnesses who knew Richard or Nathan or both. None of their testimony was particularly compelling—Loeb's former fraternity brothers spoke about his immaturity, and Leopold's friends talked about his obsession with Nietzsche. The most interesting takeaway from these witnesses was how they emphasized the disparity between Richard and Nathan. No one took the stand and recalled Richard enthusiastically talking about a moral superiority that allowed him to kill. Nathan was the one who'd repeatedly justified murder.

On August 11, Darrow concluded his case, and Crowe's rebuttal began the following day. Crowe was contemptuous of the parade of defense psychiatrists, who had stumbled over themselves to offer questionable diagnoses and peculiar opinions that stripped Leopold and Loeb of responsibility. And so he brought in his own psychiatrists who had examined and questioned the two defendants after their arrest but before Darrow was able to advise them not to cooperate.

Neurologist Hugh Patrick opened this rebuttal. Contrary to the defense psychiatrists, he testified that Leopold and Loeb had not been without emotion when questioned and cited numerous examples from the Bowman-Hulbert report demonstrating this fact. He dismissed any idea that enlarged glands or low metabolism caused mental illness. "Unless we assume that every man who commits a deliberate coldblooded, planned murder must be mentally diseased," Patrick summed up, "there was no evidence of any mental disease in any of the communication or in any of the statements the boys made regarding it, or their earlier experiences."[12] Patrick also faulted many of the report's conclusions, insisting that they were often vague, inconsistent, or had misinterpreted information to suit the defense. Under cross-examination by Benjamin Bachrach, Patrick was—as would most of the state psychiatrists who followed him to the stand—forced to admit that the conditions under which he and his colleagues had observed, and questioned Richard and Nathan on June 1 and June 2 were not ideal. They had largely listened as the confessions were read, only occasionally asking questions. And more than a dozen people had been present for much of the time—Robert Crowe and his three assistants, two stenographers, and numerous doctors. "Did you ever in your life make an examination of any person, as to his mental state, under circumstances of that kind before?" Bachrach asked. "I think not," came Patrick's reply.[13]

Archibald Church, head of the Department of Nervous and Mental Diseases at Northwestern University, was the state's next witness. Under questioning by Sbarbaro, Church testified that he had found no evidence of any mental illness in either Richard or Nathan. Richard, he said, "was entirely oriented" during his interview. "He knew who he was and where he was, and the time of day and everything about it. His memory was extraordinarily good; his logical powers as manifested during the interview were normal, and I saw no evidence of any mental disease." He gave essentially the same explanation when it came to Nathan: "There was no evidence of any mental disease. . . . He was perfectly oriented, of good memory, of extreme reasoning capacity, and apparently of good judgment within the range of the subject matter."[14]

Church said that the Bowman-Hulbert report, "which is very

carefully and thoroughly prepared, and based upon painstaking examinations, fails to present anything which is significant of mental disease." He dismissed the idea that the pair's fantasies had any significance: "Fantasies are daydreams," Church said. "Everybody has them. Everybody knows they are dreams. They are of interest in relation to character and conduct, but they do not compel conduct nor excuse it."[15] Church also pointed out that in interviews "the emotional manifestations were entirely on the part of Loeb. Leopold showed no emotion of any kind," while when asked about the crime Richard "showed distinct emotion."[16]

Crowe next called Dr. Rollin Woodyatt to rebut defense arguments that endocrine disorders had caused mental illness in Leopold and Loeb. Woodyatt said that knowledge of the effect of endocrine glands on behavior could "be compared to the interior of Africa before Stanley went there. There are many definite facts known, but they are scattered, disordered, unrelated. This field of endocrinology beyond the coastline of definite information is a field which has been exploited by romantic writers, charlatans, and others who are not to be classified as scientists."[17]

Dr. Harold Singer followed Woodyatt to the stand. Based on watching the defendants in court, he, too, agreed that neither Richard nor Nathan displayed any signs of mental illness. They were, he said, "free and easy in their movements, which were natural, easy and smooth. I have observed them especially during the early part of the trial, laughing and conversing with one another. . . . I have noticed that during the last two weeks since the alienists for the state started to testify their demeanor has been distinctly different. There has been much less laughing although occasionally they do laugh now, particularly Leopold."[18]

Crowe's final psychiatric witness was Dr. William Krohn. Richard, he declared, was "not suffering from any mental disease, either functional or structural, on May 21, 1924, or on the date I examined him. . . . The stream of thought flowed without any interruption or any break from within. There was not a single remark made that was beside the point. The answer to every question was responsive. There was no irresponsive answer to any question. There was abundant evidence that the man . . . was perfectly oriented as to time, as to place, and as to his social relations. . . . Not only that, there was excellence of attention. . . . There was not a single evidence of any defect, any disorder, any lack of development, or any disease, and by disease I mean functional as well as structural."

Nor did Krohn find anything mentally unbalanced about Nathan. "There was no evidence of any organic disease of the brain," he said. He found "no evidence of any toxic mental condition resulting from any toxicity of the body, because the pulse and the tremors that would have been incidental thereto were absent at this examination. . . . He showed remarkably close attention, detailed attention; he showed that he was perfectly oriented socially as well as with reference to time and space. . . . He had none of the modifications of movement that come with certain mental disorders."[19]

Benjamin Bachrach went on the attack against Krohn, particularly after he insisted that the circumstances under which Crowe's psychiatrists had observed Leopold and Loeb had been ideal for forming an opinion. The arguments went on for a day, but Krohn refused to back down, and finally the doctor left the witness stand. His testimony ended the sentencing hearing: all that remained were the closing arguments before Judge Caverly.

Newspapers tried to make sense of this competing psychiatric testimony. For most of the public, the conflicting opinions seemed hopelessly muddled. The doctors for the state had been emphatic: neither Richard nor Nathan was suffering from any organic condition that would result in mental illness. Darrow's alienists had insisted that traumatic childhoods or malfunctioning endocrines had left Leopold and Loeb unable to make rational choices or resist their murderous impulses.

But, as Darrow had hoped, the testimony succeeded in one thing: it altered perceptions that the two defendants were simply amoral thrill-killers. Now, the public saw them as alienated, scarred by past traumas. As historian Paula Fass notes, the defense psychiatrists "re-negotiated the terms of the crime from the satanic to the domestic. The monsters who inhabited an alien world of learning, culture and wealth, who had committed an incomprehensible crime, became just two boys."[20]

Four of the defense psychiatrists who examined Richard and Nathan—White, Healy, Glueck, and Hulbert—produced reports declaring them insane. When Darrow decided not to risk a jury trial and instead pleaded them guilty, he concealed these diagnoses. On the stand the doctors ignored their original findings, testifying that the defendants were mentally ill but not technically insane, suffering from some indefinable cocktail of abusive childhoods, personality disorders, and defective glands that had practically compelled the pair to kill. These cynical decisions call the entirety of the defense psychiatric case into question. Which opinions were valid? The private findings of insanity, or the assertion of lesser mental illness?

Until the psychiatric testimony, the public largely believed that Nathan had been the controlling mastermind behind the crimes, with Richard as his weak-willed victim. Now, and relying on simplified—and erroneous—readings of the psychiatric testimony, newspapers reported that it was Richard who had dominated the impressionable Nathan. For much of the public—and for history—Nathan became merely an accomplice, an unwilling participant, unable to resist Richard's magnetic charm and malignant influence.

Both Richard and Nathan came into the relationship emotionally and psychologically damaged. With Richard, it was his sense of alienation from his family and the constant pressure to achieve academically. Accustomed to pleasing people—his parents, his governess, his teachers—he always followed the line of least resistance and was easily influenced by stronger personalities. That weaker character came into focus throughout the plot, murder, and aftermath, from Richard's desire to abandon the plan; his refusal to pour acid on Bobby's body; his being the first to crack under pressure and confess; his fainting when identified during the investigation; and—contrary to the usual mythology of the case—his numerous expressions of emotion and re-morse over the crime.

Nathan, on the other hand, was quite different. Sexually abused as a child, isolated and having no real friends, he adopted a brittle, cynical personality as a defense mechanism to disguise deep insecurities. Even so, at heart he was arrogant and defiant; his twisted interpretation of Nietzsche allowed him to validate his own feelings of superiority. In all things—ornithology, academics, and behaviors—Nathan was ob-sessive and controlling.

Reading mysteries and detective stories didn't set Richard on the path to a life of a crime. He indulged his childish fantasies, and he cer-tainly committed more than his share of vandalism and petty thefts, but it was only after he met Nathan that Richard embarked upon more serious crimes and violence against people. This wasn't Richard escalating on his own: it is likely that Nathan provided the violent impetus. It's hard to downplay the string of evidence. Nathan was the one with fantasies of dominance; the one dreamed up ways to torture people; who enjoyed sadistic sexual encounters in puberty; the one who liked to humiliate others; the one who carried his violent sexual fan-tasies into adulthood—whether it was pretending to rape Richard or his desire to first kidnap, brutalize, and rape a young girl as part of the kidnapping plot. While people would later speak of Richard as a leader, they meant among his social circles; behind the scenes, it was Nathan, with his intelligence and stronger will, who probably con-trolled the relationship. Richard introduced Nathan to the thrill of committing crimes, but Nathan was an enthusiastic participant.

Perhaps Richard unwittingly provided Nathan with the courage and means to embrace his inner sadist. Doing so allowed him to en-act his fantasies and prove that he was indeed a superman, above all earthly laws. It's often said that neither Richard nor Nathan would have killed individually: rather, it was the coming together of their two scarred personalities that led to murder. This is certainly true of Richard, but it is more difficult to make the case where Nathan is concerned.

CHAPTER SEVENTEEN

With testimony at an end, the closing arguments began. On August 19, assistant state's attorney Thomas Marshall rose and opened for the prosecution. Leopold and Loeb, he declared, "wanted to commit the master crime; they wanted to talk about it and read about it. The master criminals wanted to commit the perfect crime that could not be detected. They did commit a most atrocious crime, and went about it with deliberation and a malice aforethought that carries with it only one punishment, and that is the extreme penalty." Marshall insisted that "nowhere in the whole history of murder in Illinois is there a crime so cruel, so brutal, so vicious, as this crime."

Marshall spoke of two recent defendants who had been sentenced to death in Illinois despite being under the age of twenty-one. They had robbed a store and in the ensuing struggle shot and killed a policeman. They hadn't intended to commit murder, as Leopold and Loeb had, but they still received the death penalty. Marshall asked why they should "go to the gallows, under the law, when men of the same age, of greater education, of better opportunity, can deliberately plan and scheme a murder and kidnapping for ransom for months and months, carry it into execution and by any possibility escape that penalty?" After speaking for two days, Marshall ended: "There is only one sentence that can be imposed upon these vile culprits that fits the act they committed, yea, the acts they committed. Twice over the law requires their lives upon their admissions of record in this court, and any lesser penalty than the extreme penalty, upon the record in this case, would make a mockery of the law itself."[1]

Richard and Nathan, according to the *Chicago Daily News*, seemed bored by Marshall's speech. They "listened with as little interest as if they were casual spectators," it reported. At one point, Nathan "leaned over Darrow's shoulder" to read a letter, laughing aloud at its content even as the assistant state's attorney called for the two defendants to be executed.[2]

Assistant state's attorney Joseph Savage followed Marshall, and painstakingly recited details of the crime. "Your Honor, at the outset of this case Mr. Darrow walks in before the court and makes a virtue out of necessity," he said. "He pleads both defendants guilty before your Honor to murder, and to kidnapping for ransom. . . . He asks your honor for mercy, and he tells your Honor that they are both youths, boys. . . . What mercy did they show that boy?" Voice rising, Savage declared, "Why, Judge, you wouldn't strike a dog four times!"

The crime, Savage emphasized, had been methodically planned and carried out. He heaped scorn on the defense psychiatrists: "I think it would be safe to say that you never before heard two murderers referred to as 'Babe' and 'Dickie.'" He dismissed the ways in which the defense had tried to link Richard's petty crimes to abnormality and mental illness—"Is there anything unnatural about a little fellow to burn shacks, wagons, fences? To steal? To lie?"[3]

Savage spared nothing: "If ever there was a case in history that deserves the most severe punishment, this is the case," he declared. "And I want to say, your Honor, that if your Honor does not hang both of these murderers, it will be a long time in Cook County before we ever hang another murderer. I want to say your honor that if we do not hang these two most brutal murderers we might just as well abolish capital punishment because it will mean nothing in our law. And I want to say to your Honor that the men who have reached the gallows prior to this time have been unjustly treated, if these two do not follow. And I know your Honor will live up to his full responsibility; and that you will enforce the law as you see it should be enforced. The people of this great community are looking to your Honor to mete out justice, that justice that the murderers in this case so richly deserve. And when your Honor metes out that justice we will have no more supermen; we will have no more men with fantasies, whose desires are to ravish young children and then murder them."[4] This last remark, about men with fantasies "to ravish young children," homed in the state's belief that one or both of the killers may have molested Bobby.

The incessant accumulation of damning facts in Savage's speech, according to the *Daily Tribune,* touched many in the courtroom: "lumps rise in throats and tears well up in the eyes. . . . The tears of mothers and sisters of other little boys like Bobby Franks were flowing. . . . It was the first time that eyes have been moist with sympathy for the victims." And where previously Nathan and Richard had laughed or looked uninterested, they pointedly gazed at the floor as Savage spoke.[5] Nathan was apparently shaken: turning around in his seat, he asked his brother, "My God, Mike, do you think we'll swing after that?"[6]

Having concluded the state's initial closing, Savage handed over the court to defense counsel Walter Bachrach; Darrow would follow with his closing, then Benjamin Bachrach would offer brief comments, and finally Robert Crowe would end the state's case.

"We raise no issue," Walter Bachrach said, "as to the legal sanity of these defendants, and make no contention that by reason of the fact that they are suffering from a diseased mental condition there should be any division or lessening of the responsibility to answer for the crime, the commission of which they have confessed. We do assert that they are suffering and were suffering at the time of the commission of the crimes with which they are charged from a diseased condition of the mind, and that such diseased mental condition of each defendant is a circumstance which should be considered by this court in the determination of the proper sentence to be imposed upon them." Bachrach dismissed the state's psychiatric testimony as "without value," contending that they had not spent sufficient time with the defendants to render reliable evaluations. Nathan, he said, "is mentally diseased . . . his mind is not functioning properly . . . he has the tendencies of what is called a paranoid personality." Richard, too, according to Bachrach, was suffering from "a schizophrenic condition of mind."

Bachrach inadvertently undermined conceptions that Nathan had been under Richard's control. Referring to the "pair of cocksuckers" letter, Bachrach noted that in it Nathan "lays down the code to be obeyed by his companion, Richard Loeb, whom he generously also allows to go under the designation of superman, but for whom he, Leopold, establishes a code of conduct."[7] Yet the idea that it was Nathan who had dictated the terms of the relationship, passed without comment.

Bachrach ended by reminding Judge Caverly: "Your Honor stands in the relationship of a father to these defendants. Every judge does. Every man in his heart knows that the judge on the bench is his father; his punisher, when he is wrong; that he must come before him and receive his chastisement. But when he comes before his legal father on a plea of guilty, that father is faced with the duty which every father has of desiring understanding of the wrongdoer, and what it was that brought about the situation, before the punishment is inflicted. It is so easy to hang; the important problem is put out of sight. It requires more intelligence to investigate. Your Honor, don't the very circumstances of this crime, the details of which we have heard recited here a number of times, recited with emphasis, with adverbs and adjectives, don't these circumstances show abnormal mental condition?"[8]

Then, at half past two that Friday afternoon, August 22, it was Clarence Darrow's turn. Anticipating a dramatic closing, thousands of people ringed the Criminal Courts Building, hoping for a seat in the courtroom. "Police reserves couldn't hold the frenzied crowd," the *Chicago Daily News* reported, adding that the "tidal wave of men and women swept over and flattened a skirmish line of bailiffs at the main entrance and poured up the stairs and elevators, sweeping all obstacles away."[9]

So long was Darrow's closing that it stretched over three days, starting Friday, continuing Saturday, and concluding on Monday. He began: "It has been almost three months since the great responsibility of this case was assumed by my associates and myself. I am willing to confess that it has been three months of great anxiety. . . . Our anxiety over this case has not been due to the facts that are connected with this most unfortunate affair, but to the almost unheard-of publicity; to the fact that newspapers all over this country have been giving it space such as they have almost never given a case before. The fact that day after day the people of Chicago have been regaled with stories of all sorts about it, until almost every person has formed an opinion. And when the public is interested and want a punishment, no matter what the offense is, great or small, they only think of one punishment and that is death."

"It was announced that millions of dollars were to be spent on this case," Darrow said. "Wild and extravagant stories were freely published as if they were facts. . . . We announced to the public that no excessive use of money would be made in this case, neither for lawyers, for psychiatrists or in any other way. We have faithfully kept that promise which we made to the public. . . . If we fail in this defense it will not be for lack of money. It will be on account of money. Money has been the most serious handicap that we have met. There are times when poverty is fortunate, and this is one of those times. I insist, your honor, that had this been the case of two boys of this age unconnected with families who are supposed to have great wealth that there is not a state's attorney in Illinois who would not at once have consented to a plea of guilty and a punishment in the penitentiary for life. . . . We are here with the lives of two boys imperiled, with the public aroused. For what? Because, unfortunately, their parents have money, nothing else."

Darrow railed against public opinion—"I have heard in the last six weeks nothing but the cry for blood." He insisted: "Neither the

parents nor the friends, nor the attorneys would want these boys released. That they are as they are, unfortunate though it be, it is true,
and those the closest to them know perfectly well that they should
be permanently isolated from society. . . . We did plead guilty before
your honor because we were afraid to submit our cause to a jury." He
laid on the flattery: a judge, Darrow said, "has more experience, more
judgment and more kindliness than a jury. . . . I know perfectly well
that where responsibility is divided by twelve, it is easy to say, 'Away
with him.' But, your honor, if these boys hang, you must do it. There
can be no division of responsibility here. You must do it. You can
never explain that the rest overpowered you. It must be your deliberate, cool, premeditated act, without a chance to shift responsibility."

Darrow attacked characterizations of the crime: "Cruel, dastardly,
premeditated, fiendish, abandoned and malignant heart—that sounds
like a cancer, cowardly, coldblooded. Now that is what I have listened
to for three days against two minors, two children, who could not
sign a note or make a deed." He then launched into an offensive di-
atribe: the real cruelty and cowardice, Darrow insisted, was the fact
that the two defendants were "handcuffed" when brought into and led
from the courtroom; that they were "penned" like rats "in a trap" in
their jail cells, and asserted that "the officers of justice, so-called," had
worked "this community into a frenzy of hate" while "planning and
scheming, and contriving, and working to take these two boys' lives."

There were frequent slips into offensive rhetoric: "This," Darrow
declared, "was one of the least dastardly and cruel of any that I have
known anything about. . . . Poor little Bobby Franks suffered very little. This is no excuse for his killing. If to hang these two boys would
bring him back to life, I would say let them go, and I believe their
parents would say it, too. . . . Robert Franks is dead, and we cannot
change that. It was all over in fifteen minutes after he got into the
car, and he probably never knew it or thought of it." This, of course,
was wrong: Bobby lived much longer than fifteen minutes, bleeding,
perhaps assaulted, in shock, gasping for air and slowly suffocating to
death on the car's rear floor for as long as several hours. But Darrow

offered a cool summation: "I am sorry for the poor boy. I am sorry for his parents. But, it is done."

Darrow insisted that, "so far as the cruelty to the victim is concerned, you can scarce imagine one less cruel." He then added insult to injury by again depicting Leopold and Loeb as the real victims: "my clients are boys, too, and if it would make more serious the offense to kill a boy, it should make less serious the offense of a boy who did the killing."

The lawyer repeatedly depicted the crime as "the senseless act of immature and diseased children . . . a senseless act of children, wandering around in the dark and moved by some emotion, that we still perhaps have not the knowledge of life to thoroughly understand. . . . There is no sort of question but what these boys were mentally diseased."

Darrow insisted that Richard and Nathan had killed Bobby "because they were made that way. Because somewhere in the infinite processes that go to the making up of the boy or the man something slipped, and these unfortunate lads sit here hated, despised, outcasts, and the community shouting for their blood. Are they to blame for it? . . . These two are the victims. I do not know what it was made these boys do this mad act, but I do know there is a reason for it." He began to lay out his theory that genetic inheritance and glands had made the crime inevitable: "I know they did not beget themselves. I know that any one of an infinite number of causes reaching back to the beginning might be working out in these boys' minds, whom you are asked to hang in malice and in hatred and injustice, because some one in the past has sinned against them." But with these words scarcely out of his mouth, Darrow dropped the subject and ended the day with yet another offensive comparison: "When you are pitying the father and the mother of poor Bobby Franks, what about the fathers and mothers of these two unfortunate boys, and what about the unfortunate boys themselves?"[10]

Court was back in session Saturday morning, and Darrow continued his rambling, disjointed closing. "There is not a sane thing in all of this from the beginning to the end," he argued. "There was not a normal act in any of it, from its inception in a diseased brain, until today, when they sit here awaiting their doom." The attorney argued that Judge Caverly should send the defendants to "a psychopathic hospital" where they would be "treated kindly and with care." Of course, Darrow had dismissed his chance to do just that by abandoning insanity pleas and thus tied the judge's hands though he seemed not to realize the contradiction.

Darrow asserted that executing Leopold and Loeb was a more brutal act than Bobby's murder: "It might shock the fine sensibilities of the state's counsel that this boy was put into a culvert and left after he was dead, but, your honor, I can think of a scene that makes this pale into insignificance. I can think, and only think, your honor, of taking two boys . . . irresponsible, weak, diseased, penning them in a cell, checking off the days and the hours and the minutes until they will be taken out and hanged. Wouldn't it be a glorious day for Chicago? Wouldn't it be a glorious triumph for the state's attorney? Wouldn't it be a glorious triumph for justice in this land? Wouldn't it be a glorious illustration of Christianity and kindness and charity? I can picture them, wakened in the gray light of morning, furnished a suit of clothes by the state, led to the scaffold, their feet tied, a black cap drawn over their heads, placed on a trap door, and somebody pressing a spring, so that it falls, under them, and they are only stopped by the rope around their necks. It would surely expiate the placing of young Franks, after he was dead, in the culvert. That would bring immense satisfaction to some people. It brings a greater satisfaction because it is done in the name of justice.

"I know that every step in the progress of the world in reference to crime has come from the human feelings of man," Darrow insisted. "It has come from that deep well of sympathy, that in spite of all our training and all our conventions and all our teaching, still flows forth in the human breast. Without it there would be no life on this weary old planet. And gradually the laws have been changed and modified, and men look back with horror at the hangings and deaths of the past. . . . I am not pleading so much for these boys as I am for the infinite number of others to follow, those who perhaps cannot be as well defended as they have been, those who may go down in the storm and the tempest, without aid. It is of them I am thinking, and for them I am begging of this court not to turn backward toward the barbarous and the cruel past."[11]

Court adjourned until Monday. And for the third day, Darrow rose and continued his closing. He had left off Saturday discussing the psychiatric testimony, but he now returned to the issues of money and genetics. "Something, or some combination of things," he argued, had forced Richard to his actions: "Dickie Loeb was a child of wealth and opportunity. Over and over in this court your honor has been asked and other courts have been asked to consider boys who have had no chance; they have been asked to consider the poor whose home had been the street, with no education and no chance; and they have done it, and done it rightfully. But your honor, it is just as often a great misfortune to be the child of the rich as it is the child of the poor. Wealth has its misfortunes. Too much, too great opportunity and advantage given to a child has its misfortunes, and I am asking your honor to consider the rich as well as the poor, and nothing else."

But he once again interrupted his own argument by returning to the subject of capital punishment: "Shall we charge them with the responsibility that we may have a hanging, that we may deck Chicago in a holiday garb and let the people have their fill of blood, that you may put stains upon the heart of every man, woman and child on that day and that the dead walls of Chicago will tell the story of blood? For God's sake, are we crazy?"

Then Darrow blamed Richard's parents: "I say to you seriously that the parents of Dickie Loeb are more responsible than he. And yet few boys had better parents. . . . I know that one of two things happened to this boy: that this terrible crime was inherent in his organism and came from some ancestor or that it came through his education and his training after he was born. . . . If he was normal, if he had been understood, if he had been trained as he should have been, it would not have happened. . . . If there is responsibility anywhere, it is back of him, somewhere in the infinite number of his ancestors, or in his surroundings, or in both. And I submit, your honor, that under every principle of natural justice, under every principle of conscience, of right, and of law, he should not be made responsible for the acts of somebody else, whether wise or unwise. And I say this again, let me repeat, without finding fault with his parents, for whom I have the highest regard, and who doubtless did the best they could: they might have done better if they had not had any money. . . . This boy needed more home, needed more love, more affection, more direction, directing. He needed to have his emotions awakened. He needed to have guiding hands along the serious road that youth must travel. Had these been given him, he would not be here today."

Darrow described Nathan as "just a half-boy, an intellect, an intellectual machine going without balance and without a governor, seeking to find out everything there was in life intellectually; seeking to solve every philosophy, but using his intellect only. Of course, his family did not understand him; few men would." Reading Nietzsche, the lawyer said, had unhinged Nathan's mind. This fell atop a psyche, Darrow insisted, already corrupted "by what has not been developed publicly in this case, perversions that were present in the boy," an unsubtle reference to Nathan's homosexuality. As if his sexuality answered all questions, this unspoken "perversion," Darrow said, proved "a diseased mind." And, if Nietzsche was to blame, Darrow argued, then so, too, was the University of Chicago, whose library held his books; its teachers who discussed his ideas in philosophy classes; and even Macmillan, the company that published his writings.

Having finished this strange excursion, Darrow again made remarks which Bobby's family must have found revolting. While insisting that the two defendants had much to offer if they were spared, the lawyer then opined: "I do not know what Bobby Franks would have been had he grown to be a man. I do not know the laws that control one's growth. Sometimes, your Honor, a boy of great promise is cut off in his early youth. Sometimes he dies and is placed in a culvert. Sometimes a boy of great promise stands on a trapdoor and is hanged by the neck until dead. . . . Perhaps the boy who died at fourteen did as much as if he had died at seventy, and perhaps the boy who died as a babe did as much as if he had lived longer. Perhaps, somewhere in fate and chance, it might be that he lived as long as he should."

Darrow continued this offensive line of argument: "Has your honor a right to consider the families of these two defendants? I have been sorry, and I am sorry, for the bereavement of Mr. and Mrs. Franks, and the little sister, for those broken ties that cannot be healed. All I can hope and wish is that some good may come from it all. But as compared with the families of Leopold and Loeb, the Franks are to be envied, and everyone knows it."

The Leopold and Loeb families, Darrow said, had already been punished enough: "Here are these two families, who have led an honest life, who will bear the name that they bear, and future generations will bear the name that they bear. Here is Leopold's father, and this boy was the pride of his life. He watched him, he cared for him, he worked for him, he was brilliant and accomplished, he educated him, and he thought fame and position animated him, as it should have. It is a hard thing for a father to see his life's hopes crumbling into the dust. Should he be considered? Should his brothers be considered? Is it going to do society any good or make your life safe or any human being's life safer that it should be handed down from generation to generation that this boy, their kin, died upon the scaffold? And Loeb's, the same. The faithful uncle and brother, who have watched here day by day, while his father and his mother are too ill to stand this terrific strain, waiting for a message which means more to them than it seems to mean to you or me. Have they got any rights? Is there any reason, your honor, why their proud name and all the future generations that bear it shall have this bar sinister attached to it?"

Darrow used poetry several times to make his points. Quoting A. E. Housman's "Now Hollow Fires Burn Out to Black," he painted a bleak picture of what lay in store for Leopold and Loeb:

Now hollow fires burn out to black,
And lights are fluttering low:
Square your shoulders, lift your pack
And leave your friends and go.
O never fear, lads, naught's to dread,
Look not left nor right:
In all the endless road you tread
There's nothing but the night.

"The easy thing and the popular thing to do is to hang my clients," Darrow summed up. "I know it. Men and women who do not think will applaud. The cruel and the thoughtless will approve. . . . I know your honor stands between the future and the past. I know the future is with me, and what I stand for here; not merely for the lives of these two unfortunate lads, but for all boys and all girls; all of the young, and as far as possible, for all of the old. I am pleading for life, understanding, charity and kindness, and the infinite mercy that forgives all. I am pleading that we overcome cruelty with kindness and hatred with love. I know the future is on my side. Your honor stands between the past and the future. You may hang these boys; you may hang them by the neck till they are dead. But in doing it you will turn your face toward the past. In doing it you are making it harder for every other boy. In doing it you are making it harder for unborn children. You may save them and it makes it easier for every child that some time may sit where these boys sit. It makes it easier for every human being with an aspiration and a vision and a hope and a fate. I am pleading for the future; I am pleading for a time when hatred and cruelty will not control the hearts of men."

For the fourth time in his closing, Darrow turned to poetry, quoting Omar Khayyam:

So I be written in the Book of Love,
I do not care about that Book above.
Erase my name or write it as you will,
So I be written in the Book of Love.[12]

And with this, Darrow sat down, his closing arguments finally at an end.

In his autobiography, Darrow insisted: "I endeavored in my address to make a plain, straightforward statement of the facts in the case, and I meant to apply such knowledge as we now have of the motives that move men. . . . When I closed I had exhausted all the strength I could summon. From that day I have never gone through so protracted a strain, and could never do it again, even if I should try."[13]

From his jail cell, Richard wrote Darrow an admiring letter: "Only the tears in my eyes as you talked and the feeling in my heart could express the admiration, the love that I have for you. I have gone thru so much of my life as a play actor—but I am sure you know when it is the heart that is speaking. A heart, Mr. Darrow, with a thick coating of deceit, of selfishness, but a heart that way down deep must, because I am the son of my father and mother, have some good in it and my message comes from there."[14] Nathan, too, later professed himself overwhelmed by the closing: "That address came through Clarence Darrow's mouth straight from his heart. Into it he distilled a half century's penetrating observation and a half century's profound reflection. Mr. Darrow was pleading not so much for Dick and me as he was pleading for the human race. For love, for charity, for understanding. Especially for understanding."[15]

Darrow's closing has assumed a mythological status in legal history. It has been described as a powerful mixture of oratory and poetry, with heartfelt pleas and soaring rhetoric. But the widespread praise rests largely on myth. After the sentencing hearing ended, Darrow borrowed the transcript so that he could republish his speech; he failed to return most of the portions chronicling his speech, leaving a void in the record. The published account he presented, upon which nearly all of the praise has been directed, was not Darrow's actual closing but instead a carefully edited version. As historian Simon Baatz noted, the attorney "rewrote the speech, cutting out long passages, correcting his syntax, and streamlining his argument."[16]

Darrow's actual closing was disorganized, jumping back and forth from one subject to the next, dangling arguments and then neglecting to follow them up. In his stream-of-consciousness rambles, Darrow repeatedly interrupted his own narrative, reiterated the same points multiple times, and left many in the courtroom confused. He took aim at first one subject then another, using a scattershot approach in an effort to save Leopold and Loeb from the hangman and perhaps to wear down Judge Caverly. The lawyer's offensive remarks about Bobby's death, his contention that the Franks family was more fortunate in having had their son killed than either the Leopolds or the Loebs, his dismissal of Bobby's future, and his equation of the murdered boy with his killers, were callous and stunning. His arguments about responsibility, or lack thereof, were absurd: Darrow blamed the killers' parents, the University of Chicago, Nietzsche, the philosopher's publisher—anyone and everyone except Richard and Nathan. They, he insisted, were victims—of their glands, their childhoods, their parents, their governesses, their wealth, their youth. And he offensively tried to lay the blame for the crime on Nathan's homosexuality.

Darrow was appealing for something that did not yet legally exist: that Leopold and Loeb had been subject to irresistible impulses that had left them unable to refrain from committing the crime.[17] But this, too, was nonsense. They were more than capable of making rational decisions when it came to the planning and execution of their scheme. Flawed though it had been, everything bespoke consideration and deliberation.

Darrow did seem prescient in at least one of his arguments: that Nathan and Richard had been so morally corrupted by an abundance of money that they were no longer able to differentiate between privilege and responsibility—probably the earliest use of the "afflu-enza defense." "They had the misfortune to be born rich," was how the *Chicago Daily News* summed up Darrow's arguments.[18] It would be left to Judge Caverly to interpret Darrow's rambling series of excuses when it came to Leopold and Loeb.

CHAPTER EIGHTEEN

On Tuesday, August 26, and after a brief statement by defense counsel Benjamin Bachrach in which he once again outlined the opinions of Darrow's alienists that Richard and Nathan were suffering from some mental disease, state's attorney Robert Crowe began his close.

It was stiflingly hot in the courtroom; nerves were on edge, and having listened to Darrow's rambling, at times incoherent, statements, Crowe was scarcely able to control his anger. The press had been transfixed by Darrow's presentation, but they were far more critical of Crowe. According to the *Chicago Daily News*, Crowe "spoke in a frenzy. He shouted and stamped and waved his arms. Now he thrust his face, purple with the strain of his apoplectic speech, into the faces of Loeb and Leopold; now he strode before Judge Caverly shaking his fist as he put all his lung power into some climax or other. It was all climax, for that matter. There were no valleys in the speech, just peaks. And Crowe's nasal voice accentuated the severity of the sentences it uttered. Into the faces of the two young defendants he hurled epithet after epithet, his eyes blazing and his voice screaming anger."[1]

Crowe began by attacking Darrow's characterization of the two confessed murderers. "We ought not to refer to these two young men, the poor sons of multimillionaires, with any coarse language. . . . We have planned, according to Mr. Darrow, for three months, and we have conspired to take the lives of two little boys who are wandering around in dreamland."

The state's attorney heaped scorn on the defense psychiatrists, calling them the "three wise men from the East." He saved a fair amount of venom for Dr. William White, calling him "Old Doc Yak," who "took me by the hand and led me into the nursery of two poor, rich young boys. . . . Then he told me some bedtime stories, and after I got through listening to them he took me into the kindergarten and he presented to me little 'Dickie' and 'Babe.'"

Crowe turned to Leopold: "I wonder now, Nathan, whether you think there is a God or not. I wonder whether you think it is pure accident that this disciple of Nietzschean philosophy dropped his glasses or whether it was an act of Divine Providence to visit upon your miserable carcasses the wrath of God in the enforcement of the laws of the state of Illinois."

"Clarence," Crowe declared, "would expound his peculiar philosophy of life, and we would meet with communists and anarchists, and Clarence would regale them with his philosophy of the law, which means there ought not to be any law and there ought not to be any enforcement of the law." Calling Darrow "an anarchistic advocate," Crowe derided him as a "kindly old nurse in this case for the two babes who are wandering in dreamland."

Referring to the defendants as "these two perverts, these two atheists, these two murderers," Crowe ridiculed Darrow's appeals for sympathy: "We ought to treat them with kindness, we ought to treat them with consideration. . . . Treat them with kindness and consideration? Call them babes, call them children? Why, from the evidence in this case they are as much entitled to the sympathy and mercy of this court as a couple of rattle snakes, flushed with venom, coiled and ready to strike. They are entitled to as much mercy at the hands of your honor as two mad dogs are entitled to, from the evidence in this case. They are no good to themselves. The only purpose that they use themselves for is to debase themselves. They are a disgrace to their honored families and they are a menace to this community. The only useful thing that remains for them now in life is to go out of life and go out of it as quickly as possible under the law."

Crowe ridiculed Darrow's claim that if the two defendants had been poor, they never would have faced the death penalty: "Their wealth, in my judgment, has nothing to do with this. It permits a defense here seldom given to men in the Criminal Court. Take away the millions of the Loebs and Leopolds, and Clarence Darrow's tongue is as still as the tongue of Julius Caesar." Crowe said that he had called in his own psychiatrists because "I knew how much money they had," and he worried that "they were going to put in some kind of fancy insanity defense." Describing the defendants as "young, egotistical smart-alecks . . . spoiled by the pampering and the petting of their folks and by the people who fawn upon them on account of their wealth," Crowe insisted on the significance of the fact that the state alienists had made their observations before the pair consulted with lawyers, "before they had been advised to invent fantasies; before they had been advised to answer certain questions in certain ways and before they had been advised to withhold even from the 'wise men from the East' certain information that might be detrimental to the defense in this case." He dismissed the Bowman-Hulbert report as "lies bought and paid for, for the purpose of defeating justice and saving these two mad dogs from the fate they so richly deserve."

Real fireworks erupted that Tuesday afternoon when Crowe suggested an unspoken motive for the crime: "These two defendants were perverts, Loeb the victim and Leopold the aggressor, and they quarreled. . . . One of the motives in this case was a desire to satisfy unnatural lust. They first wanted a little girl so that Leopold could rape her and then they decided on a little boy. What happened? Immediately upon killing him they took his trousers off. How do you undress a child? First the little coat, the collar, the tie, the shirt, and the last thing is his trousers. Yet, immediately after killing this poor little boy, his trousers alone came off, and for three hours that little dead boy, without his trousers but with all his other clothes on him, remained in that car, and they did not take the balance of the clothes off until they pushed the body into the culvert. You have before you the coroner's report and the coroner's physician says that when little Robert Franks was examined his rectum was distended."[2]

Both Darrow and Benjamin Bachrach shot up from their seats. "I take exception to that statement," Bachrach said. "The coroner's report said there was no sign of recent dilation. . . . This is the first time it has been charged in this case that the committing of an immoral act was the purpose of this crime. . . . If that is not cleared up at this time, if it goes out to the newspapers, it will do us no good unless it is cleared up at this time, and it is not a fair inference from that report."[3]

"And I," Crowe replied, "want to call your honor's attention to the fact that this little naked body lay in the water all night long with running water going over it, and that is why there wasn't any other evidence."

Bowing to contemporary sensitivities, Crowe warned that "ladies, if there are any here who do not want to hear testimony that might be embarrassing to them, to kindly step out," and called a brief recess. When the court returned, Crowe continued: "The Coroner's report says that he had a distended rectum, and from that fact, and the fact that the pants were taken off, and the fact that they are perverts, I have a right to argue that they committed an act of perversion. . . . I do not contend that the coroner's report states that an act of perversion was committed. It merely says that the rectum was distended. There was no evidence of semen, but it was washed away, I contend."

Hearing this, Judge Caverly banged his gavel and declared, "I have asked the ladies to leave the room. Now, I want you to leave. If you do not, I will have the bailiffs escort you into the hallway. There is nothing left here now but a lot of stuff that is not fit for you to hear. There will be nothing else but that to read. Why do you persist to listening? Step out into the hallway."

Once ladies had been cleared from the courtroom, Bachrach again rose and objected. Holding the autopsy report, he noted that while Bobby's "rectum was dilated," and "would easily admit one finger," the coroner had found "no evidence of a recent forcible dilation." But Crowe replied, "The evidence is that these two defendants are perverts, and when they took the body of the boy in, the first thing they took off was his trousers."[4]

This thought was left to linger as the day's session came to a close. Court was back on Wednesday morning, and Crowe resumed his closing. The state's attorney again attacked arguments that Richard and Nathan were suffering from mental illness. "In all probability the present mental disease of these two defendants would disappear very rapidly if the causes for its existence were removed. If the glasses had never been found, if the state's attorney had not fastened the crime upon these two defendants, Nathan Leopold would be over in Paris, or some other of the gay capitals of Europe, indulging his unnatural lust with the $5,000 he had wrung from Jacob Franks. If they were to be discharged today, through some technicality in the law, this present disturbance would all disappear very rapidly if the causes for its existence were removed.

"I submit," Crowe declared, "that this defense is not an honest defense. This is a defense built up to meet the needs of the case. If the State had only had half of the evidence that it did have, or a quarter of the evidence that it had, we would have had a jury in the box, and a plea of not guilty. But trapped like a couple of rats, with no place to escape except through an insanity defense, they proceed to build it up. A weird, uncanny crime? The crime is not as weird or uncanny as the defense that is put in here."

Crowe ridiculed the contradictory conclusions reached by the defense psychiatrists: "It has been argued here that because Richard Loeb told the doctors that he had no ambition in life, that he hadn't selected or thought of any profession, that is an indication he is mentally unbalanced; and because the other defendant had a definite ambition in life, he is also mentally unbalanced. A happy philosophy of medicine, especially when you are testifying in a guilty case, and trying to cheat the gallows. It is too bad that they have two defendants here. It would be so much easier to prove one insane, because anything you found in him could be a bad sign. But when you have two, and they are not exactly alike, when one has broken arches and the other has a high arch, why then, it has got to be a bad sign in one and a bad sign in the other. And if one has to shave every day, that is a bad sign; and if the other does not have to shave but twice a week that is a bad sign." He also dismissed the idea that Richard's mind had been poisoned by reading mysteries and detective stories: "A whole lot of us are in the same fix. I remember crawling under the bed to read Nick Carter. After I got through reading Nick Carter I began to read Gaboriau's French detective stories, and when I was a student of Yale I paid more attention to Raffles than I did to real property.

"All this king and slave fantasy," Crowe insisted, was "a mere figment of the imagination," dreamed up to help prove that the defendants were mentally ill. He hammered home the point that everything the defense psychiatrists knew had come either directly from the defendants or from their legal team. "I tried to get them to admit on cross-examination that boys of superior education and intellect, boys who could plan a crime of this sort stretching over a period of six months and attend to every minute detail, boys who showed such an abandoned and malignant heart as the facts in this case show that they possessed, might possibly, when caught like rats, lie just a little bit to friendly doctors who were trying to build up a defense for them to save their worthless lives. Oh, no, that is impossible. Everything they told us was true. They withheld nothing. They distorted nothing. They suppressed nothing." He then read out the sections from the Bowman-Hulbert report outlining how Richard and Nathan had frequently been caught in lies and omissions during their interviews.

"What strange hold," Crowe asked, "did this man Leopold have upon Loeb? Why did he submit himself to the unnatural practices of Leopold?" Crowe believed that the key lay in the mysterious "A, B, C, and D" crimes. He declared that Nathan "had something on" Richard. Loeb "was afraid of exposure; he contemplated murdering him, and the other one blackmailed him in the manner that I have already indicated. Loeb wanted to shut the mouth of Leopold and then break with him. Leopold had enough on him . . . and that is why he wanted Leopold to help him choke the life out of little Bobby Franks."

Crowe attacked Darrow's attempts to lay the blame on Nietzsche and the defendants' parents. "If reading this philosophy would be an excuse for this crime, how about the countless thousands who have gone before and who are still reading this philosophy who lead decent, honorable lives?" he asked. Darrow, he noted, "was not quite satisfied in blaming some remote ancestor, so he blames their parents, respectable, decent, law-abiding citizens. The only unfortunate thing that ever came into their lives was to have a snake like Leopold in that decent family. Casting blame where blame was not due, but where sympathy should go out as it does go out from the heart of every person in this community, to the respected families of these men."[5]

Thursday came, and with it the last of Crowe's closing. He again insisted that money had been the real motivating factor in the crime, reiterating the careful planning that went in to trying to obtain the ransom. If the kidnapping and murder had only been meant to provide a thrill, he argued, there was no need for Richard and Nathan to select such a high-profile victim. They could have grabbed any young boy off the street; instead, they wanted to make sure that whomever they took had parents wealthy enough to pay the ransom. Crowe scored an important point: "If they merely wanted to get the money and did not want to use it, what difference whether the bills were old; what difference whether they were marked or unmarked if they did not intend to spend them? . . . All the way through, if your Honor please, all the way through this most unusual crime runs money, money, money."

In his close, Darrow had mentioned the testimony of Detective James Gortland, who claimed Nathan had suggested he might plead guilty before a "friendly judge" and escape death—the same thing Nathan had told Crowe before he was charged. "Everybody connected with the case has laughed and sneered and jeered," Crowe now said. "And if the defendant Leopold did not say that he would plead guilty before a friendly judge, his actions demonstrate that he thinks he has got one."

Crowe then returned to attacking Darrow and his "peculiar philosophy of life." He began by reading from a 1902 address Darrow had given to prisoners in the Cook County Jail, in which the defense lawyer had suggested that there was no such thing as criminal responsibility and that prisons should be abolished. Darrow immediately objected that it was immaterial to the case; Crowe countered that Darrow had been allowed to quote poetry in his summation, poetry which was also immaterial to the case. But an angry Judge Caverly sided with Darrow.

"I want to tell you the real defense in this case, your honor," Crowe continued. "It is Clarence Darrow's dangerous philosophy of life. He said to your Honor that he was not pleading alone for these two young men. He said he was looking to the future; that he was thinking of the ten thousand young boys who in the future would fill the chairs his clients filled, and he wants to soften the law. He wants them treated not with the severity that the law of this state prescribes, but he wants them treated with kindness and consideration. I want to tell your Honor that it would be much better if God had not caused this crime to be disclosed; it would be much better if it had gone unsolved, and these men went unwhipped of justice; it would not have done near the harm to this community that will be done if your Honor, as Chief Justice of this great court, puts your official seal of approval upon the doctrines of anarchy preached by Clarence Darrow as a defense in this case. Society can endure, the law can endure, if criminals escape but if a court such as this court should say that he believes in the doctrines of Clarence Darrow, that you ought not to hang when the law says you should, a greater blow has been struck to our institutions than by a hundred, aye, a thousand murders."

The state's attorney then made his final appeal, pleading that Judge Caverly not be swayed by sentiment but instead follow the law. "I submit, if Your Honor, please, if we can take the power of American manhood, take boys at eighteen years of age and send them to their death in the front-line trenches of France in defense of our laws, we have an equal right to take men nineteen years of age and take their lives for violating those laws that these boys gave up their lives to defend." Bobby, Crowe declared, "had a right to live. He had a right to the society of his family and his friends and they had a right to his society." Crowe ended by saying, "I believe that the facts and circumstances proved in this case demonstrate that a crime has been committed by these two defendants, and that no other punishment than the extreme penalty of the law will fit it; and I leave the case with you on behalf of the State of Illinois, and I ask your Honor in the language of Holy Writ to 'Execute justice and righteousness in the land.'"[6]

The state's presentation of the murder case was over, but there remained the issue of the kidnapping charges. Once Crowe had completed his arguments, he offered up an hour-long presentation devoted to proving that the defendants were also guilty of this crime, with a handful of witnesses—including Jacob Franks—recalled to the stand to testify briefly as to the various elements. And, with this finished, Crowe finally took his seat.

It seemed that the day had fizzled out with this rather anticlimactic conclusion. But then Judge Caverly struck. Caverly had said nothing when Darrow had mentioned the testimony of James Gortland, but now he erupted in anger at Crowe—his eyes were "blazing," reported the *Chicago Daily News*.[7] Crowe's mention of the "friendly judge" had needlessly antagonized Caverly: there was an impression that if Caverly spared the defendants from death he might have been bribed to do so. The judge thundered at the state's attorney, calling his remarks "a cowardly and dastardly assault upon the integrity of this court." Crowe apologized, explaining that he had not meant to attack the judge's integrity, but Caverly was having none of it: "It could not have been used for any other purpose except to incite the mob and to try and intimidate this court," he declared. "It will be stricken from the record."[8] As one author noted, Crowe might accidentally have actually saved Leopold and Loeb from the gallows with this one remark: "Caverly seemed more concerned about showing that he could not be bullied than about the public backlash if he sent the youths to jail."[9]

Before leaving the bench, Judge Caverly announced that he would take the next ten days to consider his verdict. He set the date for his decision as September 10. "If anybody molests me during the next few days while I am deliberating on this case they will be sent to jail instantly," the judge warned.[10] It was August 28: the sentencing hearing was over. Chicago, and the nation, now waited for Judge Caverly to render his verdict.

CHAPTER NINETEEN

THE NEXT TEN DAYS PASSED AGONIZINGLY SLOWLY FOR AN ANXIOUS Chicago, and for the families of the victim and of the two defendants. But the accused seemed relieved. "I will have more opportunity to make a name for myself in the jail baseball league," Richard told a reporter. Nathan, too, was glib about their predicament. "If I am hanged," he said, "it will be a rare occasion. . . . I will arrange to have a good jazz band and plenty of hard punch." Then he offered a tantalizing statement: "I am planning the last supreme shock for the world in the form of my farewell speech."[1] Perhaps this was empty bravado, or perhaps Nathan planned to reveal the pair's other enigmatic crimes as he stepped to the gallows.

Dire warnings at the end of the hearing didn't stop threats against Judge Caverly. The courthouse would be bombed, one writer declared; if the judge didn't sentence Leopold and Loeb to death, another promised, he himself would be shot and his body hung up on a telephone pole.[2] "I tried not to mind the unkind remarks made by hundreds of cranks who wrote to me about the case," Caverly later said, "but I started to worry when they began to threaten my wife."[3]

On the morning of Wednesday, September 10, as he prepared to render his decision, Caverly was so worried about safety—that of the defendants as well as of himself—that he had the Criminal Courts Building ringed with extra police reinforcements.[4] Some five thousand people pushed around the building in never-ending waves, desperately trying to gain admittance.[5]

Caverly called the court to order at half past nine. Richard and Nathan sat between Darrow and the Bachrach brothers; behind them were Nathan's father and his brother Mike. Richard's father remained at Charlevoix with his wife Anna, but his brother Allan and his uncle Jacob Loeb were in attendance that morning. After both defendants declined to make any last statements, Caverly began reading his decision.

"In view of the profound and unusual interest that this case has aroused not only in this community but in the entire country and even beyond its boundaries," Caverly said, "the court feels it his duty to state the reasons which have led him to the determination he has reached." He noted that although Leopold and Loeb had pleaded guilty, they had done so because the state's evidence against them was overwhelming. As such, their guilty pleas could not mitigate their punishment.

"By pleading guilty," Caverly declared, "the defendants have admitted legal responsibility for their acts; the testimony has satisfied the court that the case is not one in which it would have been possible to set up successfully the defense of insanity, as insanity is defined and understood by the established law of this state for the purpose of the administration of criminal justice. The court, however, feels impelled to dwell briefly on the mass of data produced as to the physical, mental, and moral condition of the two defendants. They have been shown in essential respects to be abnormal; had they been normal they would not have committed the crime. . . . The court is willing to recognize that the careful analysis made of the life history of the defendants and of their present mental, emotional and ethical condition has been of extreme interest and is a valuable contribution to criminology. And yet the court feels strongly that similar analyses made of other persons accused of crime will probably reveal similar or different abnormalities.

The value of such tests seems to lie in their applicability to crime and criminals in general. Since they concern the broad question of human responsibility and legal punishment and are in no wise peculiar to the individual defendants, they may be deserving of legislative but not judicial consideration. For this reason the court is satisfied that his judgment in the present case cannot be affected thereby." And with this, and perhaps sensing that the arguments could never be resolved, Caverly rejected all the psychiatric testimony in the case.

The crime, Caverly continued, "was deliberately planned and prepared for during a considerable period of time. It was executed with every feature of callousness and cruelty. And here the court will say, not for the purpose of extenuating guilt, but merely with the object of dispelling a misapprehension that appears to have found lodgement in the public mind, that he is convinced by conclusive evidence that there was no abuse offered to the body of the victim. But it did not need that element to make the crime abhorrent to every instinct of human ability, and the court is satisfied that neither in the act itself, nor in its motives or lack of motives, or in the antecedents of the offenders, can he find any mitigating circumstances.

"It would have been the task of least resistance," Caverly summed up, "to impose the extreme penalty of the law. In choosing imprisonment instead of death, the court is moved chiefly by the consideration of the age of the defendants, boys of eighteen and nineteen years. It is not for the court to say that he will not, in any case, enforce capital punishment as an alternative, but the court believes it is within his province to decline to impose the sentence of death on persons who are not of full age. This determination appears to be in accordance with the progress of criminal law all over the world and with the dictates of enlightened humanity. More than that, it seems to be in accordance with the precedents hitherto observed in this State. The records of Illinois show only two cases of minors who were put to death by legal process . . . to which number the court does not feel inclined to make an addition. Life imprisonment, at the moment, may not strike the public imagination as forcibly as would death by hanging, but to the offenders, particularly of the type they are, the prolonged suffering of years of confinement may well be the severest form of retribution and expiation. The court feels it proper to add a final word concerning the effect of the parole law upon the punishment of these defendants. In the case of such atrocious crimes, it is entirely within the discretion of the department of public welfare, never to admit these defendants to parole. To such a policy the court urges them strictly to adhere; if this course is persevered in the punishment of these defendants, it will both satisfy the ends of justice and safeguard the interests of society." Caverly then announced his decision: Richard and Nathan both received life sentences for the murder of Bobby Franks, with an additional ninety-nine years added for the kidnapping charges.[6]

Hearing this, Richard and Nathan relaxed. They were seen to shake hands with Darrow.[7] "If Judge Caverly meant literally what he said in his opinion, the whole elaborate psychiatric defense presented in our behalf and the herculean efforts of our brilliant counsel were of no avail," Nathan later wrote. "The only thing that influenced him to choose imprisonment instead of death was our youth: we need only have introduced our birth certificates in evidence."[8]

The two convicted killers were handcuffed and led from the courtroom. They would spend one last night in the Cook County Jail: transfer to the state penitentiary was to take place the following morning. Aware that their lives were about to drastically change, and that they could no longer count on indulgent treatment once the state took over, Richard and Nathan enjoyed one final celebration. "Go out," Nathan ordered the sheriff, "and get us a big meal! Get us two steaks—that thick!" as he held his fingers some three inches apart. "Yes!" Richard agreed, "and be sure they are smothered in onions. And bring every side dish that you can find. This may be our last good meal." Before the sheriff left, Nathan shouted for him to "bring chocolate eclairs for dessert!"[9]

After the sentences were delivered, Darrow spoke to the press. "I have always hated capital punishment," he declared. "This decision at once caps my career as a criminal lawyer and starts my path in another direction. . . . Perhaps the sentence is worse than a death penalty for the two boys, but not for their families."[10]

Robert Crowe was furious. "The State's Attorney's duty," he told reporters, "was fully performed. He is in no measure responsible for the decision of the court. The responsibility for that decision rests with the judge alone. Like all other law abiding citizens, when the court pronounces his decision I must be content with it, because his decision in the case is final. While I do not intend and have no desire to criticize the decision of the court, I still believe that the death penalty is the only penalty feared by murderers."[11]

Caverly's decision came as a shock. "These young men should, and probably will, stay in jail for life," opined the *Herald and Examiner*. "The governor who extended any clemency to them, even twenty years from now, would be inviting his own oblivion. The public forgets many things, but a murder like this is not one of them."[12] And the *Daily Tribune* declared: "It was the opinion in legal circles that not only had Mr. Crowe's 'mountain high evidence' been displaced by Clarence S. Darrow's sage philosophizing to the extent of saving the lives of the young killers, but they go to prison with the prospect of emerging before they reach middle age."[13]

One of Caverly's most vocal critics was John Wigmore, dean of the Northwestern School of Law. He publicly denounced the decision, with its "astonishing pronouncements," calling it a "dangerous error." Caverly's opinion, Wigmore wrote, "ignores entirely" the question of punishment as deterrence and instead justified itself entirely on the age of the two defendants. "What has the twenty-one-year-old line to do with criminal law? Nothing at all, nor ever did have. The twenty-one years is merely an arbitrary date for purposes of property rights, family rights, and contract rights."[14]

While researching his book on the case in the early 1970s, author Hal Higdon spoke to Ernst Puttkammer, Nathan's old law professor at the University of Chicago. Puttkammer was skeptical that Caverly wrote his own decision. Never before, he said, had the judge "been able to voice his opinion so aptly." It seemed too articulate. Puttkammer probed and learned that Ernst Freund, a law professor at Northwestern University, had actually composed most of the decision, with contributions from Caverly, the weekend before sentencing.[15]

Caverly rarely spoke about his decision. But when he did, he justified it by erroneously insisting that Leopold and Loeb "didn't plan" what had happened. "They planned to commit the perfect crime, yes—to kidnap a boy, not harm him, write his parents, get the money and return the boy," he insisted. "It took courage to make the decision I did," he added. "I would do the same thing again. I am proud of the decision I made."[16]

Jacob Franks spoke briefly to the press after the sentencing. Although he had earlier expressed his hope that the young men who murdered his son should themselves be put to death, his position had now softened. "My wife and I," he declared, "never believed Nathan Jr. and Richard should be hanged."[17] Flora was satisfied with the verdict—"Bobby didn't believe in capital punishment," she said. "He wrote about it and read his articles at school and he told me it was wrong and somehow, after that, how could I ask for it?" And Jacob added: "I'm glad it is over, because this means the end. There can be no hearing in regard to their sanity, there can be no appeal, there can be no more torture by seeing this thing spread over the front page of the newspapers. It will be easier for Mrs. Franks and for me to be relieved of the terrible strain of all this publicity. It has kept the picture before us constantly."[18]

These quiet, dignified remarks stood in stark contrast to the statement issued by the families of both defendants: "There is but little to say," Jacob Loeb said. "We have been spared the extreme penalty. What have these families to look forward to? Nathan F. Leopold is sixty-four-years old. He has lived in Chicago practically his entire life, coming here from Michigan as a boy. He has been an exemplary citizen. His youngest son was his special pride. He justly believed that his boy was a genius, a most brilliant student, and a loving son. He honored him with his own name. He hoped that this boy of nineteen would make his mark on the world, be a comfort and a solace in his old age and accomplish tasks for the benefit of humanity. Now Mr. Leopold is crushed in spirit in his declining years. Albert Loeb, my brother, has spent his entire life of fifty-six years in the city of Chicago. He came from the ranks. He worked his way through college. He became a lawyer of repute, then a great businessman. He was always interested in every forward movement for communal welfare. His one hobby has always been his wife and children. He considered Dickie, the third boy, particularly talented. This son entered the University of Michigan at fourteen, and he was the youngest graduate of that college. He was always a most affectionate and loving son, never known in his home life to be disobedient but was thoughtful and considerate of his parents and the members of his family until this terrible tragedy overtook them. It is painful that on account of illness at a time like this the father and mother are unable to be at the side of their son. Again I say, what have these two families, whose names have stood for everything that was good and reputable in the community, to look forward to? Their unfortunate boys, nineteen years of age, must spend the rest of their lives in the penitentiary. What is there in the future but grief and sorrow, darkness and despair?"[19] There was not a word of sympathy for the Franks family or any expression of sorrow over the crime: instead, the Leopold and Loeb families seemed concerned only with their own position and feelings.

Worse was to come. After the sentence was delivered, defense psychiatrists contacted the Franks family. They wanted a "friendly conference" between the Franks and the parents of Leopold and Loeb. Dr. William White explained: "The suggestion was made that together they found an institution for the special study and understanding of problem children, and that over the entrance to this institution the profiles of these three boys be carved."[20] Bobby's family must have been appalled: an image of their murdered son, engraved on a building next to those of his killers? They rejected this insensitive and offensive idea; White professed himself surprised at their decision.

Heartbroken and exhausted, Jacob Franks and his family tried to put the tragedy behind them. They had endured months of morbidly curious crowds filling the sidewalk outside their house on Ellis Avenue. "During the last months their home has been a sort of mecca for cranks and the terrorists and curiosity's thousand eyes," the *Daily Tribune* reported. "Automobiles slow to a walk as they pass the slain boy's dwelling. Pedestrians linger to stare at it, at the lilac bushes which fringe the southern sidewalk, at the drawn blinds that hide the sorrowing family from morbid watchers. . . . The fashionable Hyde Park district has become a region of horror and chilling blight to the Franks. . . . Half a block up Ellis Avenue, within easy view of the Franks' front window, stands the magnificent Loeb residence. Its garden walls and Elizabethan roofing are forever in sight to remind the grieving family of the past. Fashionable Ellis Avenue, with its quiet homes and comfortable looking trees, has become a street of horror to the Franks. . . . It was as if the house has become . . . a sinister house of Usher, which someday might sink from sight."[21]

Bobby's family lived in a virtual state of siege that turned to agony as the weeks wore on. One night, someone crept onto the porch of a house across Ellis Avenue and erected a grisly tableau: a human skull, two decaying arms, and a leg in the form of a pirate emblem and tacked on a note: "If the court don't hang them we will." It was signed, "Ku Klux Klan."[22] Another night a cross was set on fire at the corner of 49th Street and Drexel Boulevard, apparently in an outburst of anti-Semitic violence.[23]

Cranks terrorized Bobby's already traumatized family. Letters arrived at the yellow house on Ellis Avenue threatening to kidnap Josephine and Jack, or demanding money to keep them safe. After one such threat, Jacob Franks actually followed the instructions, brought a fake ransom bundle, and met the extortionists—three eighteen-year-old boys—whom the police quickly arrested.[24] In August two more boys, eleven and nineteen, were arrested after threatening to kill Flora or Josephine unless they received $8,000.[25]

Several times Anna Loeb made the uneasy journey across Ellis Avenue from her mansion to the Franks house. She knocked on the door and asked to see her cousin Flora. Twice she was refused entry. On the third occasion, she was ushered into the parlor where Flora sat in a daze. Anna started to apologize for what her son had done, but Flora seemed confused by the mention of her dead child. "I'm sure Bobby will be coming back pretty soon," was her only comment to Anna Loeb. "She doesn't seem to understand that the boy is dead," Jacob Franks explained.[26]

Jacob finally decided that the attention was too much, and that he no longer wanted his family to live in the yellow mansion on Ellis Avenue. It had become a tourist attraction, a prison, and for his emotionally fragile wife Flora, every room held memories of her lost son. Just before the sentencing hearing, Jacob moved himself, his wife, and his two remaining children into a suite at the Drake Hotel. He put his mansion up for sale and announced that the furnishings would be auctioned off; the family would take only personal effects and the stained-glass window depicting their three children which had dominated the staircase landing.[27]

A notice in Chicago newspapers announced that the firm of Williams, Barker, and Severn would conduct the auction on September 22. Among the offerings were a Weber, Louis XV–style grand piano; furniture from the parlor; "handsome bedroom suites in walnut, mahogany, and white enamel"; Oriental carpets; silver services; lamps; curtains; and all kitchen appliances. On the preview day, reported the *Daily Tribune*, "several hundred thrill seekers crowded through the house. . . . They fought to get into the room where Robert Franks had slept before he was made the victim of Richard Loeb's and Nathan Leopold Jr.'s 'experiments.' Perhaps 1,200 were in the crowd, where gaping curiosity made it easy to understand why the Franks family no longer can live there. Of the crowd, at least eighty in every hundred were women. . . . The Franks' furniture was not of the exceptional kind."[28] The house itself was sold to cinema owner Joseph Trinz, who paid some $60,000 for the mansion.[29]

Before attempting to disappear into whatever obscurity and peace he could find, Jacob announced that he was establishing a trust that, after his own death, would actively fight any release of Leopold and Loeb from prison. All it would take, Jacob warned, was "a lenient governor, a shrewd lawyer, an indifferent public," and "in a few years" the two convicted murderers might be at liberty. "During my lifetime I shall fight every effort that they may make to defeat justice, and the creation of the trust fund will keep this battle up when I am gone."[30] In the end, though, he apparently failed to follow through on the issue.

There was one final, ignoble chapter to be concluded that early autumn. After having thrown everything into his efforts to save the lives of the two killers, Clarence Darrow had yet to be paid his full fee. He and his wife traveled up to the Loeb farm at Charlevoix to discuss the issue. Apparently, none of the defense lawyers had asked for a set fee in the case, and the defendants' families now supposedly used this to advantage. Darrow is said to have suggested $200,000 as a reasonable fee.[31] But, according to Darrow, when he mentioned this amount to the Loebs, one unnamed family member actually fainted: "When representatives of these families," Darrow said bitterly, "with an aggregate wealth of ten million dollars, came to me pleading for me to take the case . . . nobody fainted then."[32]

It is said that Richard's uncle Jacob Loeb, who had appealed to Darrow to save the defendants and insisted that their families would pay anything, now wanted to fight over the issue. "You know, Clarence," Loeb supposedly insisted, "the world is full of eminent lawyers who would have paid a fortune for the chance to distinguish themselves in this case."[33] When Darrow finally received payment, roughly six months after the trial ended, he was outraged. He apparently got $65,000 (equivalent to a little more than $1 million in 2021), a sum which included the initial retainer already paid.[34] Thinking that if he didn't accept he would never be paid, Darrow agreed to this sum. The two Bachrach brothers split between themselves an additional $65,000. In 1931, Charles Harrison published a biography of Darrow with which the lawyer had cooperated. It thus presumably reflected

Darrow's version of events. In it, he claimed that he had been forced, because of a prior agreement with his law firm, to pay his clerks, assistants, researchers, copyists, and others who had helped in the case, from his $65,000. This left him with a mere $30,000 profit.[35] Darrow was irate, complaining that "the fee was about a quarter of the amount I should have received for a case of such magnitude and exacting labor."[36]

PART V

INTO THE PAGES
OF HISTORY

CHAPTER TWENTY

On September 11, 1924, Nathan and Richard were driven to the Illinois State Penitentiary at Joliet, where Warden John Whitman received his newest prisoners. They had their heads shaved, were photographed and fingerprinted, showered, and received prison kits: underwear; blue striped shirts; pants; a pair of heavy shoes; socks; and two handkerchiefs.[1] Nathan became Prisoner No. 9305 and Richard became No. 9306.

The Illinois State Penitentiary was an overcrowded, outdated facility, described as a "hellhole."[2] The cells, four feet by eight, were damp, with narrow windows and no running water: prisoners made do with a bucket to use as a toilet.[3] "I never saw such a tiny little space," Richard commented on entering his new home.[4]

Leopold and Loeb had received indulgent treatment at the Cook County Jail; things were different at Joliet. They could send a single letter, and receive visitors, once every two weeks.[5] Using funds from their prison accounts, they could purchase tobacco, rolling papers, chewing gum, and candy from the prison commissary.[6] There were no other privileges.

Nathan was assigned a job in the fiber shop, weaving cane bottoms for chairs, while Richard worked in the furniture shop.[7] On September

17, they joined other prisoners for a concert; both, it was reported, broke down in tears at the reminder of a life now lost to them. The warden then told them that they would not be allowed to see each other again—it was prison policy to keep them separated.[8]

On October 6 Anna Loeb, who had returned to Chicago from Charlevoix with her ill husband, visited Richard. Guards listened to the conversation, and then reported it to the press. Anna embraced her son. "Dickie my boy," she supposedly said, "I want you to know and keep in mind during all the long years you are going to be here that your father and I and all the rest of us are hoping and praying for your welfare."

"I know mother," Richard allegedly replied. "I have been taken away from you for all time." At night, he said, "we get to read and write and do a lot of thinking." After some twenty minutes, the guards ended the visit; Anna embraced her son before leaving.[9]

At half past ten on the night of October 27, Richard's father, Albert, died from another heart attack in the house on Ellis Avenue at the age of fifty-six. Richard had not seen his father since the afternoon of May 29. "His death, members of the family and his physicians asserted," reported the *Chicago Daily Tribune*, "was in no sense caused and indeed was not hastened by the trial and conviction."[10] Richard could have applied for temporary compassionate release to attend the funeral, but his family apparently thought it best if he stayed away— there had been too much unwelcome attention already. Even so, an immense crowd gathered outside the house on Ellis and at the Rose-hill Cemetery, hoping for a glimpse of the late man's notorious son.[11] Albert had an estate valued at some $3 million, including some $1.2 million in Sears stock—much less than the press had previously speculated; his will, drawn up in 1918, left everything to his wife.[12]

In May 1925, following a bout with appendicitis, Nathan was transferred to Stateville Prison, a larger, new institute five miles from Joliet. Stateville had four immense round blocks, each with four tiers of cells arrayed around a central open space dominated by an interior guard tower.[13] This was more comfortable than Joliet: cells had hot and cold water; toilets; beds with spring mattresses; bookshelves; and radiators that could be controlled by the inmates.[14]

Nathan had a job in the shoe shop.[15] But the young man who held himself to be above the law was soon caught violating prison rules and sent to solitary confinement. Here, there was no running water and only a concrete bench for a bed. Nathan was handcuffed to the cell door for eleven hours a day; for meals he had bread and water.[16] In May 1926 he was reportedly caught stealing sugar and again placed in solitary confinement—there would be numerous infractions over the years.[17] Typically, Nathan attributed his punishment to the "publicity given my case," not to his own actions.[18]

More serious was Nathan's possible complicity in a 1926 escape attempt, when seven inmates overpowered guards and killed the deputy warden at Stateville. Nathan didn't flee, but a search of his cell uncovered a letter to his father, saying that he was about "to go away."[19] Nathan insisted that this reflected fears he might be killed, but this seems unlikely.[20] He had known and worked with six of the seven escapees, and one was a former cellmate.[21] Perhaps, as author Hal Higdon suggested, Nathan changed his mind about the escape at the last minute.[22] It's also possible that the other prisoners used Nathan to work out the scheme and then abandoned him. When the case went to trial, Nathan refused to testify, perhaps to protect the defendants, perhaps to protect himself.[23]

IN 1927 CHARLES REAM BROUGHT suit against Leopold and Loeb, charging them with his castration in 1923 and asking for $100,000 in damages. The trial opened at the Will County Court House in Joliet, Illinois, on January 5, 1927. The specter of Leopold and Loeb again sitting in a public court brought reporters out: they noted that both defendants laughed during the trial, as they had done in 1924. As full of himself as ever, Nathan even interrupted the proceedings with unsolicited advice to the court stenographer about the spelling of certain words.[24]

The trial lasted a mere two days. Three police officers who had originally worked on the case in 1923 testified that Ream said that he might be able to identify the man in the rear of the car. Ty Krum, a reporter who had been present in the corridor of the Criminal Courts Building on June 2, 1924, when Ream encountered Leopold and Loeb, said that Ream's identification was "not entirely spontaneous," and that a photographer had aided him.[25] It is possible that someone pointed out the pair to help Ream's identification; it is also possible that someone simply alerted a nervous Ream that the men he believed had assaulted him were about to appear. Unfortunately, the point was not resolved.

Both Richard and Nathan took the stand and denied that they had assaulted Ream. Nathan admitted to owning sharp knives that he used to skin birds. When asked if he had ever owned or used chloroform, though, Nathan said, "Not that I can think of." Had he owned or used ether? "I think not," Nathan replied.[26] Nathan was lying: he had owned and used both on his birds, and the pair had even brought along ether to use on Bobby.

Ream's lawyer David Tone summed up the evidence for the jury. He pointed out that Leopold knew the area where Ream had been dumped—on the edge of the prairie leading to Wolf Lake. After Dr. Orlando F. Scott, who had treated Ream in 1923, took the stand and described the castration as "skillful, not surgical," Tone argued that Nathan had the necessary skill to commit the assault. The lawyer insisted that Ream had been too upset and too emotional at the confrontation on June 2, 1924, to have faked his reaction. Added to Ream's identification of the pair, Tone suggested that the jury should have no doubt that Leopold and Loeb were behind the attack since they were already admitted murderers.[27]

The attorney representing Leopold and Loeb countered by reminding jurors that Ream had changed his story about being able to identify both of his assailants, as well as the location of the attack. He suggested that the former cabdriver had read about the Franks case, and, seeing Nathan's picture after his arrest, had decided, "There's the man I'll pick out. It is the logical place for him to light with his $100,000 damage suit."[28]

The case ended with a hung jury: eight of the twelve believed that Nathan and Richard had kidnapped and castrated Ream. Joseph Boylan, the jury foreman, said, "No one in the end would give ground. Eight of us were convinced that Leopold and Loeb were guilty. We believed it was perfectly possible and even probable for Ream to identify, to recognize them under all the circumstances."[29] In his memoirs, Nathan commented bitterly, "I guess it was impossible that a jury could find for us, regardless of testimony."[30]

But while Nathan dismissed the case, it seems that the evidence was more serious than he let on. The Leopold and Loeb families privately agreed to pay Ream a large cash settlement if he dropped his lawsuit.[31] Considering how they haggled over paying attorney Clarence Darrow for his services in 1924, this settlement suggests that the families, at least, believed that there was compelling evidence of their sons' guilt.

IN MAY 1928 NATHAN WAS assigned to work in the library at State-ville.[32] He did well and won praise from officials but, as Higdon noted, his "motives might not have been entirely altruistic. Working in a library was undoubtedly more pleasant for him than working in a shop. Such conduct also would be more likely to impress a future parole board."[33]

On April 4, 1929, Nathan's father died following an operation. The following morning a guard pulled Nathan aside and asked, "Did you hear anything about your old man, that he kicked the bucket?" Nathan was surprised; only now, he said, did he realize "the enormity of what I'd done. It was the first time I was ever honest to God sorry. Regretful, remorseful. It had taken five years to sink in."[34]

Yet alleged remorse brought little change in Nathan's behavior. He continued to break prison rules and got into at least four physical fights with other inmates that resulted in more visits to solitary. He later insisted that three of the fights had come when he resisted sexual advances, but this seems doubtful.[35]

AT JOLIET RICHARD ADAPTED EASILY to prison life: he befriended fellow inmates and was well liked. "People who knew Dick Loeb" in prison, wrote one reporter, "are almost unanimous in remembering him as an extraordinarily attractive young man."[36] Almost uniquely, Richard was never once caught violating prison rules, and he was never disciplined for any reason: prison officials assigned him the highest rank possible in their hierarchy of inmates, "Grade A," singling him out as exceptionally trustworthy, cooperative, and obedient.[37] Had Richard really been the sociopath depicted in the press, it isn't likely that he would have done so well in his new life.

"Loeb," one prison official said, "reads everything he can get his hands on about Arctic and Antarctic explorations. I asked him once if he hoped to go on one of his own some day. He laughed and said no, he didn't expect to go himself." On June 11, 1926, Anna Loeb again visited him in prison, this time bringing her son Ernest. It was Richard's twenty-first birthday, and the warden allowed her to give him some fruit and candy.[38]

Richard kept in minimal contact with Nathan in these years. "Once in a great while," Leopold wrote, "I would get a message from Dick in the old prison. Usually these were merely short verbal messages, little more than hellos."[39] Perhaps some feeling remained; it is also possible that Richard was constantly on guard, fearful—as he had expressed several times in 1924—of what Nathan might do or say, or that he might reveal damning details about the mysterious "A, B, C, and D" crimes. Based on his past experiences, Richard may have regarded Nathan both as a friend and as a potential threat.

In the summer of 1930 Richard, who had been working in the deputy warden's office as an assistant, won a transfer to Stateville. Nathan's actions sabotaged any reunion: he was caught forging passes with the chaplain's name and, after a week in solitary, was sent back to Joliet, just as Richard arrived at the new prison.[40] Not until 1931 were both reunited at Stateville. Officials allowed them to mix together, and even asked the pair to write a booklet explaining parole conditions to fellow inmates.[41]

Nathan said that he and Richard were "as close as it is possible for two men to be. Whatever happened to be our individual assignments, we worked together as a team. . . . No matter what our separate activities for the day might be, we made it an invariable practice to have a twenty-minute talk immediately after breakfast each day. We cut up everything, whether it concerned him, or me, or both of us. We had no secrets."[42]

Yet Richard overshadowed Nathan—"everyone knew him and everyone liked him," Nathan said. "He was one of the three or four men in the prison about whom no one had anything bad to say." Richard was thrilled when his fellow inmates asked him to represent them on a prison advisory board; it was something useful and would undoubtedly look good on his record if he ever came up for parole. But Nathan objected. Perhaps jealous or resentful, he strongly urged Richard not to take the position. And so—and against his own wishes—Richard again gave in to Nathan, refusing the offer.[43]

Father Eligius Weir, a Franciscan priest serving as prison chaplain, befriended Richard and Nathan. Weir thought that both "were trying to rehabilitate themselves."[44] Nathan attributed a growing sense of remorse to Weir's influence. "Certainly it hadn't existed when first I came to prison," Nathan admitted. "About the only thing I had been sorry about then was that I had been caught. But somewhere between then and now remorse had not only entered my mental life; it dominated it." He claimed to be "haunted" by what he had done, and declared, "How very often I've wished that I could trade places with Bobby Franks!"[45]

In the autumn of 1932 Richard tried to put his rehabilitation into practice. Shocked that many inmates were poorly educated, Richard asked Warden Frank Whipp if he could establish a high school curriculum for his fellow prisoners. "The advantages of this system are obvious," the proposal read. "It would place a high school education within the reach of any inmate industrious enough to take advantage of the privilege. To those interested in some particular subject, such as history or languages, it would offer a chance to spend their spare time pleasantly and profitably. Finally, since certificates of completion could be given, following satisfactory work in a course, the inmate would have a definite goal to strive for."[46]

Whipp approved the idea, allowing Richard to design courses with Nathan's assistance. Classes were to be conducted by correspondence, with lessons given and corrected by inmate instructors in their cells at night.[47] The Stateville Correspondence School officially opened on January 1, 1933, with twenty-eight students and a waiting list of sixty-four.[48] Richard taught history, English, and geometry, while Nathan tackled algebra and foreign languages.[49] Believing that the available materials were either too simple or too advanced, Richard wrote an English textbook. He was so proud of it that he had a copy bound in leather and sent to his mother as a Christmas gift.[50] The school proved to be such a success that it was soon expanded to Joliet and eventually across the state, with authorities praising Richard for his dedication.

IN 1935, JOSEPH RAGEN TOOK over as warden at Stateville. Previously prisoners could receive money from outside the institution to use at the commissary. Richard had always shared his fifty-dollar-a-month allowance, buying food and cigarettes for other inmates.[51] Ragen, believing the system led to corruption, cut allowances to three dollars a week.[52]

On January 28, 1936, Richard had breakfast with Nathan, then spent the morning correcting school papers.[53] After lunch, he went off to take a shower in the private bathroom attached to the school's future offices.[54] A short time later, Richard was found on the floor near the shower: he'd been attacked, and was naked and covered in blood.

Hearing of the attack, Nathan rushed to the infirmary. Richard lay on an examination table, an ether mask on his mouth and nose as four doctors hovered over him. There were four deep wounds to his throat: one had opened the jugular vein and, as Nathan recalled, "had almost severed his head from his body." Ugly gashes covered his torso, arms and legs: "Nowhere on his entire body could you go six inches without encountering a cut. He was breathing through a rubber tube inserted into his windpipe though the gaping hole in his throat."[55] In all, fifty-seven wounds had been inflicted by a straight razor.[56]

As blood flowed from the wounds, Richard took on a ghostly pallor, and doctors asked Nathan to cover his bare feet with a sheet and grab hot water bottles to raise his body temperature. Nathan offered to donate blood, but the hospital already had enough: the problem was keeping it in Richard's body. When doctors gave him transfusions, geysers of blood gushed from his neck.[57]

Prison authorities called Richard's family in Chicago; his brother Ernest arrived at Stateville about 2:45 that afternoon, bringing family physician Lester E. Frankenthal, who ironically had delivered both Richard and Nathan.[58] There was nothing to be done. "He's going any time," Frankenthal said. "Go get the priest."[59]

Nathan stepped out of the room and spoke to Father Weir. Richard hadn't been Catholic, though his mother was. Weir offered to administer last rites if Nathan thought that was what Richard or his family would want. But Nathan stopped him, saying he doubted Richard would want them.[60] Weir settled on praying for him.[61] Richard, Weir recalled, "was unconscious when I entered the operating room. He was incapable of speech."[62]

Frankenthal held Richard's hand. Within a few minutes it was cold: Richard died at 3:05 that afternoon at the age of thirty.[63] "I felt like half of me was dead," Nathan later said.[64]

"Strange as it may sound," Nathan reflected of Richard, "he had been my best pal. In one sense he was also the greatest enemy I ever had. . . . It was he who had originated the idea of committing the crime, he who had planned it, he who had largely carried it out. It was he who had insisted on doing what we eventually did." Knowing that he now had the last word, Nathan also claimed that Richard never regretted their crime: "I don't believe he ever, to the day of his death, felt truly remorseful for what we had done. . . . There persisted in his makeup to the very day of his tragic death an element of the demonic."[65]

Richard's body was taken to Donnellan's Funeral Home in Chicago, where police stood guard lest a public still outraged over Bobby's murder attempt its own vengeance on the corpse. The following day the Loeb family held a private funeral in their mansion on Ellis Avenue. Morbid groups crowded the sidewalks outside the house, waiting in vain for a glimpse of Anna Loeb or her surviving sons. Richard was taken to Oak Wood Cemetery, where Rabbi Gersen Levi of Temple Isaiah Israel conducted a brief service, after which Richard was cremated.[66] The family disposed of his ashes privately—no one knows where, although it has been speculated that they were interred on the estate at Charlevoix.

THERE WAS NO MYSTERY ABOUT who killed Richard. Twenty-three-year-old James Day had a long record of delinquencies and robberies by the time he arrived at Stateville in August 1934.[67] Until mid-December he had been Richard's cellmate. But when Richard's allowance was cut and he could no longer share food and cigarettes, Day fought with him and was finally moved to another cell.[68]

Day offered up a sensational motive, claiming that Richard had relentlessly pursued him for sex. He said that Richard had cornered him in the shower while holding a straight razor: "He grabbed at me with his free hand and slashed at me with the razor as he fell. He missed me by two inches. I hit him on the neck with my fist. . . . Loeb's hand, the one with the razor in it, hit the sill of the shower as he fell and the razor dropped. He grabbed for it as I jumped over his body and caught him by the wrist and throat and we fell together. The razor dropped again. I grabbed it this time. Loeb swung at me and hit me in the face, I slashed back at him and blood flew all over my face. I slashed at him again and he fell back against the sill of the shower.

Loeb got the razor away from me then and got on top of me, holding me by the throat. . . . I got him off me, I don't know how. The razor was in my hand when I got up. Loeb swung at me, half laughing and hollered, 'So you can fight when you have to.' I started slashing at him again and he backed into the shower. . . . I kept slashing at him. . . . After some minutes he sank into a sitting position. . . . Then Loeb got up slow. His eyes were big and starry. He put everything he had in a lunge at me. He held his hands up in front like claws. I started slashing some more and kept on until he fell. He was mumbling. . . . I heard like laughter or a groan and I turned around. Loeb was standing straight up. He lunged and knocked me down. He fell away and fell down at the door."[69]

This lurid, melodramatic account, depicting Richard as some kind of crazed, unstoppable killer out of some horror movie, was hardly convincing. Richard stood five-feet-nine-inches tall and weighed 160 pounds; Day was fifteen pounds lighter and three inches shorter. Yet Day had escaped what he described as a violent life-and-death struggle with only a few superficial scratches.[70] It was Richard who had defensive wounds on his hands and arms, suggesting that he had been the one attacked and the one who had tried to fend off the assault. Nor could Day explain how Richard's throat had been slashed from behind.

None of the prison authorities believed Day's account. Warden Ragen was convinced that Day had carried out the attack "without any provocation" and then fabricated the story about Richard having propositioned him.[71] State's attorney William McCabe, who investigated Richard's murder, concluded: "I disbelieve Day's story almost in its entirety. What he says of Loeb's morality is directly opposed to all that was known of Loeb. It is my belief that Loeb was deliberately lured to the spot where he was killed."[72] But two years passed before authorities learned that Richard had never had any razor: Day's cellmate George Bliss had stolen it from the prison barbershop and given it to him to use against Richard that morning.[73]

Day went on trial for Richard's murder in June 1936. He resorted to an early example of what would become the "gay panic defense," asserting that he'd protected himself from Richard's alleged sexual overtures. "I only did what any normal man might have done under the circumstances," Day insisted. Emmett Boyd, his lawyer, concurred, saying that Day "had the right, and should have killed Loeb." The verdict of not guilty, when it came on June 4 after less than an hour of jury deliberations, reflected both the homophobia of the time as well as a lingering desire to see Bobby Franks's death avenged. Indeed, the courtroom erupted in applause when it was announced.[74] "Nobody," commented one of the jurors many years later, "likes a queer, a homo, or a lesbian . . . so it was a good thing to get rid of such people."[75] Day later seized upon his new notoriety for financial profit, promoting himself as the man who had killed "one of America's most notorious murderers."[76]

Still, what happened, or more accurately, what was alleged to have happened, has become part of the legend. Richard's death became a morality lesson, providing justice for the death of Bobby Franks. In reporting the murder, newspapers and magazines reiterated supposed links between queerness and criminal behavior. Thus, *Time* magazine noted Richard's death by reminding readers that he had been one of "two perverted Chicago youths" who had "violated" Bobby Franks before he was killed.[77] The murder even became the subject of a persistent, lurid joke. *Chicago Daily News* journalist Ed Lahey supposedly wrote a story that began: "Richard Loeb, a brilliant college student and master of the English language, today ended a sentence with a proposition."[78] No one has ever found the alleged issue of the paper: the story seems to be apocryphal, but the lighthearted manner in which Richard's murder was dismissed underlines how attitudes against Leopold and Loeb had become deeply ingrained.

"THE REALIZATION THAT DICK WAS dead took some time to become vivid and real to me," Nathan later wrote. "It just didn't seem possible. I missed him terribly, all the more so since all the years in prison we had shared everything and planned everything together. I was very lonely."[79]

Perhaps this was true, but we have only Nathan's word for it. He refused to assist the investigation into Richard's murder.[80] "Punishing Day," Nathan claimed, "would not help Dick. It wouldn't bring him back."[81] This reticence had led to speculation that Nathan may have known more than he let on, including rumors that perhaps he arranged to have Richard killed.

On its face it seems an absurd charge. Yet Nathan, ever the smarter of the two, knew that parole was possible. Because Judge Caverly hadn't specified how the sentences were to be served, laws governing the Illinois State Board of Pardons and Paroles dictated that they run concurrently. With time off for good behavior, eventual parole was a possibility. Nathan was aware of this. He reportedly hoped that "after ten years or so public sentiment will have subsided to such an extent that it will be possible to make definite efforts to achieve freedom."[82] And he later admitted: "I felt that if I didn't die young I stood a reasonably good chance of getting out sometime, but it would be a very long time and I would make no surmises on just when it would be."[83] He knew what factors would play in to such a possibility. It may be significant, then, that after repeatedly violating prison rules, from 1931 on he at least attempted to keep his record clean.

Why would Nathan want Richard dead? In giving them identical sentences, Caverly unwittingly set Richard and Nathan up for a battle if parole ever loomed. The board would evaluate good behavior, remorse, and rehabilitation. Richard was the only one to demonstrate all three. The board would also want a complete and coherent account of the crime, which would pit Richard and Nathan against each other when it came to questions of who actually killed Bobby. To win his freedom, Nathan needed to become the sole narrator of his own story, to present himself as an unwilling victim, under Richard's malignant domination and unable to resist his magnetic personality, without objections from his former partner. For Nathan, as Hal Higdon noted,

Richard's death removed "the biggest obstacle standing between him and freedom."[84]

By autumn of 1935, the relationship between Richard and Nathan was eroding. Father Weir noticed that while Nathan admired Richard, Richard "did not have the same admiration for Leopold." Loeb began pulling away from Leopold in the months before his death. "They were not so chummy toward the last," Weir said, adding that "their contacts were less. They were not so closely associated in school, were not out for recreation at the same time."[85] State's attorney William McCabe, who investigated Richard's murder, said some "unnamed persons may have been interested in having Loeb killed." He thought that Nathan's failure to cooperate with authorities was "significant," and declared that investigation revealed that Leopold "resented his former companion's popularity." He also said that he had "secret information" from Father Weir concerning the circumstances of the murder without specifying precisely what this meant.[86]

Whatever happened between Richard and Nathan in the autumn of 1935 could potentially have served as a catalyst for action. The relationship had always been uneasy, and each man may have feared the other. There was always the possibility that one might try to reduce his sentence by cutting a deal and revealing information about their previous, uncharged crimes. What guarantee did Nathan have that his weaker-willed friend might not again break and attempt to win his own freedom, especially since the state's attorney believed that Leopold had actually killed Bobby? Richard had already done it by confessing in 1924. Several times after his arrest Nathan had suggested that he could use his family's money to avoid prison. It hadn't worked then, but money talked at Stateville: it isn't impossible that Nathan might have arranged the attack on Richard with the promise of a financial reward.

It seems unlikely for the supposedly lovesick Leopold, but back in 1923, at the height of the relationship and presumably at the height of his infatuation with Richard, Nathan had actually threatened to kill him on several occasions. If he had been willing to do so then, why would he be unwilling to consider the same action a decade later? And yet no real evidence supports such an idea.

Death deprived Richard of the redemption story Nathan would soon claim for himself. History—and increasingly Nathan—would portray Loeb as a malicious mastermind who had corrupted an adoring Leopold and led him to murder. In the coming years Nathan seized the opportunity to remake himself and revise his history, free from fear that Richard would contradict him, in an effort to enhance his own shattered image at the expense of his "best pal."

CHAPTER TWENTY-ONE

NATHAN KEPT WORKING AT THE STATEVILLE CORRESPONDENCE School in the wake of Richard's murder, at least for a time. Enrollment rose to nearly 450 students, and college courses were added. But the project had really been Richard's, and Nathan's enthusiasm soon waned—he admitted that he was "tired of it."[1] When Warden Ragen canceled the special privileges instructors had previously enjoyed, Nathan asked to be transferred to another job, although for a few years he continued reading and correcting student papers.[2]

Nathan went to work as an X-ray technician in the prison infirmary.[3] He apparently used the position to look through mugshots as if they were Grindr profiles, selecting the best-looking prisoners, calling them in for X-rays, and soliciting them for sex—it was still all about Nathan.[4] Unpopular, he had at least one fight with another inmate before taking a janitorial job in 1942, only to return to the infirmary within sixteen months.[5] "Nobody wanted me around, neither cons nor screws," Nathan later recalled.[6] He later railed against his years in Stateville, "where the People of Illinois, in their wisdom, had sent me (for the good of my soul?)," complaining about the "ignorant, bigoted, sadistic motherfuckers in the employ of the state."[7]

Most inmates avoided Nathan: he was a notorious child killer, suspected of having molested Bobby before murdering him.[8] "Almost everybody hated him," fellow prisoner Paul Warren recalled, thinking that Nathan was "a smart son of a bitch, arrogant . . . no good." Warren didn't know what to make of Nathan's strange talk of "domination and submission" and "the cultivation of tabooed pleasures," presumably an effort to entice him into a sexual relationship.[9] Another inmate, Gene Lovitz, remembered how Nathan bragged about his intelligence; complained the guards were inferior; espoused racist beliefs; and continued to extol the virtues of Nietzsche. But when Nathan made sexual overtures, Lovitz quickly ended the association.[10]

In 1944, as malaria decimated American troops fighting World War II in the Pacific, Alf Alving and his fellow doctors from the University of Chicago asked for inmate volunteers to test experimental vaccines.[11] "I wanted to work on the project so bad I could taste it," Nathan insisted.[12] At first, he merely assisted, but finally Nathan was injected with the infected glands. He later recounted suffering through days of high temperatures, and he bore scars on his legs from having the infection excised—"they're not very pretty, but I'm rather proud of them," he wrote.[13]

The experiments were dangerous, but Alving wasn't impressed. He later complained that other volunteers had done more than Leopold; that Nathan had been reluctant to serve as a guinea pig; and that he exaggerated his illness after being bitten.[14] He also accused Nathan of using the program to seduce other prisoners.[15]

Participants were told that their sentences might be reduced. This, Nathan admitted, "was a chance I could not afford to miss. . . . I felt that I had some reason to hope that public opinion in my regard might be softened to some degree."[16] He began cultivating an image as a selfless, reformed inmate with an eye toward eventual parole. Later, he admitted his habit of taking "all the credit for anything good that happens, and to disclaim responsibility for anything that blows up." It was quite easy, he wrote, to "put up a pretty convincing story" that everything he did was "for the very noblest motives," even if the opposite was true.[17]

Warden Joseph Ragen aided these efforts, promoting Nathan as an example of the rehabilitation possible with proper discipline.[18] He made Nathan available to the press; allowed him to participate in radio broadcasts; and let him pose for photographers from *Life* magazine.[19] Nathan embraced the opportunities: "Every bit of the enormous publicity I had received over a period of twenty years had been bad," he complained. "The one thing I was known for was being a kidnapper and murderer. That I was, all right, but I was more than that. I was a human being, too."[20]

Based partially on Leopold's malaria work, Illinois governor Adlai Stevenson granted Nathan a sentence reduction in 1949, making him eligible for parole in 1953. With this tantalizing hope dangling in front of him, Nathan accelerated efforts to recast history and change public perception. There was no escaping his past: Nathan had kidnapped and killed Bobby Franks; he had expressed no remorse about his crime; he had proudly used his peculiar philosophy to justify his actions; and he and Richard had been involved in a sexual relationship that contributed to widespread beliefs that he was "abnormal."

Nathan had to overcome these hurdles if he hoped to win release, and he intensified an intricate—and wildly inaccurate—revision of his life. In this quest he would blame the man who could no longer answer back or refute his claims, Richard. It was Richard's malignant influence, Nathan later insisted, that had led to a crime he had no desire to commit. He had been unable to resist his magnetic charm because he was too emotionally immature to do so. The sexual relationship had been nothing but a manifestation of this immaturity, and in no way reflected Nathan's true proclivities. "In equating heterosexuality with normality, and normality with rehabilitation," notes John Fiorini, "Leopold reinforced mid-century perceptions about the correlation between homosexuality and predatory behavior even as he argued that those prejudices should no longer apply to him."[21]

On January 8, 1953, Nathan had his first parole hearing. Former state's attorney Robert Crowe was too ill to attend, but a letter to the parole board made his opposition clear: "I thought at the time they ought to hang. There were no extenuating circumstances; it was a brutal murder."[22] John Gutknecht, who held the office of state's attorney for Cook County, agreed. "Society," he said, owed "nothing" to Nathan Leopold.[23]

"I couldn't give a motive which makes sense to me," Nathan said when asked why he and Richard had killed Bobby Franks. "It was the act of a child, a simpleton kid. A very bizarre act. I don't know why I did it. I'm a different man now. I was a smart-aleck kid. I am not any more. . . . I can only tell you that what happened in 1924 can't happen again. . . . It seems absurd to me today, as it must to you and all other people. I am in no better position to give you a motive than I was then."[24]

This was a mistake. Treating the crime so cavalierly didn't sit well with the parole board. Nathan offered no insight into his crime, and no expressions of remorse not directed at his own situation. Nathan knew it, too: he wrote two increasingly frantic letters to the board, attempting to sway opinion. He continued to describe Bobby's murder as "a completely motiveless, senseless, stupid act. . . . The damn fool act of an irresponsible and immature kid." But he now added a healthy dose of remorse: "I have been, through all these years and I am today, bitterly regretful for what I did. . . . The thought that I had cut off an innocent young life, and the knowledge of the grief I had caused both his family and mine has been present in my consciousness every day for the past quarter century. . . . I cannot undo what I did. What little I have had the opportunity of doing by way of atonement and expiation I have, within my limits, attempted to do." Then, with a deft turn, Nathan adroitly shifted blame for his previous failure to express adequate remorse from himself to the parole board. He had hesitated, he said, to "speak of my repentance" because he did not want members of the parole board to misinterpret "this expression as a maudlin bid for sympathy, or worse, a calculated and motivated piece of special pleading." He only "hesitated long to mention how sorry I am for what I did for fear that you might think it is merely talk."[25]

The decision, when it came, went against Nathan. Victor Knowles, chairman of the parole board, said that Nathan had come across as a "con man," who exaggerated his accomplishments, failed to express any real remorse, and didn't make any case why he should be freed.[26] "Not one place," Knowles declared, "in any testimony that this man ever gave the board, has he ever uttered one word of remorse for his crime. He has merely passed it off as a 'damned fool stunt,' by two irresponsible kids."[27] The board gave Nathan an unprecedented twelve-year continuance, meaning that he would not be granted automatic parole consideration. Nathan portrayed himself as a martyr: "I had hoped the board would see fit to parole me, but since it hasn't I can accept its decision as gracefully as possible."[28]

Nathan could still appeal for clemency before the parole board. Anticipating this, he spent more time reshaping his image, rearranging and omitting details as fiction came to replace fact. He gave selective interviews to friendly journalists, and only if they focused on his prison work and his rehabilitation. These articles depicted a repentant, reformed, and mature man who only wanted to contribute to society. Even so, he was unable to stop himself from boasting about his intelligence: "I have studied," he told one reporter. "I have learned a lot. . . . I read some twenty-six or twenty-seven languages—Polish, Sanskrit, Hebrew, Russian, Egyptian—as well as the more common ones. I've studied mathematics, too. I went about as far in math as it was possible to go in prison."[29]

In 1955, Nathan cooperated with writer John Bartlow Martin on a four-part profile for *The Saturday Evening Post* after being assured that he would have editorial input before publication.[30] Emphasizing the desired message, the series carried the title, "Murder on his Conscience." Nathan reduced his role in Bobby's murder to "something I'd been present at," as if he had merely been an innocent bystander.[31] He also downplayed his relationship with Richard. Thus, Martin called it a "childish" association that "did not involve acts usually thought of as adult homosexuality. Leopold was in no sense a 'true homosexual.'" And, Nathan insisted, it had been his only gay relationship.[32]

Nathan hoped that the series would help his efforts to win release, but the board rejected requests for parole in 1955 and 1956. Refusing to give up, Nathan redoubled his efforts. In 1957 Chicago lawyer Elmer Gertz took over the case. He solicited letters of support and prominent Chicago columnists used their newspapers to advocate for release. That summer, he won Nathan a new clemency hearing.[33]

On July 9, 1957, Nathan and Gertz appeared before the parole board. Gertz offered up supportive letters and several witnesses who testified on Nathan's behalf, including his old university friend Abel Brown. In his effort to win Nathan clemency, Brown gave a statement startling in its revisionist and inaccurate take. He described Richard as someone with "a sadistic streak," a "pathological liar" possessing "every bad quality," and a constant reader of detective stories—the sign, he insisted, of "a sick mind." But Nathan, Brown insisted, had merely been "a follower," who committed a single "dreadful error" only because he was "a lonely kid." Brown capped this wildly erroneous analysis with the truly stunning claim that Nathan had never been interested in Nietzsche: that, Brown said, had been "strictly a figment of a reporter's mind."[34] This didn't fool anyone, least of all the parole board, which pointed out that Brown's presentation did not agree with established facts. In the end, the board denied Nathan clemency.

Gertz decided to petition for parole, and despite their previous ruling, the board agreed to hear the case in February 1958. Gertz began by insisting that "Nathan Leopold is not now and has not been since his imprisonment a sexual deviant, or indeed a sexual problem in any respect. . . . Whatever his pre-prison infatuation for Loeb was, he completely outgrew it and there was not the slightest tinge of homosexuality from the moment he entered prison to this very moment."[35] After insisting that Loeb had been the actual killer, Gertz presented opinion polls favoring Nathan's release.[36] He ended by condemning those opposed to Nathan's parole, asserting that they were focused only on "punishment, even vengeance."[37]

Then it was Nathan's turn to speak. His answers to questioning at previous hearings had left board members unimpressed. His new statement, Gertz had warned, needed "to cover the case so completely as to obviate the number of potentially embarrassing questions that might be put to him. It would have to be contrite, unrehearsed, and spontaneous yet not glib. . . . The statement would have to explain how he could have been involved in so hideous a crime; how Loeb's role had been the greater and his the lesser. . . . It also had to persuade everyone of his remorse and rehabilitation." Gertz spent long hours editing the suggested text, and asked Leopold to memorize it so that it would seem spontaneous.[38]

"It isn't possible," Nathan began,

to compress into a few minutes the thoughts and feelings of thirty-three years and some months, especially if those years have been spent in prison. For here we have long hours to think, to think painfully, to regret bitterly, to repent fervently. A lot of those hours I have spent trying to understand how I could have possibly taken part in the horrible crime of which Richard Loeb and I were guilty. I can't explain that even to my self. . . . I admired Richard Loeb extravagantly, beyond all bounds. I literally lived and died on his approval or disapproval. I would have done anything he asked, even when I knew he was wrong, even when I was revolted by what he suggested. And he wanted very badly to commit this crime. Why, I can't be sure. Surely it was mad, irrational. It may have been some kind of juvenile protest, an overwhelming desire to show that he could do it and get away with it. . . . He spent years reading detective stories and acting the parts of both detective and criminal. . . . I had no wish to do this dreadful thing. Quite the opposite, it was repugnant to me. For weeks and weeks, until only a day or two before the crime, I was sure we would never go through with it. That it was something we would talk about and plan but never actually carry through. Loeb made certain that we would commit this mad act. I didn't, I couldn't stop him. And then it was too late. I couldn't back out of the plan without being a quitter, and without losing Loeb's friendship. Hard as it is now for me to understand it, these seemed more important to me at that time than a young boy's life. True, Loeb did the actual killing, but that does not exonerate me. . . . The only thing that bears on it that long thinking has produced is that my growth and development were unnatural. I was bright and yet undeveloped. I thought like a grown up person and felt like an undeveloped infant. . . . My emotional development was at least five years behind. . . . I was overwhelmingly attracted to Loeb, with the violence and lopsidedness that only extreme youth can know. . . . When my emotions did mature when I was about twenty-five, remorse for what I had done set in. . . . It has never left me since—not for a single day. It is with me constantly. . . . Sometimes it is in the front of my mind, so that I can think of nothing else. . . . It is not easy to live with murder on your conscience. The fact that you didn't do the actual killing yourself does not make it any easier.[39]

This statement, meant to demonstrate Nathan's acceptance of responsibility and show his remorse, was an exercise in evasion and distortion, with more words devoted to denouncing Richard than to his own supposed rehabilitation. There is little evidence that Nathan ever spent long, painfully introspective hours pondering his crime or assessing his alleged remorse. Far from being "revolted" by the scheme, it was Nathan who spent hours working out the complicated plan to obtain the ransom, and who pushed Richard when Loeb's enthusiasm waned. The bulk of the evidence suggested that it was Nathan, not Richard, who actually killed Bobby. If the crime had been so "repugnant" to Nathan, why had he been the one to continue pushing to collect the ransom after Bobby's body had been found? Why had Richard expressed remorse multiple times in 1924 while Nathan never once did so? When it came to winning his freedom, Nathan was quite willing to lie to suit his own ends.

To this, Nathan added a fair amount of self-pity. He offered expressions of remorse about Bobby's death, but his words positioned himself as victim. "My punishment," he said, "has not been light. I have spent over one third of a century in prison. During that time I have lost most of those who were near or dear to me. I never had an opportunity to say a prayer on their graves; I forfeited all home and family; forfeited all the chances of an honorable career."[40]

Nathan declared that he had begun practicing Judaism. When asked about his infatuation with Nietzsche, though, Nathan again resorted to lies. "I never had the philosophy of Nietzsche," he claimed. "Actually I don't know much about Nietzsche. I know in general I have read the history of philosophy in which the subject is outlined but I am not a follower. . . . I took a course or two in general philosophy and he must have been mentioned. I know of the theory but never read a book by him."[41]

This time, Nathan offered the board a concrete plan for his future if released. Some years earlier, he had met Dr. Harold Row, executive secretary of the Church of the Brethren, a small Christian group based in Elgin, Illinois. They operated a number of charities around the world and had established a hospital in the small town of Castañer in Puerto Rico. With his knowledge as an X-ray technician, the church promised Nathan a job in its new facility.

The board expressed concerns about Leopold's penchant for courting the media. Nathan insisted that, if he was released, he would "wince at the thought of trading on my notoriety." The very idea, he said, "would be the worst thing in the world." He ended: "All I want, if I am so lucky as to ever see freedom again, is to try to become a humble little person. . . . Gentlemen, you see before you today not the arrogant, conceited, smart-alecky boy of nineteen who came to prison. I am a broken old man, who humbly begs for your compassion."[42]

On February 20, the board granted Nathan parole. The decision came with restrictions. Nathan could not use alcohol; had to report regularly to his parole officer; have no contact with former prisoners; could not own a car or guns; and must obey a 10:30 p.m. curfew. There was nothing unusual in these, but the board added one unique condition. Nathan, the board insisted, "shall not voluntarily participate in any publicity activities or personal appearances on stage, radio, motion pictures, television, or any other publicity media."[43] An exception was made to accommodate his memoirs, which were set to be published that spring of 1958.

On Thursday, March 13, 1958, wearing a blue, prison-made suit and gray fedora, Nathan finally walked out of Stateville and faced a mob of waiting reporters.[44] Gone was the slight, fastidiously dressed young man with the caterpillar eyebrows of 1924: instead, the surviving half of Chicago's most infamous criminal duo was pudgy, balding, and looking distinctly uncomfortable. Nathan faced the media crowd and read from a prepared statement that once again put his own suffering at the forefront: "Many of you—I hope all of you—feel that a third of a century spent in prison has been severe punishment and are happy to see me free. I hope you want to see me succeed, to see me vindicate the trust reposed in me. Don't then, I beg you, add to that punishment. Don't make it impossible for me to succeed. I appeal as solemnly as I know how, to you and to your editors and to your publishers and to society at large to agree that the only piece of news about me is that I have ceased to be news. I beg, I beseech you to grant me a gift almost as precious as freedom itself, a gift without which freedom ceases to have much value, the gift of privacy. Give me a chance, a fair chance, to start life anew."[45]

It had been a long time since Nathan had ridden in a car; he climbed into the rear of a white 1958 Oldsmobile that one of his lawyers had rented and set off for Chicago. A contingent of cars crammed with reporters chased him, with photographers hanging out of the open windows trying to catch a glimpse of the newly freed man. The speed and the motion soon got to Nathan; at least six times the Oldsmobile pulled over so that he could vomit.[46]

Nathan spent his first night of freedom at his friend Abel Brown's apartment. He had wanted to go to Rosehill Cemetery where his parents (as well as Bobby Franks) were buried, but unrelenting media attention prevented the excursion. Instead, he contented himself with whiling away the hours with Brown and his family, eating sukiyaki.[47]

The following evening, March 14, Nathan boarded an airplane—his first flight since as a boy he had gone up briefly in a rickety and primitive craft during a visit to Florida—and set off for Puerto Rico.[48]

NATHAN DISAPPEARED TO THE TINY MOUNTAIN VILLAGE OF CASTAÑER, working as an X-ray technician at the small hospital run by the Church of the Brethren.[1] Inevitably he soon tired of village life, and moved to San Juan, enrolling at the University of Puerto Rico, working toward a master's degree in social work, and also teaching several classes. He took a job for the Department of Social Welfare, doing medical research on parasite transmission among humans. This brought a decent income, $5,200 a year, and allowed Nathan to live in a comfortable apartment near the city center.[2]

Nathan resented the restrictive parole conditions that were to last five years, though he constantly broke them, ignoring his curfew; communicating with former prisoners; and secretly buying guns. He justified his defiance by comparing himself to George Washington and Gandhi. In 1924 Nathan had killed Bobby because he believed that the rules governing ordinary men did not apply to him; nearly forty years later, his attitude hadn't changed. For all of his posturing about remorse, he remained convinced of his own superiority and put his own happiness above obeying the law.[3]

In 1956 Simon & Schuster had published Meyer Levin's novel *Compulsion,* which fictionalized the Leopold and Loeb case. The character of Artie Strauss stood in for Richard, while Judd Steiner paralleled Nathan. Most of the details were straightforward, though Levin offered up some heavy-handed Freudian analysis, suggesting underlying sexual motivations in every act: the chisel was a phallic symbol, the culvert a makeshift womb, and the acid poured over the body Steiner's attempt to erase, by proxy, his own Jewish identity and destroy "the girl-part of himself" that he so despised.[4]

Compulsion's success only contributed to Nathan's animus. He reluctantly admitted that the book was "amazingly accurate" and "masterfully put together," but he strenuously objected to the "fictional material," asserting that Levin had incorporated it "so cleverly, that it is impossible for the general reader to know where fact stops and fiction begins."[5] But his objections went far beyond this mingling of fact and fiction. He likely didn't want his criminal past churned up again at a time when he was trying to win parole, and he also resented the fact that someone other than himself was profiting from his history. *Compulsion* had seized his own story from him: Nathan had lost control of the narrative, at a time when he needed to present himself in the best possible light. He was also furious that his character was clearly depicted as gay: he'd spent years trying to diminish and disassociate himself from his sexual past.[6]

Nathan hoped that his own autobiography would supplant *Compulsion* as the authoritative account of his life. He spent three years on the manuscript while still in prison: not until 1957 did he find a publisher, Doubleday, willing to take the risk. *Life Plus 99 Years,* as Nathan titled the manuscript, was most notable for one thing: Nathan's absolute refusal to discuss his crime. "I don't want to think about those sordid things," he insisted.[7]

Life Plus 99 Years is a decidedly biased and inaccurate chronicle. Nathan shuffled and reshuffled details of his life to suit his own ends, omitting facts and adding claims that left the end result unreliable. He gave faint praise to Richard before depicting him as the evil mastermind behind the crime: "I thought so much of the guy that I was willing to do anything—even commit murder—if he wanted it bad enough. And he wanted to do this—very badly indeed. . . . For the commission of the crime itself I had no enthusiasm. Instead I had a feeling of deep repugnance."[8] Richard, he wrote, "had originated the idea of committing the crime . . . had planned it . . . had largely carried it out. It was he who had insisted on doing what we eventually did."[9]

"Remorse," Nathan claimed, "has been my constant companion. It is never out of my mind. Sometimes it overwhelms me completely, to the extent that I cannot think of anything else."[10] Yet his only frame of reference was to his own "grief." As John Fiorini writes, he was "portraying himself almost as a martyr for enduring his prison sentence. Leopold's refusal to discuss the act for which he claimed to feel such remorse, the formulaic nature of most of his claims about it, and his readiness to minimize his role in comparison to Loeb's all exposed him to criticisms that he used superficial humility to mask presumption, and that his claims of remorse were canned and hollow."[11]

Critical reception to *Life Plus 99 Years* was mixed. Given *Compulsion*'s success, Nathan imagined that his own book would do equal business. But while it sold well on release, interest soon waned, and sales dropped off significantly. Doubleday slashed the price and retailed copies at deep discounts, depriving Nathan of the financial windfall he had anticipated.[12]

Nathan's resentment was heightened by the release of 20th Century–Fox's film version of *Compulsion* in April 1959, starring Dean Stockwell as Judd Steiner and Bradford Dillman as Artie Strauss. He saw the film at a cinema in San Juan, sitting among an unsuspecting audience watching the essentials of his story play out on-screen.[13] An idea began forming. In his *New York Times* review of the novel, Erle Stanley Gardner had written that it "follows the established facts of the Loeb-Leopold case so closely that any libelous statement would still be actionable."[14]

This was exactly what Nathan decided to do. If he couldn't get rich from his own memoirs, he would get rich from the proceeds of Levin's book. Lawyer Elmer Gertz came up with a novel legal complaint: the book and everything that had followed from it had illegally appropriated Leopold's name for commercial purposes and violated his right to privacy. It was a way for Nathan to claim ownership of his story and restrict its telling only to versions that had his approval. Gertz explained: "If we won, Leopold would no longer have to fear the shocking excesses of fiction writers and sensationalists; they could no longer drag up again his long expiated crime whenever they decided they might make money on it or simply get some creative satisfaction from the effort."[15]

Gertz filed suit on October 2, 1959, against Levin; his publishers; 20th Century–Fox; the film's distributors; and even theaters where it had been shown. In all, it cited fifty-six defendants for the "appropriation of the name, likeness and personality of Leopold and conversion of same for their profit and gain." The complaint sought $4.3 million: $2.9 million from 20th Century–Fox, another $1.4 from various distributors and outlets, and $150,000 from Levin himself.[16]

Levin was outraged. "Leopold was now a victim, a man who had suffered thirty years of imprisonment as if in a death camp," he complained. Describing "Leopold's claim of ownership . . . of the crime itself," Levin openly questioned whether he had actually changed: "Wasn't he by this action making the very same boast that he and Dickie Loeb had made as a rationale for their murder: We are above the common laws as we are above the common run of mankind?"[17]

It took more than a decade for the lawsuit to wend its way through court. The final verdict, when it came from the Illinois State Supreme Court in May 1970, completely vindicated Levin and the other defendants. The decision rejected Nathan's claim that his right to privacy had been violated: "The plaintiff became and remained a public figure because of his criminal conduct in 1924. No right of privacy attached to matters associated with his participation in that completely publicized crime." Nathan's own actions had caused his life "to be placed in public view. . . . He cannot at his whim withdraw the events of his life from public scrutiny."[18] With this, Nathan's hopes to turn his crime into a personal financial bonanza abruptly fizzled out.

IN 1961, NATHAN MARRIED GERTRUDE Feldman Garcia de Quevedo, the American widow of a San Juan doctor. "Trudi," as she was called, said that the first time she met Nathan "he looked like he needed a friend more than anybody I had ever known."[19] Nathan admitted to Elmer Gertz that he didn't love her, but he apparently thought he could use the marriage to win release from parole.[20]

That didn't happen—Nathan had to wait until 1963 for his parole conditions to expire. Trudi called her new husband "a great humanitarian," telling the press, "I love him very much."[21] They settled into a comfortable apartment in the Santurce section of San Juan: it was, said a visitor, "bright and pleasant, although not of the standards of Chicago's Gold Coast." The first thing callers noticed was a prominently displayed, framed photograph of Richard Loeb. Trudi tried to laugh it off—"Nate wants it," she explained, adding, "and let's face it, Nate after all is complex."[22]

The photograph hinted at Nathan's enigmatic character. "Don't you subscribe to the theory about sampling every experience at least once?" he once asked a visiting reporter.[23] Far from being shy about his past, Nathan used it to promote himself—he liked being recognized, and felt no shame in mentioning that he was a notorious murderer if it got him a better table at a restaurant.[24] He remained arrogant, espoused racist beliefs, and supported selective abortion for those who might be mentally or physically infirm.[25] Psychiatrist Bernard Glueck, who had testified in his defense during the sentencing hearing in 1924, visited Nathan in Puerto Rico and chatted with him for several hours. He left convinced that Leopold was a paranoid schizophrenic.[26]

Nathan never abandoned his pursuit of men. He is said to have been discreet about these liaisons, but he didn't fool Trudi, who privately complained about the continuous trysts.[27] But she could do nothing. Her marriage to Nathan flailed along behind closed doors. They often fought, and Trudi, as she later admitted, found him extremely difficult to get along with. Nathan, she complained, "isn't one bit different than he was in 1924."[28]

An overwhelming obsession with money drove Nathan relentlessly in these years—he resented having to rely on his brother for payments from the family trust. In 1963 he published a book called *A Checklist of the Birds of Puerto Rico and the Virgin Islands,* a chronicle in keeping with his ornithological interests, and he authored several scholarly articles on prison reform, but these specialized endeavors had no widespread appeal. Ironically, the man then suing over his fictionalized depiction in *Compulsion* even suggested writing a novel about Richard Speck, who had killed eight nurses in Chicago in 1966.[29]

Nathan hoped that his autobiography would be made into a film, but not a single studio expressed interest. In 1963 he began collaborating with former actor Don Murray on a film to be called *Beyond the Night.* Conceived as a vehicle to burnish Nathan's image by focusing on his prison work and time in Puerto Rico, this, too, found no takers. Unwilling to abandon financial possibilities, Nathan started a new memoir, rather inappropriately called *Reach for a Halo.*[30] This never got beyond the first few chapters: much to Nathan's surprise, no publisher wanted his story.[31]

When the *Compulsion* lawsuit finally went against him in 1970, Nathan seemed to lose a sense of purpose. More and more, he fought openly with Trudi, and there was talk of divorce.[32] His health declined sharply: overweight, he suffered from diabetes, drank too much, and smoked incessantly. By the spring of 1971 Nathan was seriously ill. He spent much of April and May in the hospital after a series of heart attacks.

In the summer of 1971, he traveled back to Chicago. Perhaps Nathan sensed that this would be his last visit, for he did something he had always avoided. One day, he asked a friend to drive him out to Wolf Lake. Why, of all places, did Nathan want to see it again? It had figured in his bird-watching activities, but it was also the site of his crime, his greatest defeat. He found that the area had changed considerably since 1924: the prairie was still there, but roads now crossed the former woods, and development had long since erased any sign of the culvert where Nathan and Richard had hidden Bobby's body. Nathan walked around, trying to get his bearings but the march of time had erased any reminders from 1924. "I would never have recognized it," was his only comment.[33]

Just a few days later, Nathan again fell ill. He spent the next week in a Chicago hospital but finally returned to Puerto Rico. Summer came and his energies ebbed. On the morning of August 19, Nathan had trouble breathing. Trudi rushed him to Mimiya Hospital in San Juan, where he lingered for the next ten days. Doctors could do nothing: Nathan's heart was simply worn out. On August 29, Nathan Leopold Jr. died at the age of sixty-six: Trudi was at his side.[34]

Some years earlier, Nathan's brother Sam had told him that the family didn't want him to buried in their plot at Rosehill Cemetery. His presence there, even in death, would only serve to remind visitors of his infamous crime.[35] And so Nathan willed his body to the University of Puerto Rico for medical research. His eyes, as newspapers noted, were donated: one went to an elderly woman, the other to a man. "Leopold," Elmer Gertz said of his passing, "would have been pleased that, in his death, he was still news."[36]

OF THE THREE PRINCIPALS MOST concerned with the fates of Leopold and Loeb, Judge John Caverly seemed most affected by the strain of presiding over the case. Just three weeks after delivering the sentence, he suffered what was described as a nervous breakdown and was hospitalized.[37] He eventually returned to the bench but asked to be assigned lighter duties. He died in 1939.

State's attorney Robert Crowe never overcame his resentment of Caverly's sentence. He used the case to stage another successful run for office but, after frequent accusations of corruption, he returned to private practice in 1928.[38] In 1935, to mark the eleventh anniversary of Bobby's murder, the *Chicago Daily Tribune* ran a lengthy retrospective on the case. Crowe continued to describe it as "the most dastardly crime of the generation, worse than the Lindbergh kidnapping because it was committed by two intelligent fellows who had planned it for months." Although he had some choice words about Richard, calling him an "arch criminal," Crowe still believed that it was Nathan who had actually struck Bobby with the chisel.[39] He returned to the bench as a judge in 1942 but retired after a brief tenure. Crowe died in 1958 at the age of seventy-eight, having opposed Nathan's parole to the end.

Only Clarence Darrow went on to greater fame. In 1925, he defended Tennessee teacher John Scopes when the latter was charged with teaching evolution in what became one of the most famous court cases of the twentieth century. Darrow put on an impassioned defense but lost; the verdict was eventually overturned on a technicality. Darrow died in 1938. Ironically, his ashes were scattered into the lagoon at Chicago's Jackson Park, near the spot where Richard had tossed the stolen typewriter used to write the ransom note.

After her husband's death in October 1924, Richard's mother Anna lived quietly, dividing her time between the mansion on Ellis Avenue and the estate at Charlevoix. In 1929, following a trip to Europe, she had her own brush with the law, when customs officials accused her of attempting to smuggle in expensive Parisian lingerie to avoid paying duty and fined her nearly $10,000.[40] Anna continued to visit Richard in prison until his death in 1936. She died in 1950 at the age of seventy-four.

Allan Loeb, Richard's oldest brother, ran several family businesses, while his younger brother Ernest managed the farm at Charlevoix. In 1927, increasing losses forced the sale of most of the Michigan property, though the Loebs kept their immense mansion above Pine Lake; descendants still visit today. Ernest died in 1961, and Allan the following year. Tommy, Richard's youngest brother, struggled to forget the events of 1924. He died in 1991.

To escape the notoriety of Nathan's crime, his brothers Mike and Sam both changed their surname from Leopold to Lebold. "Sometimes," Mike admitted, "when I think of the irreparable harm that Babe has done to himself and all of us I could kick the guts out of him."[41] Although he married in 1936, Mike decided not to have children, lest they be tarred by their infamous uncle's actions. Mike died in 1953, but Sam, the middle Leopold son, lived on in Chicago, married twice, and had several children before his death in 1973.

After Nathan's death, his widow Trudi started writing her own book, tentatively titled, *I Married a Murderer*. She apparently planned to reveal Nathan's continued gay liaisons and assert that he hadn't reformed at all.[42] It would, she promised reveal "a lot of tough truths."[43] Trudi never finished the book: she died in 1987 in Puerto Rico.

The Franks family was forever altered by the events of May 21, 1924. Jacob Franks died in 1928. The cause was described as a heart attack, but the *Chicago Daily News* assured readers that his ill health had been caused by "grief over the murder of his son."[44]

In 1930, Bobby's mother, Flora, together with his brother Jack, helped lay the cornerstone of a new clubhouse for boys dedicated to Bobby's memory. Jacob Franks had left money in his will earmarked for construction of "a fitting memorial to perpetuate the memory of my boy." It should, he said, "be one that would give pleasure, help and encouragement to his playmates."[45] Jack took to the podium and told the gathered crowd that his brother's death had "left an aching void in our hearts. It may help to appease that pain to realize that hundreds of boys will be happy here in this structure built to his memory."[46]

Five years later, Jack gave a rare interview to the *Chicago Daily Tribune,* in which he spoke about his brother's killers. "I have no feeling of animosity," he declared. "It has been hard for the families. How my family feels about it I don't know. We never discuss it. So far as I am concerned, I just want them to stay out of my life. They're in another world from me, and I'm not interested in theirs, that's all."[47]

In 1933 the widowed Flora married Chicago attorney Albert Louer. She lived in her suite at the Drake Hotel until her death, from breast cancer, in 1937. Her only surviving son, Jack, married, divorced, and died of heart trouble just a year after his mother.[48] Only daughter Josephine lived a long life. She married Richard Glaser, her first husband, in 1927 and gave birth to three daughters. Widowed in 1954, she waited until 1976 to marry again, this time to Carl Lederer. Josephine outlived her second husband by nearly three decades, dying in October 2007 just a month before she would have celebrated her 101st birthday.

A HUNDRED YEARS ON, THERE are few tangible reminders of "the crime of the century." Nathan's infamous glasses are today stored in a temperature-controlled vault of the Chicago History Museum, to preserve their brittle frames. The area around Wolf Lake remains a marshland preserve, but the culvert where Leopold and Loeb placed Bobby's body disappeared decades ago.

Much of the once-exclusive enclave of Kenwood fell on hard times in the 1950s, when the nearby University of Chicago successfully split the neighborhood in half. North Kenwood, as one half became, disintegrated into a series of ruined buildings and low-cost housing, but South Kenwood remains an upscale place of comfortable houses and considerable affluence. Until he was elected president, Barack Obama lived with his wife and daughters in a house just a block west of those once occupied by the Loebs and the Franks.

The former Leopold house on South Greenwood Avenue is long gone, although the large garage where Nathan kept his red Willys-Knight still stands, having been transformed into a private residence. The Loeb mansion, too, has vanished. Sold in the 1930s, it became, ironically, a branch of the Illinois Protestant Children's Home, with orphaned or abandoned boys sleeping in Richard's former bedroom. In 1971 the derelict house was finally razed: all that remains is the high brick wall that once surrounded the property.

The former Franks house still stands across Ellis Avenue from the site of the Loeb mansion. It went through several owners in the decades following Bobby's murder before finally being purchased in 1936 for use as the Ffoulkes School for Boys and Girls. By 1991 it was empty and began a slide into decay, with boarded up windows and the formerly immaculate terraced garden choked with weeds. In 2007, new owners bought the house and have turned it into two luxurious condominiums. Transformation into condominiums, too, has been the fate of the Harvard School for Boys. The building remains a Kenwood landmark, the school having closed in 2003 after more than a century of operation.

Some ten miles across Chicago, far from the school he left on the afternoon of May 21, 1924, Bobby's body rests in the Franks family mausoleum at Rosehill Cemetery, along with those of his father, mother, brother, and sister. The Loeb family plot is nearby, with the white stone obelisk marking the Leopold family graves just beyond. In 1924, fate brought the three families together in tragedy; now, they share the same ground for eternity.

ACKNOWLEDGMENTS

The Leopold and Loeb case has horrified and haunted us both for many years. It was one of the first true crime cases that captured our interests, long before we had ever met. Part of that fascination undoubtedly stemmed from its enigmatic quality. It remains a true historical mystery on many levels: why they committed the crime; who actually killed Bobby Franks; and how the tumultuous relationship between Leopold and Loeb eventually led to murder. Probing deeper into the personal and sexual dynamic that existed between these two immature teenagers seemed to offer a promising avenue forward. Here, we have tried our best to get at these issues by taking the case back to original sources and reconstructing events, in much the same way we did in *The Fate of the Romanovs,* our 2003 book on the murder of the Russian imperial family.

Even so, we hadn't planned for this to be our next book. A conversation with Charles Spicer, our editor at St. Martin's Press, changed our minds. A reanalysis of the Leopold and Loeb case, coming just before the hundredth anniversary of the case, he argued, was a fantastic idea. His enthusiasm erased any doubts we might have had, and allowed us to move forward with a book that intrigued us both and challenged us to rethink accepted history. Dorie Simmonds, our agent, agreed and pushed hard to make this book happen. They both have our grateful thanks for the support and belief in our ability to breathe life into this notorious case. And once again, Sarah Grill, associate editor at St. Martin's, has patiently guided us through the technological complexities of manuscript delivery and illustrative demands.

We were fortunate, indeed, to have conducted most major research for this book before the onset of the COVID-19 pandemic. Having been able to access important materials, including the transcripts of the sentencing hearing and the various psychological reports on Leopold and Loeb, before institutions were forced to shut down, gave us breathing room and allowed us more time to examine and analyze both the dynamic between them as well as attempt to address outstanding questions that might otherwise have gone unexplored.

Many people helped in the research and writing of this book, offering advice, information, and guidance. We received assistance, as well as support, throughout the process from numerous archives, institutions, and a multitude of individuals. We therefore would like to thank Dominic Albanese; Mark Andersen; Janet Ashton; Arturo Beeche; Antonio Perez Caballero; Simon Donoghue; Annette Fletcher; Jake Gariepy; Coryne Hall; Emma Hampton and Sally Criddle; Christopher Kinsman; Chuck and Eileen Knaus; Angela and Mark Manning; Barton Maxwell; Eugene Mejia; Susanne Meslans; Ilana Miller; Michael Revis; Jennifer Rider; Charles Stewart; Katrina Warne; Sue Woolmans; and Kelly Wright. We would especially like to thank Rachel Dailey and Laura Lechowicz from the Office of the Coroner, Cook County, Illinois, for their extensive research on not only the murder of Bobby Franks but also on the previously unexplored mysterious death of Melvin Wolf. We would also like to thank the helpful and patient staff at the Chicago History Museum, for stepping in at the last minute, and under the difficult circumstances of the pandemic, to assist us with the selection of photographs; particular thanks go to Katie in rights reproduction. Historian Brandon Whited provided valuable insight and information during our research.

Penny's husband, Tom Wilson, has remained a steadfast supporter through all our historical endeavors, and assisted in this case with new computer installation and patience. As always, he has our grateful thanks.

The writing of this book unfortunately coincided with a sharp decline in the health of Greg's father, Roger King. After two years of distressing developments, he was diagnosed with a fatal form of leukemia, which resulted in his passing on January 24, 2022, at the age of eighty-nine. Throughout this period, Greg acted as his sole caregiver, and relied heavily not only on Penny and the kindness of our agent, Dorie Simmonds, and editor, Charles Spicer, but also on the invaluable support of several close family members, including his aunt and uncle Virginia and Willard Pearson, and cousins Diane Eakin, Jeannine Evans, and Jardene Platt, all of whom have been there for him in important ways. Their continued encouragement has given enormous relief, comfort, and reassurance when, at times, uncertainties threatened to overwhelm any attempts at telling the story of Leopold and Loeb.

Our biggest debt is to Erik Rebain. Erik operates the best and most authoritative website on the case, and has spent years researching the case for his forthcoming biography of Nathan Leopold. His knowledge of the minute details is extraordinary, and he has freely shared information and advice, even taking time out of his schedule to photograph the Franks mausoleum and mansion in their current states for inclusion here. His insight as we worked through the manuscript and the numerous questions that arose has been invaluable to us, even if he sometimes disagreed with our conclusions. He has our gratitude, and we are eager to read his own take on the case.

Should anyone wish to follow our future projects and talk about history, please join us on our Facebook group: King and Wilson History: The Romanovs and Beyond.

NOTES

INTRODUCTION

1. Fass, *Making and Remaking*, 920.

CHAPTER ONE

1. J. T. Seass testimony, July 24, 1924.
2. CDT June 1, 1924.
3. RL Report, 25.
4. J. T. Seass testimony, July 24, 1924.
5. Higdon, 32.
6. Johnny Levinson testimony, July 28, 1924.
7. Carl Ulving testimony, July 24, 1924. The trial testimony and newspaper reports give his surname as Ulvigh, but research by Leopold and Loeb historian Erik Rebain has found that he went by Ulving.
8. Higdon, 168.
9. CEA May 23, 1924.
10. CDT May 24, 1924; Higdon, 32, 46.
11. CEA May 23, 1924.
12. CDT June 23, 1996.
13. Ibid., December 25, 1910.
14. Ibid., May 29, 1924.
15. Ibid., May 23, 24, 25, 1924.
16. Higdon, 33.
17. Ibid., 32.
18. CHE June 11, 1924.

19. CDT May 23, 1924.
20. Higdon, 342.
21. CDJ June 4, 1924.
22. AP report, June 5, 1924.
23. NL Report, 30.
24. Flora Franks testimony, July 23, 1924.
25. Jacob Franks testimony at Robert Franks Inquest, May 23, 1924.
26. Jacob Franks testimony, July 23, 1924.
27. Asher.
28. Higdon, 35; CDT May 23, 1924.
29. Lucille Smith testimony, July 24, 1924.
30. CDT May 23, 1924.
31. Jacob Franks testimony at Robert Franks Inquest, May 23, 1924.
32. Higdon, 36.
33. CDT May 23, 1924.
34. Flora Franks testimony, July 23, 1924.
35. CDT May 23, 1924.
36. Ibid.
37. Bernard Hunt testimony, July 24, 1924.

CHAPTER TWO

1. Sellers, 12–13; CDT May 22, 1924.
2. CDT May 23, 1924.
3. Jacob Franks testimony, July 23, 1924; Higdon, 43–44; CDT May 23, 1924.
4. CDN May 31, 1924.
5. Tony Minke testimony, July 24, 1924. Authors have used variations of Minke's name, sometimes rendering it as Manke. In fact, testifying at Bobby's inquest on May 23, 1924, he spelled out, letter by letter, his last name as Minke. See Minke at Robert Franks Inquest, May 23, 1924.
6. Ibid.
7. John Kaleczka testimony, July 24, 1924.
8. Tony Minke testimony, July 24, 1924; CHE May 23, 1924; Paul Korff testimony, July 24, 1924; CDT May 23, 1924.
9. John Kaleczka testimony at Robert Franks Inquest, May 23, 1924.
10. CDT May 23, 1924.
11. Tony Shapino testimony, July 24, 1924; CDT May 24, 1924.
12. CDN May 23, 1924.
13. Ibid.
14. Edwin Gresham testimony, July 23, 1924.
15. CDT May 23, 1924.
16. Jacob Franks testimony, July 23, 1924.
17. CHE May 23, 1924.

18. Charles Robinson testimony, July 28, 1924.
19. James Kemp testimony, July 25, 1924.
20. Percy Van de Bogert testimony, July 25, 1924.
21. Alvin Goldstein testimony, July 25, 1924.
22. CEA May 23, 1924.
23. CDT May 23, 1924.

CHAPTER THREE

1. CHE May 23, 1924.
2. CDT May 23, 1924.
3. CDT May 23, 1924; Higdon 50.
4. CHE May 26, 1924.
5. CDN May 23, 1924.
6. Lewis, 461.
7. Higdon, 78.
8. Ibid., 46, 70.
9. CDT May 24, 25, 1924.
10. CDN May 28, 1924.
11. CDT May 24, 1924.
12. Franklin, 123.
13. CDT May 24, 1924.
14. Ibid.
15. Ibid.
16. Ibid., May 29, 1924.
17. Ibid., May 30, 1924.
18. Ibid., May 24, 1924.
19. Howard Mayer testimony, July 25, 1924.
20. Ibid.
21. Higdon, 53.
22. Howard Mayer testimony, July 25, 1924; James Mulroy testimony, July 25, 1924.
23. CDT May 24, 1924.
24. Autopsy Report, Robert Franks Inquest, May 23, 1924.
25. Ibid.
26. Joseph Springer testimony, July 23, 1924.
27. William McNally testimony, July 24, 1924.
28. Autopsy Report, Robert Franks Inquest, May 23, 1924.
29. CDT May 24, 1924.
30. CEA May 27, 1924.
31. CDT May 23, 1924; Higdon, 71.
32. Ibid., May 29, 1924.
33. Lowe, 116.

34. CDT June 2, 1924.
35. Ibid., June 7, 1924.
36. Ibid., June 2, 1924.
37. Ibid., May 26, 1924.
38. CHE June 11, 1924.
39. CDT May 26, 1924.
40. Higdon, 62.
41. CDT May 26, 1924.
42. Ibid., August 31, 1924.
43. Ibid., May 26, 1924.
44. RL Report, 113.
45. CDT May 26, 1924.
46. Ibid., June 1, 1924.

CHAPTER FOUR

1. CDT June 7, 1924.
2. Thomas Wolfe testimony, July 25, 1924.
3. Ibid.
4. Thomas Wolfe testimony, July 25, 1924; Leopold, 30; Higdon, 64.
5. NL Statement, May 25, 1924, entered into trial transcript July 25, 1924.
6. CDT May 30, 1924.
7. Leopold, 33; William Crot testimony, July 25, 1924; Frank Johnson testimony, July 25, 1924.
8. Frank Johnson testimony, July 25, 1924.
9. William Crot testimony, July 25, 1924.
10. NL interrogation, May 29, 1924.
11. NL Report, 111–12.
12. NL interrogation, May 29, 1924; CDT May 31, 1924; William Crot testimony, July 25, 1924; James Gortland testimony, July 25, 1924.
13. Leopold, 40.
14. See William Crot testimony, July 25, 1924; James Gortland testimony, July 25, 1924.
15. William Crot testimony, July 25, 1924.
16. Frank Johnson testimony, July 25, 1924.
17. William Crot testimony, July 25, 1924.
18. William Crot testimony, July 25 1924; James Gortland testimony, July 25, 1924.
19. William Crot testimony, July 25, 1924.
20. Higdon, 79.
21. NL interrogation, May 29, 1924.
22. CDT May 31, 1924.
23. James Gortland testimony, July 25, 1924; William Shoemacher testimony, July

28, 1924; Frank Johnson testimony, July 25, 1924; William Crot testimony, July 25, 1924.

24. NL interrogation, May 30, 1924.
25. Leopold, 43.
26. Higdon, 87; CDT October 28, 1924.
27. RL interrogation, May 29, 1924.
28. Howard Mayer testimony, July 25, 1924.
29. CDT May 30, 1924.
30. Ibid.
31. Ibid., May 31, 1924.
32. CDJ May 30, 1924.
33. CDN May 30, May 31, 1924.
34. Arnold Maremont testimony, July 24, 1924.
35. CDN May 31, 1924.
36. William Shoemacher testimony, July 28, 1924.
37. CDT June 6, 1924.
38. Ibid., May 31, 1924.
39. NL to RL, letter of October 9, 1923, in Leopold and Loeb Collection, Northwestern University, Box 19, Volume 2. The *Chicago Daily Tribune* published the letter on May 31, 1924, omitting the word "cocksucker."
40. RL interrogation, May 30, 1924.
41. NL interrogation, May 30, 1924.
42. Ibid.
43. Sven Englund testimony, July 24, 1924.
44. RL interrogation, May 31, 1924.
45. Robert Crowe opening statement July 23, 1924.
46. William Healy testimony, August 6, 1924; Laurence Cuneo testimony, August 12, 1924.
47. Robert Crowe opening statement, July 23, 1924.
48. Leopold, 47.
49. Robert Crowe opening statement, July 23, 1924.

CHAPTER FIVE

1. CDN May 31, 1924.
2. CHE June 1, 1924.
3. CDT June 1, 1924.
4. Ibid.
5. CDJ May 31, 1924.
6. CDT June 1, 1924.
7. CHE June 1, 1924; CDT June 1, 1924.
8. CDT June 4, 1924.
9. Ibid., June 1, 1924.

10. NL Report, 44.
11. Leopold, 31.
12. NL Report, 4–5.
13. Martin, Part 1, 18.
14. Ibid.
15. NL Report, 43.
16. Ibid., 32.
17. Ibid., 5–7.
18. Ibid., 21.
19. Ibid., 86.
20. CDT June 4, 1924.
21. Martin, Part 1, 18.
22. McKernan, 55.
23. NL Report, 23–24.
24. Ibid.
25. NL interrogation, May 30, 1924; NL Report, 23.
26. NL Report, 23–24.
27. Martin, Part 1, 86.
28. NL Report, 14, 40, 46.
29. Dr. William Healy testimony, August 9, 1924.
30. Leopold, 241.
31. NL Report, 40–41.
32. CDT June 1, 1924.
33. Dr. William Healy testimony, August 4, 1924.
34. NL Report, 18.
35. Ibid., 20.
36. Ibid., 18–20.
37. Ibid., 21.
38. Ibid., 137.
39. Ibid., 51.
40. Ibid., 54–55, 65–66.
41. Ibid., 56, 137, 150.
42. Ibid., 67.
43. Ibid., 53–55.
44. Ibid., 56–57.
45. Ibid., 60.
46. Ibid., 25.
47. Martin, Part 1, 86.
48. NL Report, 65, 68.
49. NL Report, 56, 68; White, Healy, Glueck, and Hammill, 368.
50. Dr. William White testimony, August 1, 1924; NL Report, 63–65; Dr. William Healy testimony, August 4, 1924.
51. NL Report, 25–26; Dr. Harold Hulbert testimony, August 8, 1924.

52. NL Report, 51, 57, 137.
53. Ibid., 27.
54. McKernan, 127.
55. Weinberg and Weinberg, 314.

CHAPTER SIX

1. Benjamin and Cohen, 306.
2. CDT June 1, 1924; CDT October 28, 1924.
3. Ascoli, 170.
4. CDT June 1, 1924.
5. Hendrickson, 244.
6. Higdon, 118.
7. RL Report, 3, 6, 40.
8. White, Healy, Glueck, and Hammill, 372.
9. CDJ June 6, 1924.
10. RL Report, 6, 34, 40; Dr. William White testimony, August 1, 1924.
11. RL Report, 40, 132.
12. Previous accounts have called her "Emily" and said that she was twenty-eight; census records confirm her name and date of birth.
13. RL Report, 12, 40.
14. Ibid., 15.
15. Dr. William White testimony, August 1, 1924.
16. RL Report, 14.
17. Ibid., 13, 15.
18. Ibid., 20.
19. Dr. William Healy testimony, August 4, 1924; RL Report, 20.
20. RL Report, 14.
21. Ibid., 42.
22. Theodore, 5.
23. Cited, Ibid.
24. RL Report, 13.
25. Ibid., 73.
26. Ibid., 72–75.
27. Ibid., 74.
28. Ibid., 79.
29. Ibid., 81–82.
30. John Abt testimony, August 7, 1924.
31. Dr. William Healy testimony, August 4, 1924.
32. RL Report, 17, 81–82.
33. Dr. William White testimony, August 1, 1924.
34. RL Report, 68.

35. Higdon, 17.
36. RL Report, 22, 36, 41.
37. University of Chicago High School *Correlator* 1919, 56.
38. RL Report, 24.
39. Ibid., 20.
40. Ibid., 24.
41. AP report, March 3, 1931; *Pittsburgh Post-Gazette*, March 4, 1931.
42. RL Report, 15, 17.
43. Dr. William White testimony, August 1, 1924.
44. RL Report, 36–37.
45. Ibid., 16.
46. Ibid., 8.
47. Ibid., 45.
48. Ibid., 46.
49. Ibid., 77, 134.
50. See Castle Farm website.
51. Ibid.
52. McKernan, 59.
53. Ibid.
54. Ibid., 62.
55. Dr. Robert Bruce Armstrong testimony, August 8, 1924; RL Report, 9; McKernan, 62.
56. McKernan, 62.
57. CDT June 2, 1924.
58. Theodore, 5.
59. Baatz, 139.
60. Dr. William Healy testimony, August 4, 1924.

CHAPTER SEVEN

1. Dr. William Healy testimony, August 4, 1924.
2. Ibid., August 5, 1924.
3. NL Report, 67.
4. Dr. William Healy testimony, August 6, 1924.
5. Ibid., August 5, 1924.
6. Deposition of Nathan Leopold, November 15, 1960, in the Robert Bergstrom Archive, Newberry Library, Box 10, Folder 54; also in Higdon, 329–30.
7. Dr. William Healy testimony, August 5, 1924.
8. NL Report, 59–60, 100.
9. Leopold, 269.
10. Ibid., 26–27.
11. Dr. Harold Hulbert testimony, August 9, 1924.

12. Deposition of Nathan Leopold, November 15, 1960, in the Robert Bergstrom Archives, Newberry Library, Box 10, Folder 54; also in Higdon, 329; Martin, Part 1, 86.
13. Dr. William White testimony, August 1, 1924.
14. NL Report, 68–70.
15. Leopold, 26.
16. Dr. William White testimony, August 1, 1924.
17. NL Report, 93.
18. Ibid., 83–85, 89–90.
19. Ibid., 85, 92.
20. Dr. Archibald Church testimony, August 14, 1924; Dr. William Krohn testimony, August 18, 1924.
21. NL Report, 60.
22. Dr. William Krohn testimony, August 18, 1924.
23. CDT May 31, 1924.
24. Ibid., July 14, 1974.
25. RL Report, 26–27.
26. NL Report, 45.
27. Ibid., 138.
28. Ibid., 46, 37.
29. NL interrogation, May 30, 1924.
30. NL Report, 46.
31. Higdon, 18.
32. Fass, *Damned and the Beautiful*, 149.
33. Angell, 8.
34. Dr. William Krohn testimony, August 18, 1924; NL Report, 90; CHE June 3, 1924; CDT June 9, 1924.
35. Higdon, 146.
36. RL interrogation, May 29, 1924.
37. NL Report, 90.
38. Edwin Meiss testimony, August 7, 1924.
39. Max Schrayer testimony, August 7, 1924; Bernard Kolb testimony, August 8, 1924.
40. Theodore Schimberg testimony, August 8, 1924.
41. Edwin Meiss testimony, August 7, 1924; Max Schrayer testimony, August 7, 1924.
42. RL Report, 26.
43. Fass, *Damned and the Beautiful*, 46.
44. RL Report, 30–32.
45. NL Report, 114, 119–21, 124.
46. NL interrogation, May 30, 1924.
47. CDT June 4, 1924; CDT June 1, 1924.
48. NL interrogation, May 30, 1924.

49. Higdon, 19.
50. Dr. William Healy testimony, August 6, 1924.
51. Higdon, 305.
52. Ibid., 20.
53. Arnold Maremont testimony, August 7, 1924.
54. Harry Booth testimony, August 8, 1924.
55. John Abt testimony, August 7, 1924.
56. Higdon, 209.
57. NL Report, 68.
58. NL to RL, letter of October 10, 1923, in Leopold and Loeb Collection, Northwestern University, Box 19, Volume 2.
59. RL Report 127.
60. Fitzgerald, 304.
61. CDT June 4, 1923.
62. NL Report, 30.
63. Ibid., 37.
64. Ibid., 41.
65. NL interrogation, May 30, 1924; Sven Englund testimony, July 24, 1924.
66. McKernan, 86.
67. Theodore, xiii.
68. Baatz, 139.
69. Fitzgerald, 30.
70. Lorraine Nathan testimony, August 7, 1924.
71. *Washington Post*, July 11, 1982.
72. Dr. Harold Hulbert testimony, August 9, 1924.
73. John Abt testimony, August 7, 1924.
74. Arnold Maremont testimony, August 7, 1924.
75. NL Report, 51.
76. Leopold, 30.
77. CDT June 2, 1924; Leopold, 32; Martin, Part 1, 90.
78. Loeb interrogation, May 29, 1924.
79. RL Report, 86.
80. Leon Mandel testimony, July 24, 1924.
81. Robert Crowe closing arguments, August 27, 1924.
82. Katherine Fitzgerald testimony, August 12, 1924.
83. RL Report, 91–92; NL Report, 93–94.
84. RL Report, 92–93.
85. CDT May 30, 1924; Jacob Weinstein testimony, July 26, 1924; Emil Deutsch testimony, July 24, 1924.
86. NL Report, 10.
87. RL Report, 78.
88. McKernan, 115.
89. Dr. Harold Hulbert testimony, August 9, 1924.

90. RL Report, 123–25.
91. NL interrogation, May 30, 1924.
92. NL to RL, letter of October 9, 1923, in Leopold and Loeb Collection, Northwestern University, Box 19, Volume 2.
93. NL to RL, letter of October 10, 1923, in Leopold and Loeb Collection, Northwestern University, Box 19, Volume 2.

CHAPTER EIGHT

1. NL Report, 95.
2. RL Report, 88–89.
3. RL Report, 89; NL Report, 96.
4. NL Report, 97–98; RL Report, 94–96.
5. NL Report, 97–98; Dr. William Healy testimony, August 5, 1924.
6. RL confession, May 31, 1924.
7. NL statements, June 1–2, 1924.
8. NL Report, 100.
9. RL Report, 101.
10. Douglas, xvii.
11. Dr. William Healy testimony, August 4, 1924; RL Report, 129–30; Dr. Harold Hulbert testimony, August 12, 1924.
12. Dr. William Healy testimony, August 4, 1924.
13. RL confession, May 31, 1924.
14. NL Report, 98–99.
15. Dr. William White testimony, August 2, 1924.
16. Ibid., August 1, 1924.
17. NL Report, 99.
18. NL Report, 99; RL Report, 96.
19. NL confession, May 31, 1924.
20. NL Report, 100; RL Report, 99, 105; Robert Crowe opening statement, July 23, 1924.
21. RL Report, 99; See Fass, *Kidnapped*, chapter 1 for a brief overview of the Ross case.
22. Higdon, 97.
23. RL Report, 101; NL Report, 98.
24. RL Report, 102.
25. RL confession, May 31, 1924.
26. RL Report, 103.
27. NL Report, 100.
28. Higdon, 98; Baatz, 10.
29. RL Report, 98.
30. NL Report, 111.
31. RL Report, 121.

32. Ibid.
33. *Pittsburgh Post-Gazette*, September 10, 1996.
34. RL confession, May 31, 1924; NL confession, May 31, 1924.
35. Higdon, 32.
36. Dr. William White testimony, August 1, 1924.
37. RL Report, 116.
38. Dr. Hugh Patrick testimony, August 13, 1924.
39. RL confession, May 31, 1924.
40. Foreman Mike Leopold testimony, August 12, 1924; Leopold, 139.
41. Dr. Harold Hulbert testimony, August 9, 1924.
42. RL Report, 99.
43. Clara Vinnedge testimony, July 23, 1924.
44. J. D. Cravens testimony, July 23, 1924.
45. NL confession, May 31, 1924; CDT June 1, 1924; RL confession, May 31, 1924.
46. Walter Jacobs testimony, July 23, 1924.
47. David Barish testimony, July 23, 1924.
48. Walter Jacobs testimony, July 23, 1924.
49. NL confession, May 31, 1924.
50. Ibid.
51. Ibid.
52. Asher.
53. Ascoli, 360.
54. CDT October 28, 1924.
55. RL Report, 116.
56. Dr. Harold Singer testimony, August 15, 1924.
57. RL Report, 126.
58. Ibid., 104.
59. RL confession, May 31, 1924; NL confession, May 31, 1924.
60. RL statements, June 1–2, 1924.
61. Aaron Adler testimony, July 24, 1924; Robert Crowe opening statement, July 23, 1924.
62. RL confession, May 31, 1924.
63. RL confession, May 31, 1924; NL confession, May 31, 1924.
64. Hokan Stromberg testimony, July 24, 1924.
65. Leopold, 169.
66. RL Report, 116.

CHAPTER NINE

1. Sven Englund testimony, July 24, 1924.
2. William Herndon testimony, July 23, 1924; NL confession, May 31, 1924.
3. Walter Jacobs testimony, July 23, 1924.
4. NL confession, May 31, 1924; RL confession, May 31, 1924.

5. NL confession, May 31, 1924; RL confession, May 31, 1924.
6. Sven Englund testimony, July 24, 1924; NL confession, May 31, 1924.
7. RL confession, May 31, 1924; NL confession, May 31, 1924.
8. RL confession, May 31, 1924.
9. Ibid.
10. RL confession, May 31, 1924; NL confession, May 31, 1924.
11. Ibid.
12. Ibid.
13. NL confession, May 31, 1924.
14. Dr. Hugh Patrick testimony, August 14, 1924.
15. NL confession, May 31, 1924.
16. CDT June 2, 1924.
17. NL confession, May 31, 1924.
18. Autopsy Report, Robert Franks Inquest, May 23, 1924.
19. Dr. Hugh Patrick testimony, August 14, 1924.
20. Autopsy Report, Robert Franks Inquest, May 23, 1924.
21. NL statements, June 1–2, 1924.
22. RL confession, May 31, 1924.
23. NL statements, June 1–2, 1924.
24. RL statements, June 1–2, 1924.
25. Ibid.
26. NL confession, May 31, 1924; NL statements, June 1–2, 1924.
27. Carl Ulving testimony, July 24, 1924.
28. RL confession, May 31, 1924.
29. Ibid.
30. Autopsy Report, Robert Franks Inquest, May 23, 1924.
31. Robert Crowe closing statement, August 26, 1924.
32. Autopsy Report, Robert Franks Inquest, May 23, 1924.
33. Dr. William McNally testimony, July 24, 1924; Autopsy Report, Robert Franks Inquest, May 23, 1924.
34. Ernst Puttkammer testimony, July 25, 1924.
35. RL confession, May 31, 1924.
36. Ibid.
37. Ibid.
38. Dr. Archibald Church testimony, August 13, 1924.
39. NL Report, 103; Dr. Archibald Church testimony, August 13, 1924.
40. RL confession, May 31, 1924.
41. NL confession, May 31, 1924.
42. RL confession, May 31, 1924.
43. NL confession, May 31, 1924.
44. Ibid.
45. RL Report, 108.
46. Leopold, 24, 33.

47. RL statements, June 1–2, 1924.
48. RL confession, May 31, 1924.
49. NL confession, May 31, 1924.
50. Ibid.
51. Ibid.
52. Ibid.
53. Dr. William McNally testimony, July 24, 1924.
54. NL confession, May 31, 1924.
55. Sven Englund testimony, July 24, 1924.
56. CDT June 1, 1924.
57. RL confession, May 31, 1924.
58. Ibid.
59. Robert Crowe opening statement, July 23, 1924.
60. NL confession, May 31, 1924.
61. RL confession, May 31, 1924.
62. NL confession, May 31, 1924.
63. Ibid.
64. RL Report, 110–11.
65. Higdon, 63.
66. Leopold, 28.
67. Higdon, 63.
68. Leopold, 30.
69. RL confession, May 31, 1924.
70. Leopold, 39.
71. NL Report, 106.
72. CDT June 2, 1924.
73. Ibid., June 10, 1924.
74. Ernst W. Puttkammer testimony, July 25, 1924.

CHAPTER TEN

1. NL confession, May 31, 1924.
2. RL confession, May 31, 1924.
3. CDN May 31, 1924.
4. Dr. Hugh Patrick testimony, August 12, 1924.
5. RL statements, June 1–2, 1924.
6. RL confession, May 31, 1924; RL statements, June 1–2, 1924.
7. Dr. William Healy testimony, August 6, 1924.
8. NL statements, June 1–2, 1924.
9. RL statements, June 1–2, 1924.
10. William Shoemacher testimony, July 28, 1924.
11. William Shoemacher testimony, July 28, 1924; Thomas O'Malley testimony, August 12, 1924; CDT June 1, 1924.

12. Dr. William Healy testimony, August 6, 1924.
13. Higdon, 120.
14. William Shoemacher testimony, July 28, 1924.
15. CDT June 1, 1924.
16. William Shoemacher testimony, July 28, 1924.
17. CDT June 1, 1924.
18. Ibid., June 2, 1924.
19. Ibid., June 3, 1924.
20. Ibid., June 2, 1924.
21. Wallace Sullivan testimony, July 28, 1924.
22. CDT June 2, 1924.
23. CHE June 2, 1924.
24. Frank Johnson testimony, July 25, 1924.
25. Wallace Sullivan testimony, July 28, 1924.
26. CDT June 2, 1924.
27. CHE June 2, 1924.
28. Wallace Sullivan testimony, July 28, 1924.
29. Leopold, 48–49.
30. CDT June 2, 1924.
31. Dr. Hugh Patrick testimony, August 12, 1924.
32. William Shoemacher testimony, July 28, 1924.
33. CDT June 2, 1924.
34. CDT June 2, 1924; William Shoemacher testimony, July 28, 1924.
35. Dr. Archibald Church testimony, August 13, 1924.
36. RL statements, June 1–2, 1924.
37. Ibid.
38. Abrahamsen, 247; Fass, *Kidnapped*, 70; Douglas, 367.
39. Baatz, 265.
40. McKernan, 168.
41. Dr. Archibald Church testimony, August 13, 1924.
42. Dr. Harold Singer testimony, August 15, 1924.
43. Dr. Archibald Church testimony, August 13, 1924.
44. Dr. Hugh Patrick testimony, August 13, 1924.
45. Dr. Archibald Church testimony, August 14, 1924.
46. Ibid., August 13, 1924.
47. Dr. Harold Singer testimony, August 15, 1924.
48. RL statements, June 1–2, 1924.
49. CDT May 19, 1935.
50. NL statements, June 1–2, 1924; RL statements, June 1–2, 1924.
51. Dr. Hugh Patrick testimony, August 12–13, 1924; Dr. Archibald Church testimony, August 13, 1924.
52. CHE June 1, 1924.

53. CDT June 1, 1924.
54. Higdon, 129–30.
55. James Gortland testimony, July 25, 1924.
56. Frank Johnson testimony, July 25, 1924.
57. Leopold, 78.
58. William Crot testimony, July 25, 1924.
59. James Gortland testimony, July 25, 1924.

CHAPTER ELEVEN

1. CDT June 1, 1924.
2. Darrow, *Story*, 211.
3. Barrett, 265.
4. Stone, 430–32.
5. Darrow, *Story*, 232; Kersten, 196.
6. Kersten, 193.
7. Farrell, 278; Kersten, 146.
8. Hecht, 56.
9. Darrow, *Crime*, 29.
10. Stone, 433.
11. Leopold, 54–55.
12. Darrow, *Story*, 231.
13. McRae, 52.
14. CDT June 3, 1924.
15. Franklin, 135.
16. CHE June 4, 1924.
17. CDT June 2, 1924.
18. Ibid., June 7, 1924.
19. Leopold, 51.
20. CDT June 4, 1924.
21. Higdon, 132–34; Leopold, 58–59.
22. CDT June 2, 1924.
23. CDT June 6, 1924. Nathan in his memoirs claims this only took place some six weeks after their arrests, which he insisted was the first time they had an opportunity to speak. But they were together on numerous occasions prior to this. See Leopold, 57.
24. Leopold, 57.
25. Dr. William McNally testimony, July 24, 1924.
26. CDT June 6, 1924.
27. Ibid., June 11, 1924.
28. Ibid.
29. CHE June 1, 1924; CHE June 7, 1924.

30. CDT June 5, 1924.
31. CHE June 9, 1924.
32. Ibid., June 1, 1924.
33. Ibid., June 5, 1924.
34. CDT June 16, 1924.
35. Ibid., June 2, 1924.
36. Levin, *Obsession*, 104.
37. Levin, *In Search*, 27.
38. Eliassof, 65; Leopold, 112–13; Theodore, 115; Baatz, 139.
39. CDT June 2, 1924.
40. Ibid., June 1, 1924.
41. Ibid., June 4, 1924.
42. Ibid., June 8, 1924.
43. Ibid., June 4, 1924.
44. Ibid., June 2, 1924.
45. Ibid., June 4, 1924.
46. CHE June 1, 1924; CDT May 31, 1924.
47. CDT June 4, 1924; CHE June 3, 1924.
48. Franklin, 122–23.
49. CHE June 1, 1924.
50. CDT June 1, 1924.
51. Ibid., May 31, 1924.
52. CDN June 2, 1924.

CHAPTER TWELVE

1. Darrow, *Story*, 234.
2. Ibid., 237.
3. CDJ July 12, 1924.
4. Ibid., July 18, 1924.
5. Darrow, *Story*, 235.
6. Nietzsche, 14.
7. NL Report, 143.
8. Darrow, *Crime*, 144–45.
9. Torrey, 150.
10. Leopold, 63.
11. RL Report, 1.
12. NL Report, 1.
13. Riniolo, 82.
14. Darrow, *Crime*, 145.
15. NL Report, 110.
16. RL Report, 38.
17. Ibid., 67.

18. Dr. William White testimony, August 1, 1924; Dr. William Healy testimony, August 5, 1924.
19. NL Report, 109.
20. Ibid., 48.
21. Cassity, 56.
22. Higdon, 144–45.
23. RL Report, 20, 37.
24. Ibid., 20–22.
25. Dr. Harold Hulbert testimony, August 12, 1924.
26. NL Report, 14.
27. Ibid., 42.
28. Ibid., 40.
29. Ibid., 37.
30. Ibid., 139.
31. Ibid., 98.
32. White, Healy, Glueck, and Hammill, 365.
33. NL Report, 107–08.
34. RL Report, 118.
35. Ibid., 103–04.
36. Ibid., 119, 128.
37. Ibid., 107, 110–11, 128.
38. AP report, June 20, 1924.
39. RL Report, 119.
40. White, Healy, Glueck, and Hammill, 377.
41. NL Report, 137.
42. Ibid., 63.
43. Martin, Part I, 86; Deposition of Nathan Leopold, November 15, 1960, in the Robert Bergstrom Archive, Newberry Library, Box 10, Folder 54; also in Higdon, 329.
44. Darrow, *Crime*, 174–75.
45. RL Report, 10.
46. Ibid., 52.
47. NL Report, 84, 147–48.
48. CDT May 19, 1935.
49. White, Healy, Glueck, and Hammill, 361, 379.
50. Fass, *Kidnapped*, 81.
51. Barrett, 186–87.
52. Ibid., 186.
53. *The Loeb-Leopold Murder*, 347.
54. Darrow, *Story*, 237.
55. CHE June 18, 1924.
56. Shapiro, Golden, and Ferguson, 23, 55.
57. Ibid., 40, 54.

CHAPTER THIRTEEN

1. RL Report, 67.
2. Higdon, 22–23.
3. Ibid., 260.
4. Leopold, 124; CDJ June 5, 1924.
5. CHE June 6, 1924; Baatz, 230.
6. CDT September 1, 1924.
7. Ibid., September 2, 1924.
8. Ibid., November 23, 1923; June 3, 1924.
9. Ibid., June 3, 1924.
10. Ibid., January 8, 1927.
11. Ibid., November 23, 1924; June 3, 1924.
12. CDT November 23, 1924; CDN November 21, 1923; CHE November 22, 1923.
13. CDT June 3, 1924.
14. CDT November 22 and 23, 1924; CHE November 22, 1923.
15. CDT November 23, 1923.
16. Ibid., January 7, 1927.
17. Ibid., November 23, 1923.
18. Ibid., January 6, 1927.
19. Ibid., November 23, 1923.
20. Higdon, 255; CDT November 24, 1923.
21. CDT November 26, 1923.
22. Ibid., November 28, 1923.
23. Ibid., November 26 and 28, 1923.
24. Ibid., November 26, 1923.
25. Ibid.
26. Ibid., November 28, 1923.
27. Ibid., June 3, 1924; November 26, 1923.
28. Ibid., November 26 and 27, 1923.
29. Ibid., November 27, 1923.
30. Ibid., November 28, 1923.
31. *Irvington Gazette* June 13, 1924.
32. Melvin Wolf Inquest, May 7, 1924; CDT September 2, 1924; *New York World* June 4, 1924.
33. CDT June 3, 1924.
34. Ibid.
35. RL Report, 94.
36. *Irvington Gazette* June 13, 1924; *DeKalb Daily Chronicle* October 15, 1924.
37. *Irvington Gazette* June 13, 1924.
38. CDT August 29, 1924; *DeKalb Daily Chronicle* October 15, 1924.
39. Cited in Higdon, 253.
40. Robert Crowe closing argument, August 27, 1924.

41. CDT June 3, 1924.
42. *Irvington Gazette* June 13, 1924.
43. *New York Times* June 4, 1924.
44. *Irvington Gazette* June 13, 1924; CDN June 21, 1924.

CHAPTER FOURTEEN

1. CHE June 1, 1924.
2. Darrow, *Story*, 226, 233.
3. Gertz, *Handful*, 104.
4. CDT July 17, 1924.
5. Higdon, 159, 167; CDT July 22, 1924.
6. Kahr, 367–68.
7. CDT July 21 and July 22, 1924.
8. Higdon, 169.
9. CHE July 22, 1924.
10. CDT July 22, 1924.
11. Ibid., October 28, 1924.
12. Stone, 445.
13. CDT July 3, 1924.
14. *New York Times* June 29, 1924.
15. Stone, 445.
16. Waterman, 750.
17. Higdon, 171.
18. Waterman, 750.
19. Higdon, 171.
20. Higdon, 171; Baatz, 240.
21. CDT July 22, 1924.
22. Clarence Darrow opening statement July 21, 1924; CDT July 22, 1924.
23. Ibid.
24. Darrow, *Story*, 237.
25. Farrell, 338.
26. UP report, July 21, 1924.
27. CDT July 22, 1924.
28. Higdon, 181.
29. CDN July 23, 1924.
30. Higdon, 172.
31. Ibid., 169.
32. UP report July 23, 1924.
33. Robert Crowe opening statement, July 23, 1924.
34. UP report, July 23, 1924.
35. Clarence Darrow opening statement, July 23, 1924.
36. Ibid.

37. Jacob Franks testimony, July 23, 1924; CDN July 23, 1924.
38. CDT July 24, 1924.
39. Flora Franks testimony, July 23, 1924.
40. Dr. Joseph Springer testimony, July 23, 1924.
41. Clarence Darrow sentencing hearing, July 23, 1924.
42. Robert Crowe sentencing hearing, July 23, 1924.
43. Dr. William McNally testimony, July 24, 1924.
44. CDT July 26, 1924.
45. RL letter to his parents, July 28, 1924, cited in Baatz, 227–28; also in slightly different form in Stone, 444–45.
46. CDT July 26, 1924.
47. Ibid.
48. Carl Ulving testimony, July 24, 1924.
49. CDT July 25, 1924.
50. Carl Ulving testimony, July 24, 1924.
51. Leopold, 66–67.
52. James Gortland testimony, July 25, 1924.
53. Leopold, 70.
54. James Gortland testimony, July 25–28, 1924.

CHAPTER FIFTEEN

1. AP report, July 28, 1924.
2. Farrell, 344.
3. Robert Crowe sentencing hearing, July 30, 1924.
4. Sentencing hearing transcript, July 30, 1924.
5. Walter Bachrach sentencing hearing, July 30, 1924.
6. O'Kelly, 34.
7. Shapiro, Golden, and Ferguson, 14, 29.
8. Clarence Darrow sentencing hearing, July 31, 1924.
9. Robert Crowe sentencing hearing, August 1, 1924.
10. Judge John Caverly sentencing hearing, August 1, 1924.
11. Dr. William White testimony, August 1, 1924.
12. Wigmore, 405.
13. Dr. William White testimony, August 1, 1924.
14. Robert Crowe sentencing hearing, August 1, 1924.
15. Dr. William White testimony, August 1, 1924.
16. Ibid., August 2, 1924.
17. CHE August 12, 1924.
18. Sentencing hearing transcript, August 2, 1924.
19. Sentencing hearing transcript and Dr. William Healy testimony, August 4, 1924.
20. Dr. William Healy testimony, August 5, 1924.

21. Ibid., August 6, 1924.
22. Ibid.
23. Ibid., August 4, 6, 1924.
24. CDT May 31, 1924.
25. CHE June 3, 1924.
26. Levin, *Compulsion*, 38.
27. CDT July 28, 1924.
28. Ibid., August 10, 1924.
29. Franklin, 136.

CHAPTER SIXTEEN

1. McKernan, 71.
2. Leopold, 86.
3. CDT September 2, 1924.
4. Dr. Bernard Glueck testimony, August 6, 1924.
5. Ibid., August 7, 1924.
6. Dr. Harold Hulbert testimony, August 8, 1924.
7. Ibid., August 12, 1924.
8. Ibid., August 9 1924.
9. Ibid., August 8, 1924.
10. Ibid., August 9, 1924.
11. Ibid., August 11, 12, 1924.
12. Dr. Hugh Patrick testimony, August 12, 1924.
13. Ibid., August 13, 1924.
14. Dr. Archibald Church testimony, August 13, 1924.
15. Ibid.
16. Ibid., August 14, 1924.
17. Sellers, 39; Dr. Rollin Woodyatt testimony, August 15, 1924.
18. Dr. Harold Singer testimony, August 15, 1924.
19. Dr. William Krohn testimony, August 18, 1924.
20. Fass, *Making and Remaking*, 929.

CHAPTER SEVENTEEN

1. Thomas Marshall closing statement, August 20, 1924.
2. CDN August 19, 1924.
3. Joseph Savage closing statement, August 20, 1924.
4. Ibid., August 21, 1924.
5. CDT August 21, 1924.
6. Ibid.
7. Walter Bachrach closing statement, August 21, 1924.
8. Ibid., August 22, 1924.

9. CDN August 22, 1924.
10. Clarence Darrow closing statement, August 22, 1924.
11. Ibid., August 23, 1924.
12. Ibid., August 25, 1924.
13. Darrow, *Story*, 242.
14. Richard Loeb letter to Clarence Darrow, August 23, 1924, cited in Farrell, 351.
15. Leopold, 72.
16. Baatz, 458.
17. Douglas, 368.
18. CDN August 25, 1924.

CHAPTER EIGHTEEN

1. CDN August 26, 1924.
2. Robert Crowe closing statement, August 26, 1924.
3. Benjamin Bachrach sentencing hearing, August 26, 1924.
4. Robert Crowe closing statement and sentencing hearing transcript, August 26, 1924.
5. Robert Crowe closing statement, August 27, 1924.
6. Ibid., August 28, 1924.
7. CDN August 28, 1924.
8. CDT August 29, 1924.
9. Farrell, 358.
10. CDT August 29, 1924.

CHAPTER NINETEEN

1. *Philadelphia Inquirer,* August 29, 1924.
2. Ibid.
3. *New York Sun*, October 2, 1924.
4. Higdon, 261.
5. CDT September 11, 1924.
6. Judge John Caverly, opinion, sentencing hearing, September 11, 1924.
7. CDT September 11, 1924.
8. Leopold, 78.
9. CDT September 11, 1924.
10. CDN September 10, 1924; Higdon, 267.
11. CDN September 12, 1924.
12. CHE September 11, 1924.
13. CDT September 11, 1924.
14. *Symposium of Comments from the Legal Profession*, 395.
15. Higdon, 268.
16. CDT May 19, 1935.

17. Ibid., September 14, 1924.

18. CHE September 11, 1924.

19. CDT September 11, 1924.

20. Higdon, 213.

21. CDT August 31, 1924.

22. Ibid.

23. Ibid., June 19, 1924.

24. Ibid., June 24, 1924.

25. Ibid., August 31, 1924.

26. Ibid., August 12, 1924.

27. Ibid., September 22, 1924.

28. Ibid., September 23, 1924.

29. Ibid., August 31, 1924.

30. *Lancaster Enterprise*, October 23, 1924.

31. CDT December 30, 1924; Stone, 474.

32. Farrell, 360.

33. Stone, 474.

34. Farrell, 360.

35. Kersten, 203.

36. Quoted at loebandleopold.wordpress.com/2019/04/30/the-myth-of-darrows-monetary-snub/

CHAPTER TWENTY

1. Leopold, 81–84; Martin, Part I, 88.

2. Martin, Part I, 88.

3. Martin, Part I, 88; Leopold, 88; Fiorini, 99.

4. Leopold, 111.

5. Ibid., 122.

6. Leopold, 92; *The Post*, Ellicottville, NY, September 17, 1924; Martin, Part 1, 88.

7. CDT September 16, 1924.

8. *The Post*, Ellicottville, NY, September 17, 1924.

9. CDT October 7, 1924.

10. Ibid., October 28, 1924.

11. Ibid., October 30, 1924.

12. Ibid., October 31, 1924; March 25, 1925.

13. Jacobs, 16.

14. Leopold, 133–34.

15. Martin, Part 2, 32.

16. Ibid., 33.

17. Leopold, 160; CDT May 19, 1935.

18. Leopold, 151.

19. Higdon, 285; Leopold, 160.
20. Martin, Part 2, 33.
21. Leopold, 155–59.
22. Higdon, 285.
23. *New York Times*, November 21, 1926; Leopold, 161.
24. CDT January 5, 1927.
25. Ibid., January 6, 7, 1927.
26. Ibid., January 7 1927.
27. Ibid.
28. Ibid.
29. CDN January 8, 1927.
30. Leopold, 125.
31. Deposition of Nathan Leopold, November 15, 1960, in the Robert Bergstrom Archive, Newberry Library, Box 10, Folder 54; also in Higdon, 287; CDT September 18, 1927.
32. Martin, Part 2, 68.
33. Higdon, 290.
34. Martin, Part 2, 72.
35. Ibid., 68.
36. Martin, Part 3, 36.
37. Leopold, 242; Erickson, 80.
38. CDT May 19, 1935.
39. Leopold, 169.
40. Martin, Part 2, 68.
41. Martin, Part 3, 198; Leopold, 237; Gertz, *Handful*, 87–88.
42. Leopold, 243.
43. Ibid., 215.
44. Gertz, *Handful*, 77.
45. Leopold, 239.
46. Pittman, 7.
47. Ibid.
48. CDT January 12, 1933.
49. Leopold, 227.
50. Ibid., 230–31.
51. CDT February 1, 1936; Leopold, 302.
52. Erickson, 52–57, 80; Leopold, 302.
53. Erickson, 78; Leopold, 266.
54. CDT January 29, 1936.
55. Leopold, 267.
56. Erickson, 77.
57. Leopold, 267.
58. CDT January 29, 1936.
59. Martin, Part 3, 198.

60. Ibid.
61. CDT January 29, 1936.
62. Ibid., January 31, 1936.
63. Ibid., January 29 1936.
64. Martin, Part 3, 198.
65. Leopold, 269.
66. CDT January 30, 1936.
67. Ibid., January 29, 1936.
68. Erickson, 80.
69. CDN January 29, 1936.
70. Erickson, 79.
71. Ibid., 79, 86.
72. UPI report, January 31, 1936.
73. Erickson, 86.
74. CDT June 5, 1936.
75. Higdon, 301.
76. Day, 52–55, 78–80.
77. *Time* magazine, Volume 27, Issue 6, February 10, 1936, 15.
78. Higdon, 298.
79. Leopold, 278.
80. CDT January 29, 1936.
81. Leopold, 275.
82. *Seattle Daily Times*, January 16, 1927.
83. Martin, Part 3, 202.
84. Higdon, 297.
85. Gertz, *Handful*, 77.
86. UPI report, January 31, 1936.

CHAPTER TWENTY-ONE

1. Martin, Part 3, 201.
2. Martin, Part 3, 36–37; Leopold, 293; Von Pittman, 21.
3. Leopold, 293–94.
4. Higdon, 309.
5. Leopold, 301, 304; Martin, Part 3, 201–202.
6. Leopold, 301.
7. Nathan Leopold to Elmer Gertz, letter of March 4, 1962, in Leopold and Loeb Collection, Northwestern University, Box 20, Folder 22; also in Barrett, 282–83.)
8. Martin, Part 2, 65.
9. Warren, 146, 163.
10. Higdon, 305–9.
11. Harcourt, 3.

12. Leopold, 308.

13. Ibid., 320.

14. Gertz, *Handful*, 43–44.

15. Higdon, 308.

16. Leopold, 332.

17. Nathan Leopold to Elmer Gertz, letter of March 4, 1962, in Leopold and Loeb Collection, Northwestern University, Box 20, Folder 22; also in Barrett, 283–84.

18. Fiorini, 215.

19. Leopold, 327.

20. Leopold, 332.

21. Fiorini, 22.

22. CDT January 9, 1953.

23. Martin, Part 4, 135.

24. CDT January 9, 1953.

25. Nathan Leopold to parole board, letter of May 8, 1953, in Leopold and Loeb Collection, Northwestern University, Box 3, Folder 13; also in Barrett, 262–63.

26. CDT May 5, 1953.

27. Martin, Part 4, 136.

28. CDT May 15, 1953.

29. Ibid., August 11, 1952.

30. Fiorini, 178.

31. Martin, Part 2, 72.

32. Martin, Part 1, 87.

33. Fiorini, 205, 218.

34. Abel Brown, parole hearing testimony, July 9, 1957, in Leopold and Loeb Collection, Northwestern University, Box 32, Folder 16; also in Barrett, 268–71.

35. Gertz, *Handful*, 62–63.

36. Ibid., 58, 83.

37. Ibid., 84.

38. Ibid., 98.

39. Barrett, 276–77; and in slightly different form in Gertz, *Handful*, 98–99.

40. Gertz, *Handful*, 100.

41. Barrett 278; Gertz, *Handful*, 102.

42. Parole board stenographic report, February 5, 1958, in Leopold and Loeb Collection, Northwestern University, Box 33, Folder 2; also in Gertz, *Handful*, 103.

43. Gertz, *Handful*, 113–14.

44. Higdon, 322.

45. Gertz, *Handful*, 116.

46. Gertz, *Handful*, 117; CDN March 13, 1958.

47. Gertz, *Handful*, 117–18.

48. Ibid., 120.

EPILOGUE

1. CDT August 30, 1971; Gertz, *Handful*, 125; Higdon, 334.
2. Lyons, 67.
3. Nathan Leopold to Elmer Gertz, letter of March 4, 1962, in Leopold and Loeb Collection, Northwestern University, Box 10, Folder 7; also in Fiorini, 321; and in Barrett, 285.
4. Levin, *Compulsion*, 445–49.
5. CDT June 2, 1957.
6. Barrett, 267.
7. Leopold, 23, 25.
8. Ibid., 49.
9. Ibid., 269.
10. Ibid., 33.
11. Fiorini, 192.
12. Ibid., 283.
13. Gertz, *Handful*, 187.
14. *New York Times*, October 28, 1956.
15. Gertz, *Handful*, 150, 166.
16. Gertz, *Handful*, 160; *New York Times*, October 4, 1959; CDT October 3, 1959; Larson 142.
17. Levin, *Obsession*, 225–27.
18. CDN May 27, 1970.
19. CDT August 31, 1971.
20. Nathan Leopold to Elmer Gertz, letter of June 21, 1960, in Leopold and Loeb Collection, Northwestern University, Box 29, Folder 1; also in Fiorini, 368.
21. CDT January 13, 1961.
22. Lyons, 67–68.
23. Ibid., 68.
24. Higdon, 338; Fiorini, 318.
25. Gertz, *To Life*, 195, 198; Lyons, 68.
26. Higdon, 339.
27. Cited in Fiorini, 369.
28. Fiorini, 369.
29. Ibid., 341.
30. Lyons, 68.
31. Fiorini, 334.
32. Higdon, 339.
33. Barrett, 290.
34. CDT August 30, 1971.
35. Fiorini, 352.
36. Gertz, *To Life*, 198.
37. *New York Times*, October 2, 1924.

38. Lewis, 466.
39. CDT May 19, 1935.
40. Ibid., June 13, 1929.
41. Gertz, *Handful*, 6.
42. Cited in Fiorini, 367–69.
43. *Leader-Herald*, Johnstown, NY, July 3, 1974.
44. CDN April 19, 1928.
45. Ibid., September 18, 1929.
46. CDT May 19, 1935.
47. Ibid.
48. Ibid., July 12, 1938.

BIBLIOGRAPHY

In writing this book, we have relied heavily on the records of the court case, the People of the State of Illinois versus Nathan Leopold, Jr., and Richard Loeb, Circuit Court Case Nos. 33623 and 33624, 1924. Although this chronicles the sentencing hearing, it is equivalent to a trial transcript. Copies of the transcript can be found in the Leopold and Loeb Collection, in the Charles Deering McCormick Library of Special Collections at Northwestern University in Evanston, Illinois. The seven bound volumes are located in Box 1 (Folders 1–2), Box 2 (Folders 1–2), and Box 3 (Folders 1–3), and run to some 3,500 pages. Copies of the sentencing transcript are also available at the Newberry Library in Chicago, in the Robert W. Bergstrom Archive, Midwest Manuscript Special Collection, dispersed between Box 1 (Folders 1–6), Box 2 (Folders 7–11), Box 3 (Folders 12–17), Box 4 (Folders 18–23), and Box 5 (Folders 24–25). References to the sentencing hearing are given in the source notes as "Name of witness, testimony, and date of testimony" rather than by volume/page number.

One important note on the sentencing hearing transcripts: Clarence Darrow borrowed the original transcript containing his closing argument and never returned it. That gap, which encompasses some of his arguments on the first day and all of them on the second and third days, remains in the legal record. In reassembling the closing arguments in the case, therefore, we have relied on the partial legal record; on contemporary newspaper accounts, which gave most of Darrow's speech verbatim; and on the published version, which appeared in 1924 and which can be found listed in the bibliography below under Darrow.

The sentencing hearing transcript also includes the interrogations, confessions, and statements made by Leopold and Loeb between May 29 and June 2, 1924. In source notes, we have relied on the following, using the standard abbreviations of NL for Nathan Leopold and RL for Richard Loeb:

NL Interrogation, May 29, 1924, entered into sentencing transcript July 28, 1924.

RL Interrogation, May 29, 1924, entered into sentencing transcript July 28, 1924.

NL Interrogation, May 30, 1924, entered into sentencing transcript July 28, 1924.

RL Interrogation, May 31, 1924, entered into sentencing transcript July 28, 1924.

RL Confession, May 31, 1924, entered into sentencing transcript July 29, 1924.

NL Confession, May 31, 1924, entered into sentencing transcript July 29, 1924.

NL Statements, June 1–2, 1924, entered into sentencing transcript July 29, 1924.

RL Statements, June 1–2, 1924, entered into sentencing transcript July 29, 1924.

The psychological reports compiled by Dr. Karl Bowman and Dr. Harold Hulbert include *The Preliminary Psychiatric Examination of Nathan Leopold, Jr.* (cited in source notes as NL report), and *The Preliminary Neuro-Psychiatric Examination of Richard Loeb* (cited in source notes as RL report). Copies of these can be found at Northwestern University in the Harold Hulbert Papers, Series 55/23, Box 4 (Folders 1–2). Copies are also contained in the Robert W. Bergstrom Archives at the Newberry Library, Box 5 (Folders 26–27). *The Psychiatrists Report for the Defense (Joint Summary)* was published in 1924 (see in the bibliography below under White et al).

The inquest conducted on the death of Melvin L. Wolf took place on May 7, 1924. It can be found under the heading "Inquest on the Body of Melvin L. Wolf," Case 115009, 1924, and is kept in the Office of the Medical Examiner, Cook County, Illinois.

The autopsy conducted on Bobby Franks was read into both the transcript of the inquest into his death on May 23, 1924, and into the sentencing hearing transcript on July 23, 1924. It can be found in full, however, only in the inquest transcript. The documents are grouped under the heading "Inquest on the Body of Robert Franks," Case 6034, 1924, and are kept in the Office of the Medical Examiner, Cook County, Illinois.

BOOKS

Abrahamsen, David. *Psychology of Crime*. New York: Columbia University Press, 1960.

Angell, Robert. *The Campus: A Study of Contemporary Undergraduate Life in the American University*. New York: D. Appleton and Company, 1928.

Ascoli, Peter. *Julius Rosenwald*. Indianapolis: Indiana University Press, 2006.

Baatz, Simon. *For the Thrill of It: Leopold, Loeb, and the Murder that Shocked Chicago*. New York: HarperCollins, 2008.

Barrett, Nina. *The Leopold and Loeb Files: An Intimate Look at One of America's Most Infamous Crimes*. Chicago: Midway/Agate, 2018.

Benjamin, Susan, and Stuart Cohen. *Great Houses of Chicago, 1871–1921*. New York: Acanthus Press, 2008.

Cassity, John. *The Quality of Murder*. New York: Julian Press, 1959.

Darrow, Clarence. *Crime: Its Causes and Treatment*. New York: Crowell, 1922.

———. *The Story of My Life*. New York: Da Capo Press, 1996.

Darrow, Clarence, and Robert E. Crowe. *Attorney Clarence Darrow's Plea for Mercy and Prosecutor Robert E. Crowe's Demand for the Death Penalty in the Loeb Leopold Case: The Crime of a Century*. Chicago: Wilson Publishing Co., 1924.

Douglas, John. *Mindhunter*. New York: Gallery Books, 2017.

Eliassof, Herman. *German-American Jews*. Chicago: German-American Historical Society of Illinois, 1916.

Erickson, Gladys. *Warden Ragen of Joliet*. New York: E. P. Dutton, 1957.

Farrell, John. *Clarence Darrow: Attorney for the Damned*. New York: Doubleday, 2011.

Fass, Paula. *The Damned and the Beautiful: American Youth in the 1920s*. New York: Oxford University Press, 1977.

———. *Kidnapped: Child Abduction in America*. New York: Oxford University Press, 1997.

Fitzgerald, F. Scott. *This Side of Paradise*. New York: Charles Scribner's Sons, 1920.

Franklin, Paul. "Jew Boys, Queer Boys: Rhetorics of Antisemitism and Homophobia in the Trial of Nathan 'Babe' Leopold and Richard 'Dickie' Loeb." In Daniel Boyarin, Daniel Itzkovitz, and Ann Pellegrini, editors. *Queer Theory and the Jewish Question*. New York: Columbia University Press, 2003.

Gertz, Elmer. *A Handful of Clients*. Chicago: Follett Publishing, 1965.

———. *To Life*. New York: McGraw-Hill, 1974.

Hecht, Ben. *Gaily, Gaily*. New York: Doubleday, 1963.

Hendrickson, Robert. *The Grand Emporiums*. New York: Stein and Day, 1979.

Higdon, Hal. *The Crime of the Century: The Leopold and Loeb Case*. New York: Putnam, 1975.

Jacobs, James B. *Stateville: The Penitentiary in Mass Society*. Chicago: University of Chicago Press, 1977.

Kersten, Andrew. *Clarence Darrow: American Iconoclast*. New York: Hill and Wang, 2011.

Leopold, Nathan. *Life Plus 99 Years*. Garden City, NY: Doubleday, 1958.

Levin, Meyer. *In Search: An Autobiography*. New York: Horizon Press, 1950.

———. *Compulsion*. New York: Simon & Schuster, 1956.

———. *The Obsession*. New York: Simon & Schuster, 1973.

Lewis, Lloyd. *Chicago: The History of Its Reputation*. New York: Harcourt, Brace and Company, 1929.

Lowe, David. *Lost Chicago*. New York: Watson-Guptill, 2000.

McKernan, Maureen. *The Amazing Crime and Trial of Leopold and Loeb*. Chicago: Plymouth Court Press, 1924.

McRae, Donald. *The Great Trials of Clarence Darrow: The Landmark Cases of Leopold and Loeb, John T. Scopes, and Ossian Sweet*. New York: HarperCollins, 2010.

Nietzsche, Friedrich. *Daybreak*. Cambridge: Cambridge University Press, 1996.

Sellers, Alvin. *The Loeb-Leopold Case, with Excerpts from the Evidence*. Brunswick, GA: Classic Publishing Co., 1926.

Shapiro, David, Charles Golden, and Sara Ferguson. *Retrying Leopold and Loeb: A Neuropsychological Perspective*. Middletown, DE: Springer, 2018.

Stone, Irving. *Clarence Darrow for the Defense*. New York: Doubleday, 1971.

Theodore, John. *Evil Summer: Babe Leopold, Dickie Loeb, and the Kidnap-Murder of Bobby Franks*. Carbondale, IL: Southern Illinois University Press, 2007.

Torrey, E. Fuller. *Freudian Fraud: The Malignant Effect of Freud's Theory on American Thought and Culture*. New York: HarperCollins, 1992.

Warren, Paul. *Next Time Is For Life*. New York: Dell, 1953.

Waterman, A. N. *Historical Review of Chicago and Cook County*. Chicago: Lewis Publishing, 1908.

Weinberg, Arthur, and Lila Weinberg. *Clarence Darrow: A Sentimental Rebel*. New York: G. P. Putnam's Sons, 1980.

ARTICLES

Day, James. "Why I Killed Richard Loeb." In *True Detective* 73, no. 1 (May 1960): 52–55, 78–80.

Fass, Paula S. "Making and Remaking an Event: The Leopold and Loeb Case in American Culture." In *The Journal of American History* 80, no. 3 (December 1993): 919–51.

Harcourt, Bernard E. "Making Willing Bodies: Manufacturing Consent among Prisoners and Soldiers, Creating Human Subjects, Patriots, and

Everyday Citizens—The University of Chicago Malaria Experiments on Prisoners at Stateville Penitentiary." University of Chicago John M. Olin Law & Economics Working Paper No. 544, 2011, at law.uchicago.edu /academics/publiclaw/index.html.

Kahr, Brett. "Why Freud Turned Down $25,000: Mental Health Professionals in the Witness Box." In *American Imago* 62, no. 3 (Fall 2005): 365–71.

"The Loeb-Leopold Murder of Franks in Chicago." In *Journal of Criminal Law and Criminology* 15, no. 3 (1924): 347–404.

Lyons, Leonard. "The Rehabilitation of Nathan Leopold." In *Saturday Evening Post* 236, no. 21 (June 1, 1963): 66–68.

Martin, John Bartlow. "Nathan Leopold's Desperate Years: Murder on his Conscience." In *Saturday Evening Post.* Part I: vol. 227, no. 40 (April 2, 1955): 17–19, 86–88, 90; Part 2: vol. 227, no. 41 (April 9, 1955): 32–35, 65, 68, 71–72; Part 3: vol. 227, no. 42 (April 16, 1955): 36, 198, 201–02; Part 4: vol. 227, no. 43 (April 23, 1955): 28, 135–38.

O'Kelly, Kevin. "Leopold & Loeb: The Case that Capped Darrow's Career as a Criminal Lawyer. In *Experience: The Magazine of the Senior Lawyers Division, ABA* 19, no. 2 (2009): 24–31, 34.

Pittman, Von. "Correspondence Study and the Crime of the Century." In *Vitae Scholasticae* 26, no. 2 (Fall 2009): 5–16.

Riniolo, Todd C. "The Attorney and the Shrink: Clarence Darrow, Sigmund Freud and the Leopold and Loeb Trial." In *Skeptic* 9, no. 3 (2002): 80–83.

"Symposium of Comments from the Legal Profession: The Loeb-Leopold Murder." In *Journal of the American Institute of Criminal Law and Criminology* 15, no. 3 (November 1924): 393–97.

White, William A., William J. Healy, Bernard Glueck, and Ralph Hammill. "Psychiatrists Report for the Defense (Joint Summary)." In the *Journal of the American Institute of Criminal Law and Criminology* 15, no. 3 (November 1924): 360–79.

Wigmore, John. H. "To Abolish Partisanship of Expert Witnesses, as Illustrated in the Loeb-Leopold Case." In *Journal of American Institute of Criminal Law and Criminology* 15, no. 3 (November 1924): 401–5.

NEWSPAPERS AND PERIODICALS

(Dates are referenced within specific source notes)

AP, various reports

Chicago Daily Journal (cited as CDJ)

Chicago Daily News (cited as CDN)

Chicago Daily Tribune (cited as CDT)

Chicago Evening American (cited as CEA)

Chicago Herald and Examiner (cited as CHE)

DeKalb Daily Chronicle, DeKalb, Illinois

Irvington Gazette, Irvington, New York

Lancaster Enterprise, Lancaster, Ohio

Leader-Herald, Johnstown, New York

New York Sun

New York Times

New York World

Philadelphia Inquirer

Pittsburgh Post-Gazette

The Post, Ellicottville, New York

Seattle Daily Times

Time magazine

UP, various reports

UPI, various reports

Washington Post

OTHER MEDIA

Asher, Robert. Interview, November 10, 2000. At tile.loc.gov/storage
-services/service/mss/mfdip/2004/2004ash01/2004ash01.pdf.

Castle Farms, website at castlefarms.com.

Correlator, Chicago: University of Chicago High School, 1919.

Fiorini, John Carl. *Deviants of Great Potential: Images of the Leopold Loeb Case.* Master's thesis, College of William & Mary, 2013. At pdfs .semanticscholar.org/d296/b255fac4f4e2361491ca290e0996089a9411 .pdf.

The Lives and Legends of Richard Loeb and Nathan Leopold, at loebandleopold .wordpress.com/2019/04/30/the-myth-of-darrows-monetary-snub/

INDEX

Jacobs, Walter, 104
Jewishness of the Leopold-Loeb case, 3
Jews
    German, 149
    immigrant, 149, 169
    not responsible for the Leopold-Loeb
        crime, 149–50
Jimmy Dale character, 65
Johnson, Frank, 36–38, 138, 192
judge. *See* "friendly judge"
Jung, Carl, 135
jury trial, 152–53

Kenwood neighborhood, Chicago, 9–12,
    25–26, 51, 61, 172, 289
kidnapping
    boy or girl choice of, 95
    a capital crime in Illinois, 123–24
    charges in the case, 239
    phone calls from kidnapper, 13–14,
        21–22
killer of Bobby Franks, unknown after
    100 years, 111–13
Knowles, Victor, 273–74
Korff, Paul, 19
Kramer's Restaurant, 108
Krohn, William O., 136, 212–13
Krum, Ty, 258
Ku Klux Klan, 248

Lahey, Ed, 266
Lambda Chi Alpha, 79
lap rug, burning of, 122
Lederer, Carl, 288
Leopold, Florence Foreman, 52–54, 79
Leopold, Florence Michael "Mike," 38,
    41–42, 52, 56–57, 181, 287–88
Leopold, Nathan
    alibi of, 37, 40–41, 121
    arrogance of, 55
    autobiography, 146, 281–82
    bird guidebook written by, 285
    bird interest (ornithology, taxidermy),
        53, 88
    bird-watching by, 34–35
    boasts of the crime, 131
    as celebrity, 207
    characteristics, 12, 51
    chloroforming knowhow, 112
    college studies, 82–83
    college years, 79–83
    confession of, 45–46, 127–29

death (1971), 286
degree from University of Chicago,
    youngest in history, 85
drive to Ann Arbor to rob a fraternity,
    93–95
early life, 51–60
endocrinologic basis of crime, 159–60
at end of trial, awaiting sentencing,
    241
eye trouble and headaches, 89
fantasy life, 58–59, 74, 76
father of, 52–53, 118
friendships, few, 54–55
grownup looks, 87
homosexuality of, 57–59, 225
intellect of, 225
interviews and profiles of, 274–75
Judaism practice, claimed, 278
life after parole, in Puerto Rico,
    280–86
married Gertrude Feldman, 284–86
master-slave fantasies, 58–59, 76,
    158–59, 198, 204, 236
on May 21, 1924, 108
May 21, 1924, evening of, 12
May 23, 1924, out dancing, 31
memoirs of, 278
modern psychiatric assessment of, 162
money as motivation for crime, 102–3
moved to Stateville Prison, 256
named Freudenthal Jr., called "Babe,"
    52
name used for commercial purposes,
    therefore libelous, 283
Nietzschean philosophy, 204, 225
non-emotional life of, 209
paranoid psychology of, 208, 284
parole granted (1958), released,
    278–79
parole pursued by, 271–78
passed his law examinations, 123
personality of, 75, 87
petty criminality of, 53, 59, 77
physical pathologies, 209–10
plan to enter Harvard Law School, 98
plan to travel to Europe in June 1924,
    97
precocious as child, 53
preferred death penalty to life impris-
    onment, claim, 138
psychiatric evaluation of, 156, 162
pursuit of men, 284